D0787040

1000
Monuments
of Genius

Author: Christopher E. M. Pearson

Design:
Baseline Co Ltd.
33 ter – 33 bis Mac Dinh Chi Street
Star Building, 6th Floor
District 1, Ho Chi Minh City
Vietnam

© 2009 Parkstone Press International, New York, USA
© 2009 Confidential Concepts, Worldwide, USA

Credits:

Parkstone Press International would like to thank Klaus Carl for graciously letting us use his picture library.

For the other photographers:

© Alexandra Gnatush-Kostenko - Fotolia.com (n° 600)
© Ali Ender Birer - Fotolia.com (n° 767)
   Casa Mila, La Pedreda (Barcelona). Thanks to Fundació Caixa Catalunya (n° 629)
© Daniel BOITEAU - Fotolia.com (n° 405)
© Delphine - Fotolia.com (n° 83)
© domi4243 - Fotolia.com (n° 238)
© Dreef | Dreamstime.com (n° 549)
© Fedor Sidorov - Fotolia.com (n° 426)
© Frédéric GUILLET - Fotolia.com (n° 404)
© gRaNdLeMuRieN - Fotolia.com (n° 381)
© 2009, GRUENER JANURA AG, Glarus, Swizerland (n° 729)
© Haider Yousuf - Fotolia.com (n° 81)
© Inavanhateren | Dreamstime.com (n° 409)
© Jacques Evrard and Christine Bastin for the photographs of pictures n°606, 607, 608
© jerome DELAHAYE - Fotolia.com (n° 882)
© Jgz - Fotolia.com (n° 60)
© Joachim Wendler - Fotolia.com (n° 91)
© Lullabi | Dreamstime.com (n° 581)
© maccoyouns - Fotolia.com (n° 891)
© Marie-Jo Golovine - Fotolia.com (n° 231)
© Martin Atkinson - Fotolia.com (n° 855)
© Masterlu | Dreamstime.com (n° 111)
© Mikejroberts| Dreamstime.com (n° 301)
© m8k - Fotolia.com (n° 673)
© Nicolas Van Weegen - Fotolia.com (n° 499)
© pat31 - Fotolia.com (n° 120)
© 2009, Peter Mozden (n° 778)
© Phillipminnis | Dreamstime.com (n° 176)
© Pierdelune | Dreamstime.com (n° 865)
© Posztós János - Fotolia.com (n° 552)
© Preckas | Dreamstime.com (n° 221)
© Rostislavv - Fotolia.com (n° 529)
© Sds2003196 | Dreamstime.com (n° 727)
© Sebastien Windal - Fotolia.com (n° 462)
© Sedmak | Dreamstime.com (n° 333)
© Snowshill - Fotolia.com (n° 308)
© Starper | Dreamstime.com (n° 129, 519)
© Taiwan National Cultural Assiciation (n° 190)
© Timehacker | Dreamstime.com (n° 591)
© Typhoonski | Dreamstime.com (n° 869)
© UNESCO (n° 131, 205, 290, 814, 831)
© UNESCO/ Ariane Bailey (n° 588)
© UNESCO/ C. Manhart (n° 262)
© UNESCO/ Dominique ROGER (n° 694)
© UNESCO/ E. de Gracia Camara (n° 87)
© UNESCO/ F. Bandarin (n° 43, 49, 50, 59, 97, 133, 144, 154, 191, 244, 836)
© UNESCO/ G. Boccardi (n° 104, 106, 160)
© UNESCO/ J. Williams (n° 45, 820)
© UNESCO/ Messe. Meyer (n° 348)
© UNESCO/ Peter. Sare (n° 320)
© UNESCO/ V. Vujicic-Lugassy (n° 119)
© unflushable - Fotolia.com (n° 113)
© Valeria73 | Dreamstime.com (n° 461)

ISBN: 978-1-84484-463-0

Printed in India.

1000
Monuments
of Genius

PARKSTONE
INTERNATIONAL

CONTENTS

Introduction

What is Architecture?

Among the major visual arts, architecture has always had something of a reputation for being difficult to appreciate. This is not solely because it would seem to require a large degree of professional skill both to design and to understand, at least in a technical sense. Unlike a painting or a sculpture, a building does not tell an easily decipherable narrative or attempt to 'represent' some aspect of reality in artistic terms. Rather, the nature of architecture is at least in part utilitarian, serving to shelter various human activities. At the same time, architecture dignifies our daily actions by giving them a distinctive public presence in the form of a building envelope or façade, one that in the case of many historical edifices may present us with a bafflingly complex articulation. In this sense, the busy external appearance of, say, Chartres Cathedral (n° 315) or the Pompidou Centre (n° 716) may indeed prove intimidating to the visitor who encounters them for the first time. In many cases, the means of creation of a given building, including its structural techniques and even its materials, may not be immediately evident or easily comprehended by the casual viewer. Its stylistic, historical and iconographic points of reference may be obscure and unfamiliar. Should one know, or care, for example, that the colossal Ionic columns fronting the 19th-century British Museum (n° 564) are based on those of the Temple of Athena Polias at Priene from the 4th century BCE? What insight might such an observation give us into the nature of the later edifice? Moreover, the very function of a building may often be inaccessible from a purely visual inspection, especially if its original purpose has been forgotten or has changed over time: what was Stonehenge (n° 191) used for, and what does one do inside a basilica, a pagoda or a martyrium, for instance? On the other hand, unlike our encounter with a work of art in a museum, we generally experience architecture in a state of distraction: as the German philosopher Walter Benjamin once noted, we do not see and appreciate buildings so much as we simply use them or walk past them or through them. Buildings become invisible to us. This points, however, to the major reason why the study of architecture should never be daunting to the beginner: it is the art we all use every day, and each of us has a lifetime of experience with it. In this sense, as we move from home to office to shopping mall to museum to hotel, we are all architectural experts, formed by a quotidian process of the visual assessment, navigation, tactile engagement and habitation of three-dimensional spaces that have been designed by professional builders or architects.

Most of the structures in this book, however, could not be described as everyday. Rather, they are exceptional for various reasons, and on these grounds could be designated as 'monuments'. (The term 'monument' in this context does not refer simply to those constructions of a largely symbolic or commemorative character—the Washington Monument, for example, or London's Monument to the Great Fire of 1666—but to any building of fundamental architectural distinction.) Here we are largely concerned with edifices that required much time, money, labour and ingenuity in their creation. The architectural historian and theorist Geoffrey Scott wrote that civilisation 'leaves in architecture its truest, because its most unconscious record', and it is a truism worth repeating that architecture is inevitably an index of power—secular, religious and economic. Architecture, by this definition, is represented by large, formal buildings, often of a showy appearance, crafted of permanent materials and dedicated to high purposes. A Greek temple, a Gothic cathedral or a palatial residence like Versailles (n° 468), the Alhambra (n° 49) or White Heron Castle (n° 137) might come to mind. It is clear that the planning and construction of such impressive structures only become feasible with the emergence of large concentrations of wealth and influence, whether in the hands of a single ruler or a ruling caste. The resulting monuments, whose enduring nature has allowed them to far outlive their designers, patrons and originating cultures, bespeak an ability to marshal and deploy dozens or perhaps even thousands of workers over long periods of time, using forced, salaried or (most rarely) volunteer labour. This is as true of the Great Pyramids of Giza (n° 4) as it is of the latest awe-inspiring skyscraper in Beijing or Dubai. Architecture, like history, is created on behalf of those who have prevailed through the wielding of power, those who are able to command the spoils of war and to reap the profits of commerce. As with all such manifestations of power, the great monuments of the world are in this sense more often than not the products of despotic rule, inhumane value systems or an unfair division of resources, and could certainly be condemned as such. The Victorian art critic John Ruskin, for example, could even launch a contrarian attack on the ancient Greek temples—erstwhile symbols of fledgling democracy, humanistic culture and refined aesthetic sensitivity—as oppressive and dehumanising. Ruskin particularly objected to the Classical buildings' demand for monotonously repetitive carved ornament (such as mouldings, dentils or capitals), the manufacture of which would seem to have demanded a machine-like subservience on the part of the stonemasons. Even today a visit to the Colosseum in Rome (n° 231) or the great Mesoamerican pyramid-temples (n° 814; n° 821; n° 823) may well arouse uneasy thoughts of the mass slaughter that occurred there over the centuries, if not the backbreaking labour that went into their creation. The world's largest church, the Basilica of Our Lady of Peace (1985-90) in Yamoussoukro, Côte d'Ivoire, is generally seen as a self-indulgent folly on the part of that impoverished country's onetime president rather than as an architectural masterpiece of the first order. More often than not, however, and especially in the case of the venerated relics of older civilisations, we have an understandable tendency to set aside the questionable morality of their patronage and simply to appreciate the splendour, mystery and ingenuity of their built creations. With the passage of time, even the survivals of Nazi architecture, those morally repugnant but undeniably impressive reminders of recent atrocities, have gone some distance towards being the subject of dispassionate academic interest and even a measure of professional (rather than political) admiration from some practising architects, who see in them the evidence of a continuing European debt to the still-relevant legacy of Greece and Rome. Ideologically offensive regimes, it can easily be demonstrated, do not automatically produce either good or bad results in architecture, and from a purely aesthetic or technical standpoint the question of politics might even be left out of the discussion altogether—a rationalisation that continues to allow some contemporary architects to work for politically suspect patrons. More generally, as the Maltese architect Richard England has observed: 'When all is said and done there remains the building.'

Perhaps a more basic—though equally unsatisfactory—aspect of the 'elite' definition of architecture lies in its inherent bias towards monumentality: what about those cultures that, for whatever reason, chose not to build durable or extravagant monuments? Would not this definition exclude the extraordinarily skilful but often small-scale or impermanent structures of many Native American, Oceanic or African tribal groups, the domestic buildings of the ancient Greeks, or any number of localised traditions making use of fragile materials or given to humble, everyday uses? This perhaps unrealistic discrimination lies behind architectural historian Nikolaus Pevsner's famous comparison of a cathedral and a bicycle shed in his *Outline of European Architecture* (1943): the former was held to represent 'architecture' (perhaps even with a capital A) with distinct 'aesthetic appeal' while the latter was seen as mere 'building' of a strictly functional character. As this example suggests, the question is at the same time complicated by the professional divide between architecture and engineering (and indeed building and contracting). Can purely utilitarian structures, whatever their technical merits, be seen as architecture? The success of the modern movement in deliberately merging or blurring the parameters of both fields has perhaps rendered the question less pressing in the present day, but the status of ancient shelters, barns, warehouses and the like has yet to be dealt with.

Having laid out this series of caveats, we can now see that this book presents a selection of monuments that fits a more traditional definition of architecture. (The number of houses included in the later sections, reflecting a growing theoretical interest in the dwelling over the last few centuries, may represent a countercurrent.) Illustrated here are some of the most prominent examples of historical architecture to have survived above ground. Eschewing monuments that have vanished without a trace or which have left only scanty remains on the surface, the guiding principle has been to choose buildings that are still visible, even in mutilated or partial form, and which can be serviceably represented by a photograph. Apart from the fact that increasing world population and affluence over the last century has dramatically increased the sheer amount of monumental (or at least large-scale) architecture being erected, this editorial decision may help to explain why relatively few pre-medieval structures appear here while the number of buildings from after 1900 is so great. In consequence, this book cannot give a full account of, say, Hellenistic architecture, many of whose masterworks—like the Mausoleum at Halicarnassus or the Pharos of Alexandria—have disappeared from view almost entirely, leaving only a few scattered stones and shattered statues to evidence their onetime existence.

The definition of architecture also raises the question of the classification and sequencing of monuments. Older texts on architecture tended to simplify the process of historical classification by creating only two basic categories: ancient and modern. This has long been overlaid by the historiographical investigations of the last two centuries, and has further been complicated by a growing understanding of non-Western building traditions. A complete global chronology of architecture, though highly complex, can now be established. The beginning student of Western art and architecture soon learns that a great number of specialised terms—'Renaissance', 'Neo-Palladian', 'Churrigueresque', 'Postmodern' and so on—are used to describe historical buildings. (Similarly, the study of non-Western architectural cultures demands the assimilation of another set of historical labels, such as the Heian period in Japan, the Qing dynasty in China, or the Umayyad dynasty in Muslim countries.) These pigeonhole terms are at once chronological, regional and stylistic in character. But in any modern text on architecture, the introduction of such terms is immediately followed by qualifications: none is absolute, and their value lies primarily in their usefulness rather than their innate truth or accuracy. The chronological division between the Middle Ages and the Renaissance, for example, is notoriously difficult to gauge with any degree of accuracy: classicising tendencies can be traced far back into medieval thought and practise, while medieval building traditions continued long into the 17th century in many parts of Europe. The Baroque, which is generally held to run from the later 1600s to about 1750 in Europe and the Americas, is untidily overlapped on either end by the Renaissance and the Neoclassical age, and indeed can even be held to define a stylistic tendency toward exuberant formal experimentation that cuts across historical or cultural divisions: it is quite possible to talk of 'Baroque' tendencies in late Roman provincial architecture or in Japanese shrines of the early Edo period, for example. It is therefore wise to see such labels as indicating relatively loose architectural affinities rather than as airtight categories in the manner of botanical taxonomy.

Structure and Materials

The earliest buildings that have been revealed by archaeological investigation are relatively simple shelters of mud, stone, wood and bone—well suited, indeed, to William Morris's primal definition of architecture as 'the moulding and altering to human needs of the very face of the earth itself' (1881). Perhaps the most interesting aspect of many of these prehistoric buildings is the intimation that practical concerns played only a secondary role in so many of them: just as the magnificent but largely inaccessible cave paintings at Lascaux and Altamira may appear to have served no immediate ends in terms of basic survival, the great monolithic constructions of Stonehenge (n° 191) and Carnac (n° 194)—which clearly demanded inordinate amounts of sheer

physical labour—were intended purely for ritual usage. Many elaborate tomb structures would also fit this definition. Even domestic space, as suggested by foundations excavated in the very ancient Neolithic city of Çatalhöyük in Anatolia, is often indistinguishable from spaces of a sacred character. This observation perhaps serves simply to underline that a putative distinction between those activities associated with day-to-day existence and those connected with spirituality and the supernatural was by no means as clear in earlier times as it may seem to be today.

The mud ziggurats and palaces of the Mesopotamian civilisations set the precedent for the more durable stone architecture of ancient Egypt. This, in turn, was to inspire the limestone and marble temples of the Greeks, who evolved that elegant and aesthetically sophisticated mode of building that we have come to term the Classical. Based on the basic building unit of the column and making use of a complex and finely-tuned canon of proportions and ornaments, the Classical system of design that was first evolved by the Greeks for the articulation and embellishment of their religious buildings proved irresistibly appealing to later generations. The Classical Orders—Doric, Ionic, Corinthian and a few other variations—thus established their architectural pre-eminence in the West, and have been endlessly imitated by later cultures in Europe and the Americas. That the initially arbitrary or culture-specific nature of the Classical system—one attuned to the ritual needs of a particular religion focused on offering animal sacrifices to a pantheon of nature-related deities—was soon to be obscured by an impenetrable wall of unquestioned authority is largely due, of course, to the Romans, who imitated the Greek manner of building as they did most aspects of Greek culture. From the Romans, the Classical legacy was then taken up and reinterpreted intermittently throughout the Middle Ages, re-embraced actively in the Italian Renaissance, and thence handed down to the modern world. The Greeks thus bequeathed a legacy of Classical building that has lasted some two and a half millennia and still shows signs of life in the 21st century.

The enduring nature of the Classical system, which is almost entirely based on the principles of masonry construction, may again serve to underline the fact that until the last two hundred years builders could rely only on naturally-occurring materials to construct durable shelters. (Concrete, requiring the sourcing, preparation and admixture of such specialised materials as ash and quicklime, may be a partial exception.) Here the list of serviceable substances is a short one: earth (tamped, mixed with water, dried or baked), sand (for foundations), stone, wood, and—more rarely—animal parts (bone, leather) and various organic materials that are susceptible to weaving (reeds, twigs, bark). Wood has the advantage of being both relatively easy to process into framing units and relatively sturdy, though it is always vulnerable to rot, fire and insects; few ancient buildings using timber construction survive today. As the following pages will confirm, it is stone, because of its durability and great compressive strength, which has remained the material of choice for monumental buildings over many thousands of years. (And it might even be argued that concrete, which has supplanted stone in almost all modern constructions, presents itself simply as a more liquid, and hence more easily malleable, form of stone.) The most conservative method of masonry construction, as in a conventional load-bearing wall or the Egyptian pyramids, is simply to lay brick on brick or stone on stone; this can be done to some height before the foundations are crushed by the increasing weight. If the building is of multiple stories, however, this simple technique tends to demand extremely thick walls with small openings, allows little or no scope for useable internal space, and is wasteful of materials and labour. The driving technical question through much of architectural history has therefore been: how can we come up with a structural method that will allow a stone building to have both larger openings and spacious interiors? The greatest liability of stone is its heaviness and brittleness, and much ingenuity has been spent trying to find methods to get stone to span greater and greater distances without the danger of collapse. Likely drawing on now-vanished timber prototypes, one early solution was trabeation, the structural basis of Classical architecture: in conjunction with solid wall construction for the inner sanctuary, Greek temples relied almost exclusively on a simple post-and-beam method. The greatest danger here is in proposing bays of excessive length; i.e., leaving too much space between upright supports, which risks cracking the horizontal members that are made to span them. In large rooms, the low tensile strength of stone necessitates the use of either a grid of vertical supports (posts or piers) to hold up the ceiling, or a lighter timber superstructure, though the latter will again be subject to fire or other hazards. Preferentially, therefore, roofs and ceilings were often to be built using masonry, and various methods of vaulting were developed. An early technique, known as corbelling, simply extends each successive layer of stone slightly beyond the one below until a ceiling of tapered section is formed. The true arch, making use of a semicircle of voussoirs (individual blocks of trapezoidal form) and secured on top by a keystone, was much used by the Romans in both honorific and utilitarian contexts. The extension of an arch in a single direction in space results in a semicircular barrel vault (a half-cylinder), while its rotation through 360 degrees creates a hemispherical dome. Such forms provided the best method of vaulting into the early medieval period, though they often required the use of lighter materials (usually brick) and heavy buttressing in order to counteract the lateral thrust that was thrown onto the external walls. It remained for the master masons of the Gothic period to perfect a more daring and effective form of stone vaulting, one which took the material to the limits of functionality. Making use of a pointed arch for both arcades and interlacing rib vaults, as well as a series of flying buttresses to provide lateral stability, the Gothic builders were able to realise elegantly skeletal constructions that made minimal use of load-bearing wall construction and soared to unprecedented heights.

The story of architectural technique from the late 18th century through the present day is largely one of the increasing mastery of metallic construction. Following the innovations of the Industrial Revolution, first iron and then steel were pressed into use for utilitarian structures: warehouses, factories, stores and other commercial buildings could be erected quickly and cheaply, using cast-iron elements for internal framing and external cladding. Increasingly, iron framing also began to be used for larger public buildings, notably the new Houses of Parliament in London (n° 566), but these were inevitably clad in a veneer of stone or terracotta to gave the impression of traditional load-bearing construction, thus catering to genteel notions of how architecture was supposed to look. This was also true of the early skyscrapers of Chicago and New York, whose façades did not begin to make clear formal acknowledgement of their internal steel frame construction for some decades. Later in the 19th century the first experiments began to be made with reinforced concrete, which optimally combined the tensile strength of iron or steel rebar with the compressive strength of concrete. At the same time, the development of such new building technologies introduced a vexing split into architectural practise: the field of engineering was now emerging as a specialised discipline in its own right, and techniques and aesthetics thus became estranged. A telling comparison might be made between two prominent buildings erected in Paris after the mid-19th century: Charles Garnier's new Opera house (n° 580) (1861-1875) and the Eiffel Tower (n° 602) (1889). The Opera, designed by an academically trained architect, epitomised the French belief that Paris was the centre of world culture, and that its major opera house should exemplify the grandest formal design and the most sophisticated and allusive veneer of sculptural and painted ornamentation, both inside and out. Stylistically, the Opera synthesises over two thousand years of Classical architecture, drawing on the formal vocabulary of the Greeks and Romans as filtered through the Renaissance and Baroque, and thus presented itself as a summation, if not an apotheosis, of the European cultural tradition. The Eiffel Tower, on the other hand, designed as a temporary structure for a world fair, had aims that were technical and commercial rather than strictly cultural in nature, namely: reaching an unprecedented height, minimising weight and wind resistance, and making a dramatic demonstration of the new techniques of iron construction that had been developed by French engineers. Obeisance to historical precedent or accepted canons of taste played no part in this venture, and upon its erection the tower was roundly condemned as a brutal monstrosity by a coalition of prominent French artists and writers. The question seemed clear: was architecture to be a matter of good design in the humanistic tradition, or was it instead to be a technologically-driven search for scale, economy and efficiency?

It was left to the ideologists of the Modern movement in the early 20th century to attempt to forge a reconciliation between art, architecture and industry. The key ingredient, as it turned out, was modern painting and sculpture, which provided architects with a new language of abstract form and space creation that seemed suited both to the Fordian and Taylorian exigencies of modern industry and to the increasingly collective (i.e., anti-individualistic) nature of contemporary society. This is not to say that modern architecture was conceived as simply cheap, functional, expedient or anonymous, but rather that it evinced a carefully considered 'machine aesthetic' that was seen to be in tune with the modernist *Zeitgeist* of mass production, standardisation and collectivism. At the same time, modern architects made great inroads into the creative deployment of newer materials—notably glass, steel and reinforced concrete—to fashion envelopes and spaces of compelling beauty and originality. In the work of contemporary modernists like Norman Foster or Santiago Calatrava, the line between technology and art has been completely effaced, and whether a given architectural element can be seen to have a technical or aesthetic motivation within the building as a whole necessarily becomes a moot question. What can also be said with certainty is that architecture has reforged a vital partnership with engineering that has allowed tectonic forms of unprecedented complexity and irregularity to be realised. In recent years this process has been accelerated to blinding speed by the introduction of computers into the design, construction and costing processes, and the expressionist fantasies of a Frank Gehry or a Daniel Libeskind can now be achieved within reasonable parameters of time and expense.

Architecture as Theory

Architecture, as distinguished from building, might further be characterised by its reliance on written theory rather than on established folk traditions. In this light, the history of architecture is as much a matter of texts as it is of actual structures. It may not be coincidental that the emergence of formal, monumental architecture in the Fertile Crescent of Mesopotamia was accompanied by the development of the first writing systems, and architecture is in this sense always a product of literate cultures. The composition of self-consciously theoretical manuals on architecture is at the same time a record of the growing status and social aspirations of the architectural profession. Such texts are rare before Roman times, and the first real landmark we have in this field is the famous treatise written by the Roman architect Vitriuvius in the 1st century BCE. Though largely technical in nature, incorrect or obscure in certain passages and often rather dull, Vitruvius' *De Architectura* is the lone survivor of the architectural texts of antiquity, and as such necessarily remained a touchstone for practise in the West for some two thousand years. Vitruvius covered the basics of construction, the correct plans and proportions of public and religious buildings, and set out the details of the Classical orders. The organisation and subject matter of Vitruvius' text set the precedent for the Renaissance treatises of Alberti (*De Re Aedificatoria*, 1442-52), Cesariano (*Di Lucio Vitruvio Pollione de Architettura*, 1521), Serlio (*Tutte l'opere d'architettura et prospettiva*, 1537 and later), Vignola (*Regola delli cinque ordini d'architettura*, 1562) and others. European architectural theory at this time tended towards promulgating refinements to the Classical system rather than mounting any serious challenge to its hegemony, and we further begin to sense a growing divide between practise (on-site constructional expertise) and theory (the essentially intellectual or antiquarian debates underpinning the study and practise of Classical architecture). Ultimately, the most influential of all Renaissance architectural texts was that of the Venetian Andrea Palladio. His *I Quattro Libri dell'Architectura* of 1570 had the advantage of clear woodcut illustrations showing the details and proportions of the Orders, reconstructions of Roman buildings, and numerous villas and city buildings of his own design. Notable for his characteristic addition of Roman-style temple fronts to the façades of relatively modest domestic buildings, Palladio bequeathed to amateurs, architects and common builders a simplified but elegant version of Classicism that could be applied to many different typologies with minimal expense. The Palladian legacy was to persist throughout the eighteenth century and beyond in both Europe and America.

The Enlightenment saw the emergence of a new kind of architectural treatise in Europe, one that was less technical and more theoretical or speculative in nature, and which attempted to reconcile the new faith in reason with the traditional reliance on Classical precedent. Most notable here is the *Essay on Architecture* (1753) of Abbot Laugier, who put forward the idea that the Classical system derived from the most ancient building type, a hypothetical construction of tree trunks which has often been termed the 'primitive hut'. This entirely conjectural proposal served to anchor Classicism in both reason and nature, thus ensuring its continuing intellectual attractiveness. Other writers of a Neoclassical persuasion continued to subject Classicism to the new forces of reason, a process which nevertheless acted only to reinforce its supremacy. This was further confirmed by the many folio volumes of etchings put out by the Venetian architect Giovanni Battista Piranesi, who aimed to demonstrate the superiority of Roman architecture solely on the basis of its great size, complexity and engineering prowess. Almost unwittingly, however, Piranesi's unforgettably dense and moody depictions of the monumental ruins of Rome also served to affirm that Classical architecture could be turned to ends of pure emotion rather than strict rationalism, thus laying the ground for the Romanticism of Soane, Ledoux, Boullée, Schinkel and others.

The 19th century nevertheless witnessed new challenges to the Classical monopoly from architects who espoused a return to medieval building practises.

This initiative was taken, as often as not, on the basis of moral or religious principles rather than on technical grounds. John Ruskin, who had no professional or technical training in building whatsoever, proposed that the most important aspect of architecture was its ornamentation, which could engage the uncoerced and creative talents of a variety of people in society. His model was the Gothic churches and cathedrals of Europe, and most particularly the highly ornate and colourful version of Gothic to be found in Venice. As laid out in his *Seven Lamps of Architecture* (1849) and *The Stones of Venice* (1851-1853), Ruskin's emphasis on the dignity of the craft traditions was soon to inspire many writers and practitioners of the Arts and Crafts school, led by the socialist philosopher William Morris. Their goal was to recapture the timeless vernacular building traditions of a given region, which automatically foregrounded an appreciation of the inherent beauty of simple, natural materials. This idealistic line of thinking was ultimately to serve as the foundation of Frank Lloyd Wright's personal conception of an 'organic' architecture, one that drew inspiration from natural growth, responded directly to the nature of materials and the structures and forms they suggested, and which took root in a distinct region and socio-cultural environment—in this case, American capitalism, individualism and democracy. A rather different stream of thought, though one equally indebted to the precedent of the Middle Ages, was represented by the voluminous writings of the French architect and architectural restorer Eugène Viollet-le-Duc, who asserted that the true lesson of the Gothic cathedrals was to be found in their innovative construction techniques, and that these might even be applicable to modern constructions in cast iron.

The true literary proponents of the Industrial Revolution in architecture, however, were only to make an appearance after the turn of the twentieth century. The writings of Walter Gropius, Sigfried

Giedion, and above all those of the Swiss-French architect Le Corbusier, set the basic agenda for the modern movement: the harmonisation of art, design, industry and architecture. Taking cues from modern art as well as the rational and calculating attitude of the engineer, Le Corbusier proposed that architecture should make use of the abstract language of geometry, eschewing all historicising forms in favour of a fresh and unbiased approach to the fundamental questions of building; e.g., what is a house? Le Corbusier's famous response was that a house is, in essence, a 'machine for living in', just as a sewing machine is a machine for sewing, an airplane a machine for flying in, and so forth. At the same time, Le Corbusier's discourse could often veer off into unexpectedly idealistic or mystical territory, proposing that the visual effect of finely handled geometrical volumes transcended the merely aesthetic to access realms of emotion and even spirituality. Le Corbusier's thought —provocative, engaging and fundamentally dialectical in nature— was to prove inspiring to generations of modern architects, and to this day the most-thumbed volumes in architectural libraries are usually those of the eight volumes of his *Oeuvre complète*. A perhaps unexpected by-product of Le Corbusier's polemical success was the reactivation of the architectural treatise as an instrument of philosophical reflection, as well as a means by which architects could make their mark in the profession without the necessity of actually building anything. Following in the wake of Le Corbusier, the next most important body of writings was arguably that of the American Robert Venturi and his associates, whose ironic and self-consciously 'complex and contradictory' take on building design was informed by an academic familiarity with historical buildings as well an appreciation of contemporary Pop Art. The larger trend that eventually took wing from these ideas came to be known as Postmodernism, and from its origins in

architecture it came to permeate all of the creative arts and Humanities through the 1980s. More recent architectural theory, though not infrequently hermetic to the point of incomprehensibility, has tended to be less cohesive and single-mindedly polemical in nature, and the idea of establishing a particular avant-garde school or position presently seems to have fallen by the wayside. This may in part be attributable to an understandable fatigue with tracing the putative rise and fall of categorical 'movements' in architecture, but also to the increasing tempo of electronic media, which barely allows readers the time to absorb a new design concept before it is replaced by an even newer one. Perhaps for this reason, contemporary architectural treatises, such as those of Rem Koolhaas, tend to rely just as much on dense layerings of photographic or computer imagery than on pure text. This, in turn, again calls into question our definition of the architectural monument: in a time when the computer threatens to dematerialise the most stable social traditions, architecture, too, appears to be moving into a virtual phase, one in which the previously inert and (literally) concrete products of architectural design may soon become indissociable from the flow of digitised information and the unending manufacture of virtual realities. The prospects for the future of monumental architecture are indeed dizzying, not to say disorienting, for all boundaries have become fluid. Perhaps even more than we realise, traditional architecture has provided the existential matrix for our lives, the reliability of four solid walls granting us a sense of belonging, stability and orientation in a world of change and apparent chaos. As we contemplate the great building achievements of past civilisations and the exhilarating but often bewildering presentiments of the future represented by contemporary practise, we might do well to recall Walter Gropius's reminder that 'there is no finality in architecture, only continuous change.'

AFRICA AND THE MIDDLE EAST

It may seem curious that monumental architecture was first developed in a land that was so poor in such building resources as timber and stone. But from the 4th millennium BCE a series of diverse and warring civilisations residing in the 'Fertile Crescent' between the Tigris and Euphrates Rivers succeeded in inventing both writing and urban society, including mankind's first essays in architectural building on a monumental scale. That these Mesopotamian cultures were able to accomplish this using only sun-dried mud bricks is remarkable, and is perhaps a testament to the extreme degree of social control wielded by their rulers. The exact sequence of peoples who inhabited and fought over this region over many hundreds of years constitutes a notoriously complex historical patchwork, yet archaeology has revealed a recognisable consistency among them, especially in regard to architectural and urbanistic form.

The monumental architecture of the ancient Sumerians, who established a series of city-states near the Tigris-Euphrates delta, was largely religious in nature. The Mesopotamian temple soon came to assume a standardised arrangement, consisting of a taller central chamber (cella) flanked by lower spaces. As the older mud temples crumbled and were replaced by new ones on the same foundations, these shrines came to be set on tall hills, and these, ultimately, took on the form of stepped pyramids, or ziggurats—the real-life inspiration, in fact, for the Biblical Tower of Babel. Lifting the holy sanctuary as close to the sky as possible, the profile of ziggurats was further meant to recall that of a mountain, a vertical axis by which the supernatural realm could be accessed. After the Akkadian conquests of the mid-3rd millennium BCE, we find early (though limited) use of the round arch, the dome and the vault. Perhaps just as importantly, there also appear the first aesthetic impulses in monumental building: the external appearance of temples, whose simple, load-bearing masonry construction meant that they were necessarily massive, cubic and closed, came to be modulated by the addition of evenly spaced pilasters or decorative buttresses, thus creating a sculptural sense of strength and an attractively regular patterning of light and shade in the strong sunlight. In societies ruled by god-kings, in which little distinction was made between secular and religious powers, temples came to form larger precincts with royal palaces and administrative buildings. Much of this architecture was defensive in function and appearance, though often clad with fired or glazed terracotta tiles for both aesthetic and practical reasons. Individual domestic buildings, such as those comprising the city of Ur on the Euphrates, were again inwardly focused, and consisted of an inner courtyard surrounded by smaller rooms, thus serving as a prototype for Middle Eastern and Mediterranean houses for millennia to come.

From the 9th through the 7th centuries BCE the warlike Assyrians built palaces of immense size at their successive capital cities of Nimrud, Khorsabad and Nineveh. The fortified citadel of Khorsabad, erected during the 8th century BCE by Sennacherib, consisted of some 25 acres of palaces, courtyards, temple chambers and a tall ziggurat. Technically, the Assyrians made no great strides beyond their Sumerian predecessors, but their temples became increasingly large, lavish and colourful. The last great surge of monumental building in Mesopotamia took place after the fall of the Assyrians, with the erection of Nebuchadnezzar's great city of Babylon in the 7th century BCE. Its palaces and temples, their external walls decorated by glazed terracotta tiles of animals and mythological beasts, were arranged along a great processional way. In the following century the accomplishments of the Assyrians would come to be rivaled by those of the neighbouring Persians, as epitomised by the great royal palace at Persepolis (n° 12), built atop a broad terrace of native rock.

◀1. *The Great Sphinx*, Giza, c. 2530 BCE (Egypt)

Every element of architecture and relief sculpture here served to glorify the ruler, and the great audience chamber (apadana, or hypostyle hall) and nearby throne hall were notable for their numerous tall stone columns set in grid formation, some topped with addorsed bulls' heads.

While the Sumerian culture was rising, further to the west the pharaohs were consolidating their power in Upper and Lower Egypt. Here an architecture of extraordinary monumentality and stability emerged, founding a tradition that was to last almost three thousand years. Though favouring structurally conservative techniques, the Egyptians created the world's first large-scale buildings in finely carved stone, and developed stonemasonry to a peak of skill that has rarely been surpassed. It has nevertheless been demonstrated that Egyptian honorific architecture was to a large extent modelled on the forms and building materials of their much more modest domestic constructions of mud, timber and papyrus, and traces and reminiscences of these older techniques can be discovered in many temple structures. Most monumental buildings were religious and/or funerary in character, beginning with the great pyramid of Djoser at Saqqara (n° 2) and the unprecedentedly colossal Old Kingdom pyramids (n° 4) at the edge of the desert at Giza, both dating from the mid-3rd millennium BCE. There was a relative lull in monumental construction during the Middle Kingdom period (1991-1650 BCE), but from the beginning of the New Kingdom (1570 BCE) the freestanding temple again came to the fore and assumed a standardised typology, rarely departed from afterwards: as at Luxor, a central axis leads through a monumental gateway (pylon), a forecourt and a columned hall towards a smaller sanctuary in which the cult image was kept, inaccessible to all but a handful of upper-caste individuals. Egyptian tombs, like the pyramids, were inevitably associated with nearby temples. One of the most notable temple-tombs is that of Queen Hatshepsut (n° 7) in the 18th Dynasty, which was partly set on ramped terraces and partly cut into a stone cliff. Cult temples, which usually took shape gradually over many centuries, were places of holy dread, for they were seen as the literal dwelling place of the Egyptian deities. In all cases the desire of Egyptian architecture was to evoke a sense of religious mystery and awe, an effect heightened by the necessarily thick walls and dark interiors. A secondary aim, as in the Pyramids, was to foil tomb robbers through the inclusion of internal portcullises, false chambers and corridors and the like, though such strategies almost always proved ineffective and virtually all Egyptian funerary architecture has long since been looted. The Egyptians apparently felt little need to expand their interior spaces, and large enclosed areas were only made possible, as in the great hypostyle hall at Karnak (n° 6), by the insertion of a closely-spaced forest of thick columns to support the roof. Externally, walls were often battered (canted inwards) so as to give a greater effect of strength, and could be covered with large areas of intricately incised hieroglyphics and low-relief scenes, thus leaving us a vivid record of the beliefs and everyday life of Egyptians of all classes. With only a little exaggeration one might say that down through the millennia Egyptian architecture was to remain essentially unchanged, mirroring—if not a lack of intellectual curiosity or desire for innovation—the underlying stability of social life and religious belief. The Egyptians built for eternity, and their architecture is correspondingly massive, stable and timeless.

Until recently the study of the historical architecture of sub-Saharan Africa was largely the province of the anthropologist rather than the architectural historian. This is because few of the building traditions of the continent's innumerable ethno-linguistic groups matched Western notions of monumentality. Even by this rather limited definition of architecture, however, sub-Saharan Africa has produced some remarkable but still lesser-known architectural masterpieces. In early times we find traces of skilled stonemasonry being practised in Ghana, by the Kush civilisation in Sudan, and in the Ethiopian kingdom of Aksum. In the medieval period the spread of Islam produced major monuments throughout East and West Africa, most notably the Great Mosque of Djenné in Mali (n° 43). And in southern Africa, the curvilinear stone walls of Great Zimbabwe (n° 47) make up the largest medieval city of sub-Saharan Africa. The Royal palaces at Abomey, Benin (1625-1900) constitute one of the most historic sites in West Africa; built over many years as part of the capital of the ancient kingdom of Dahomey, the elaborately decorated edifices record the history and religion of their builders. Although such international bodies as UNESCO have taken up the cause in recent years, it has to be said that much remains to be done in the archaeological investigation, scholarly study, and popularisation of African achievement in architecture, and historical preservation has now become a pressing need at many sites.

Moving once again to the east, we encounter in the Arabian Peninsula the birthplace of the Islamic religion, which began its remarkable expansion through the Middle East, Asia, Africa and Europe from the 7th century. As a largely tribal and nomadic people, the first Muslims had few real architectural traditions of their own, but took over local building forms and techniques in every country they conquered. The Muslim house of worship, or mosque, can be found in its most essential form as early as 622, when the Prophet's own mosque was built in Medina. Here, based around an extensive colonnaded courtyard with a central fountain for ritual cleansing, we find the basic elements of Islamic typology: the large prayer room, the mihrab (prayer niche indicating the direction of Mecca), the minbar (elevated stand), the muhajar (balustrade), the pulpit, the midha (purification room) and one or more minarets (tall towers from which the call to prayer is made, a feature originally derived from converted church towers in Syria).

Islam's first great ruling dynasty, the Umayyads, were based in Damascus, and oversaw the creation of some of the most enduring monuments of Islam, including the Dome of the Rock (n° 29) (technically a sanctuary or shrine rather than a mosque) and the Al-Aqsa Mosque in Jerusalem (n° 39), as well as the Great Umayyad Mosque at Damascus (n° 32), which incorporated a Classical temple that had since been converted into a church. Typically Islamic building features, such as the horseshoe arch and barrel-vaulted masonry tunnels, as well as a love of rich ornamentation, emerged here. At about the same time, the Tulunids in Cairo initiated a great program of mosque-building in that city, and by the 9th century monumental mosques were being erected across North Africa. The Seljuks in Persia introduced several innovations in mosque design at the start of the second millennium, notably the incorporation of a huge iwan (giant arch) on each side of the courtyard, a feature taken from the earlier Sassanian culture. The extraordinarily beautiful mosques at Isfahan, Iran (n° 38), built from the 11th century, exemplify the Islamic genius for colourful and geometrically complex tilework. In the meantime the last of the Umayyads, expelled from the east, had taken up residence in Spain, and the Great Mosque of Córdoba (n° 31), with its famous forest of arcaded columns, was built and rebuilt from the 8th century. In conquered Constantinople, now renamed Istanbul, the Muslims took the church of the Hagia Sophia (n° 254) as the pre-eminent prototype for new mosque design, and the 16th-century structures of the architect Sinan, which draw clear lessons from Byzantium, are among the most masterful and attractive of all mosques. In terms of domestic architecture, the Alhambra palace in Granada, Spain (n° 49), bears eloquent witness to the high level of Muslim architecture and taste in the last century and a half before their expulsion. Another important Muslim typology, dating back at least to the 12th century, is the madrasa, or religious school, consisting of a large central courtyard surrounded by the students' rooms. Recent study of traditional Islamic architecture, as carried out by Hassan Fathy and others, has revealed a wealth of practical knowledge regarding ventilation, heat regulation, economy and social aptitude, factors which can only become increasingly relevant in an energy-conscious future. And as particularly seen in Saudi Arabia and the wealthy states of the Persian Gulf, Islamic architecture continues to grow and evolve, even to the extent that Western architects (like the American firm of Skidmore, Owings & Merrill) have been hired to take charge of religious buildings, and modern aesthetics and construction techniques have comfortably found their place in mosques of ever-increasing scale, comfort and sophistication.

2. *Pyramid of Djoser*, Saqqara, c. 2750 BCE and later (Egypt)

3. *Funerary Temple of Mentuhotep*, Deir el-Bahri, c. 2061-2010 BCE (Egypt)

4. *Great Pyramids of Giza*, Giza, c. 2600 BCE and later (Egypt)

Khufu, like his successors, was concerned to supervise the construction of his own funerary monument during his lifetime. Each pyramid was originally connected to a temple on the banks of the Nile, where the body of the dead ruler would be held before burial. In the long and labour-intensive construction process, blocks of rough stone were unloaded from arriving boats, shaped on the riverbank, then hauled up huge temporary ramps to add a new layer of masonry to the rising structure. With their angles aligned to the cardinal directions, the pyramids betray a geometrical precision that confirms the Egyptian mastery of calculation. Weighing more than 5 million tons and comprising some 2 million stone blocks, the Great Pyramid of Khufu is the largest of all Egyptian pyramids, and the only surviving 'Wonder' of the ancient world; it was, in fact, the tallest building on earth for a period of almost 4000 years. The pyramids' present appearance is very dilapidated: they would originally have had a veneer of smooth limestone, and the Great Pyramid had sheets of gold covering its summit. Ironically, no trace of Khufu's mummy was ever found in the Great Pyramid, and only one image of him is known to exist.

5

5. *Great Ziggurat*, Ur, c. 2100 BCE (Iraq)

6

6. *Great Temple of Amun*, Karnak, c. 1550 BCE and later (Egypt)

7

7. *Funerary Temple of Queen Hatshepsut*, Deir el-Bahri, c. 1473-1458 BCE (Egypt)

This great tomb-temple dedicated to the sun god Amun dates from the 18th dynasty, the first of Egypt's New Kingdom, but it continues an older Middle Kingdom tradition of rock-cut tombs. The general typology of Hatshepsut's monument was borrowed from the earlier and smaller temple-tomb of Mentuhotep, which is immediately adjacent. The visible part of the temple consists of three superimposed terraces fronted by rows of square piers; backed by fluted round columns, these are often interpreted as predecessors of the Doric Order that would later be developed by the Greeks. Accessed by ramps, the terraces were once irrigated and the site of lush plantings of scented trees. The temple is partly carved into the rocky cliff behind. As with earlier rock-cut tombs, the actual grave of the Queen was located on the far side of the mountains, in the Valley of the Kings; this step was taken as part of the never-ending battle against grave robbers. This is one of the few ancient monuments for which we have the name of a specific builder: its design is sometimes attributed to Senmut, a courtier, and also to Hatshepsut herself, making her history's first known woman architect.

8. *Temple of Ramses II*, Abu Simbel, begun c. 1280 BCE (Egypt)

8

9. *Temple of Amun*, Luxor, Thebes, c. 1408-1300 BCE (Egypt)

10

10. *Temple of Isis*, Philae, 500-164 BCE (Egypt)

11. *Temple of Horus*, Edfu, 237-57 BCF (Fgypt)

12

12. *Palace complex at Persepolis,* 6th-5th century BCE (Iran)

13

13. *Ishtar Gate,* Babylon (now in the Pergamon Museum, Berlin), c. 600 BCE (Iraq)

Rising from the banks of the Euphrates and covering some 10 square kilometres, Babylon was the capital of a sprawling empire. The city was extensively rebuilt in the reign of Nebuchadnezzar II, who is mentioned in the Bible. This fortified gateway, some 12 metres high, is constructed of mud bricks. It has a veneer of fired and glazed ceramics featuring many bas-relief images of stylised lions, bulls and mythological creatures; the latter, with their scaly bodies, snake heads, scorpion tails, front legs of a cat and rear legs of a bird, are associated with the god Marduk, *to whom the city's great ziggurat temple—likely the inspiration for the Tower of Babel—was dedicated. Named for the Babylonian goddess of love and war, the Ishtar Gate originally guarded the entrance to the main processional way of Babylon, some 800 metres long, which ran past the famous Hanging Gardens. Babylon was later conquered and largely destroyed by the Persians. The Ishtar Gate was discovered during German archaeological campaigns from 1899-1917 and reconstructed in Berlin. Partly restored under the regime of Saddam Hussein, the site of Babylon in modern-day Iraq has since been damaged once again under the American occupation.*

14

14. *Gymnasium*, Cyrene, 5th century BCE and later (Libya)

▶15. *The Treasury*, Petra, c. 60 BCE (Jordan)

16. *City of Timgad*, founded c. 100 CE (Algeria)

17. *Temple of Bel*, Palmyra, 32 CE (Syria)

18. *Temple of Bacchus*, Baalbek, c. 150 CE (Lebanon)

19. *Temple of Jupiter Heliopolitan*, Baalbek, c. 200 CE (Lebanon)

20. *City of Leptis Magna*, 2nd-4th century CE (Libya)

21. *City of Sabratha*, 2nd-4th century CE (Libya)

22. *Palace of Ctesiphon*, near Baghdad, c. 6th century (Iraq)

23. *Nubian pyramids at Meroë*, Meroë, 300 BCE-300 CE (Sudan)

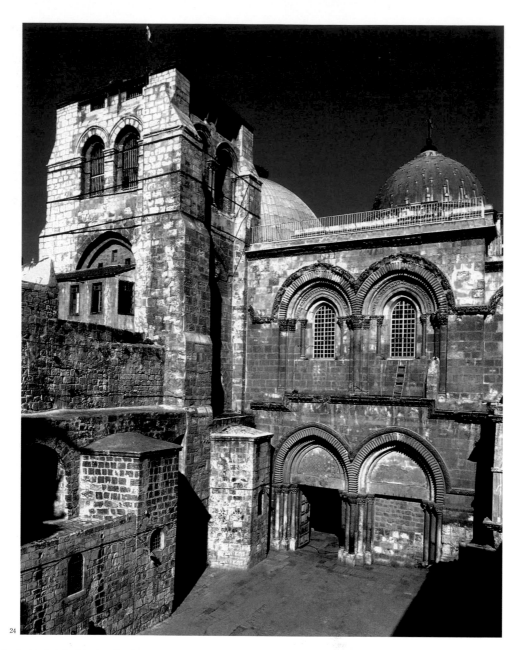

24. *Church of the Holy Sepulchre*, Jerusalem, begun c. 325 with many later rebuildings (Israel)

This famous church, the ultimate goal of Crusader zeal, has been many times destroyed and rebuilt. Since it is supposed to have been erected on the actual site of Jesus' Passion and Resurrection, the Church of the Holy Sepulchre is of central importance to Christianity: among several other holy areas which are reputed to be contained within its walls is the Hill of Calvary, where the Crucifixion took place, as well as the rock-cut tomb of Christ. In its original form, a large rotunda covered the latter site, a feature that was often imitated in later European churches. The location of the building is said to have been determined by the Empress Helena, mother of the Emperor Constantine, who came to the Holy Land and miraculously discovered the True Cross lying discarded in a pile of rubbish. The present building is a patchwork of different styles and historical periods, and the control of every square centimetre is fought over by a variety of Christian sects. For this reason, the keys to the Church have long been held by a prominent Muslim family of Jerusalem.

25. *Khirbat al-Mafjar palace complex*, Jericho, 8th century (Palestine)

26. *Qasr Amra desert castle*, c. 711-715 (Jordan)

7. *St. Catherine's Monastery*, Mount Sinai, 527-565 and later (Egypt)

▶28. *Arg-é Bam (Bam citadel)*, before the 2003 earthquake, Bam, 5th century BCE-1850 (Iran)

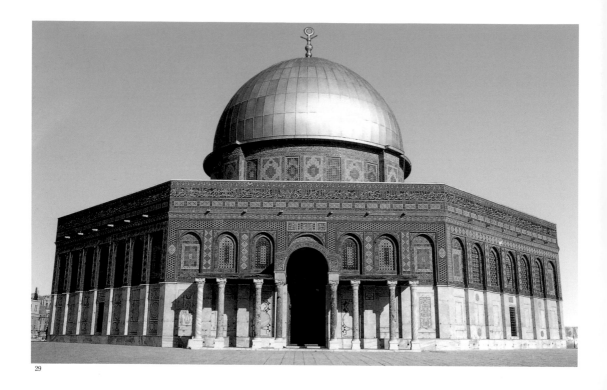

29

29. *Dome of the Rock*, Jerusalem, c. 687-692 (Israel)

Often incorrectly called a mosque, this very early Muslim shrine was erected by the rulers of the Umayyad Caliphate atop the rock from which Mohammed is said to have ascended to heaven. Its location is in fact one of the most fiercely disputed pieces of territory in the world, for it sits atop the rocky bluff, Mount Moriah, where Abraham is said to have offered his son Isaac to God, and where the great Jewish temple was erected by Solomon and later rebuilt by Herod, only to be destroyed by the Romans. The centralised form of the Dome of the Rock was inspired by early Christian churches, perhaps the rotunda of the nearby Church of the Holy Sepulchre. Its octagonal plan, generated by geometrical means, is covered by a double-shelled wooden dome set on a tall drum. The interior, with its rich mosaic decoration, has a double ambulatory to allow easy circulation for pilgrims. The shrine was re-covered in multicoloured tiles in the 17th century, and its resplendent gold leaf-covered dome stands as a familiar landmark in the troubled cityscape of Jerusalem.

30. *Al-Masjid al-Haram*, Mecca, 7th century with later rebuildings (Saudi Arabia)

30

31. *Great Mosque*, Córdoba, begun in 785-786 (Spain)

The Mezquita of Córdoba is one of the oldest mosques in existence, and bears eloquent witness to the early Islamic presence on the Iberian Peninsula. It was one of the first buildings erected in Spain by the Umayyad dynasty, which had been uprooted from its former stronghold in Damascus. Built over a 7th-century Visigothic church, the mosque was begun by Emir Abd ar-Rahman I. It was originally connected to the Caliph's palace by a raised walkway. At the time of its construction, this was the second-largest mosque in the world. Fronted by an open courtyard, the huge prayer hall is supported by a forest of columns in various stones, many taken from older Roman buildings. These support polychromatic double arches, which are horseshoe-shaped below and semicircular above; this was a structural innovation that helped to carry the high ceiling. Elsewhere in the building are complex vaulted and ribbed domes, likely showing the influence of Persian architecture. The mosque has an unorthodox orientation, with the mihrab facing south. After the Spanish reconquest of Córdoba in 1236, the mosque was turned into a Catholic church.

32. *Ummayad Mosque*, Damascus, 706-715 (Syria)

33

33. *Mosque of Al Mutawakkil (Great Mosque of Samarra)*, Samarra, 847-851 (Iraq)

34. *Al Azhar Mosque*, Cairo, 970-972 (Egypt)

35. *Mosque of Uqba*, Kairouan, 670 (Tunisia)

36. *Al Hakim Mosque*, Cairo, 990-1013 (Egypt)

34

35

36

37

37. *Kutubiya Mosque*, Marrakesh, 1158 and later (Morocco)

38. *Friday Mosque*, Isfahan, rebuilt after 1121-1122 (Iran)

38

39. *Al-Aqsa Mosque*, Jerusalem, rebuilt 1033 (Israel)

39

40

40

40. *Krak des chevaliers*, Qalaat al Hosn, c. 1100-1200 (Syria)

Greatest of the Crusader fortresses in the Holy Land, Krak des chevaliers, or the "fortress of the knights," served as the headquarters of the Knights Hospitaller. T. E. Lawrence found it to be "perhaps the best preserved and most wholly admirable castle in the world." One of several such strongholds that formed a huge defensive ring around the territory that had been conquered and controlled by the Crusaders, Krak des chevaliers was erected on top of an older Muslim fortress on a hill overlooking the main route to the Mediterranean. The Hospitallers greatly expanded the original fortress to reflect the latest French ideas on fortification. The main building, surrounded by two ranks of thick walls with twenty towers, had extensive storage facilities, stables, a chapel and a meeting hall. Water cisterns allowed it to withstand long sieges, perhaps up to five years. At its height, the castle housed a garrison of some 2000 men. After a series of unsuccessful sieges through the 12th century, it was eventually taken by Sultan Baibars in 1271, forcing the Knights to depart for Rhodes. The interior features rare frescoes from the Crusader period. It is now owned by the Syrian government and was made a UNESCO World Heritage Site in 2006.

41. *Citadel of Saladin*, Cairo, 1183 and later (Egypt)

42. *Bahla Fort*, Oasis of Bahla, 12th-15th century (Oman)

41

42

43. *Great Mosque*, Djenné, 13th century (rebuilt in 1907) (Mali)

44. *Citadel of Aleppo*, Aleppo, 1230 (Syria)

Djenné, which was converted to Islam in 1240, was a major city in the Mali and Songhai Empires. Built on the site of an earlier palace, this huge religious complex eloquently reflects the incursion of Islam into West Africa. The mosque is constructed largely of bricks of sun-dried mud coated with mud plaster, and as such is the largest adobe building in the world. The rounded appearance of its envelope reminds many people of a giant sand castle. As with all such structures, its thick walls serve to regulate the temperature, protecting the interiors from heat during the daytime and radiating stored warmth at night. Ostrich eggs, symbols of purity and abundance, provide a covering for its towers and spires. The prayer hall is supported by 90 wooden columns. Because of regular flooding the mosque is built on a raised platform. The present structure dates from a rebuilding of 1907. Its custodians have resisted any modernisation, allowing only the installation of a loudspeaker system. The mosque is kept in good condition by means of an annual festival, in the course of which any damage is repaired. It was declared a UNESCO World Heritage Site in 1988.

45. *Stelae and capitol of Aksum*, Aksum, 0-1250 (Ethiopia)

46. *Ruins of Kilwa Kisiwani*, Kilwa, 13th-16th century (Tanzania)

47

47. The Great Enclosure and other stone ruins at Great Zimbabwe, c. 1200-1440 (Zimbabwe)

The mysterious stone ruins at Great Zimbabwe are some of the oldest and most impressive monuments of southern Africa. Great Zimbabwe, or the "house of stone," is an extensive area containing hundreds of such structures. Archaeology has shown this to have been an important trading centre, with a network of contacts stretching across the continent. The Enclosure may have held as many as 18,000 inhabitants at its height. The ruins are notable for their eschewal of rectilinearity: their walls form a series of fluent and elegant curves. Most impressive of all the sites is the Great Enclosure, whose walls extend for some 250 metres and reach 11 metres in height. The first Europeans to see the ruins were Portuguese traders in the 16th century. During the subsequent imperialist era, the notion that the structures were the work of Africans was widely discredited for racial and political reasons, but excavations have since proved that they were indeed an indigenous production, probably built by a people belonging to the Bantu linguistic family. It is unclear why the settlements were abandoned, but drought, disease or a decline in trade are current theories. The modern-day nation of Zimbabwe is named for the ruins.

48. *Madrasa Al-Firdaws*, Aleppo, mid-13th century (Syria)

49

49. *The Alhambra, Granada, 13th-14th century (Spain)*

The royal citadel of the Alhambra was the centre of Muslim power in southern Spain. It was begun in the 13th century by Muhammad I Ibn al-Ahmar and added to piecemeal over a number of decades. The Alhambra comprises both a great fortress with 23 towers as well as a cool and luxurious retreat for the Caliphs, with many spacious rooms, courtyards and gardens. A variety of media, including stucco, colourful mosaic tiles, marbles and bas-relief sculpture, was used to ornament its walls. In many of the Alhambra's interior spaces we find muqarnas *vaulting, a decorative ceiling treatment in carved plaster that has a purely visual rather than a structural function. The most famous of the Alhambra's outdoor spaces is the gracefully arcaded Lion Court: with its central fountain and four sunken water channels it is said to represent an earthly manifestation of paradise. Some of the complex was destroyed and built over when the Christians retook the region in 1492, but much remains. The Alhambra's name means "red" in Arabic, referring to the colour of the bricks of its outer defensive walls.*

50. *The Church of St. George,* Lalibela, c. 1250 (Ethiopia)

51. *Great Mosque of Divrigi,* Divrigi, c. 1299 (Turkey)

52. *Sultan Qala'un funerary complex,* Cairo, c. 1285 (Egypt)

53. *Mosque-Madrassa of Sultan Hassan,* Cairo, 1356-1363 (Egypt)

54

54. *Topkapi Palace*, Istanbul, 1459 and later (Turkey)

This immense palace, which served as the official residence of the Ottoman Sultans from 1465 to 1853, is set on a prominent point overlooking the Golden Horn. Built on the site of the ancient Greek city of Byzantium, it was begun shortly after the conquest of Constantinople by Sultan Mehmed II. Insulated from the outer world, the palace was largely self-sufficient, having its own water supply, cisterns and kitchens. As many as 4000 people lived here at its height. Its plan is roughly rectangular, organised around four main courtyards, but frequent extensions and alterations resulted in an asymmetrical complex of hundreds of rooms, interspersed with gardens. Life in the palace was carried out according to strict ceremony, and speaking was forbidden in the inner courtyards. The innermost spaces were the private and inviolable sanctum of the Sultan and his harem. In 1921, with the end of the Ottoman Empire, the Topkapi Palace was turned into a museum. Its name, which dates only from the 19th century, means "cannon gate," after a portal once located nearby.

55

55. *Chinli Kiosk, Topkapi Palace*, Istanbul, 1473 (Turkey)

56

56. *Fortress city of Fasil Ghebbi*, Gondar, c. 16th-17th century (Ethiopia)

57

57. *Bayezid II Mosque*, Istanbul, 1501-1506 (Turkey)

58. *Tomb of Askia*, Gao, c. 1550 (Mali)

59. *Sankore Mosque (University of Sankore)*, Timbuktu, 1581 (Mali)

60. **Mimar Koca Sinan ibn Abd al-Mannan**, also known as **Sinan**, *Mosque of Sultan Suleiman the Magnificent*, Istanbul, 1550-1558 (Turkey)

This spectacular mosque, which occupies a prominent location near the harbor, is only one part of a larger religious complex featuring a cemetery, madrasas, shops, a caravanserai and many social services. Typical in many respects of Ottoman religious buildings, it is one of the masterworks of the architect and engineer Koca Sinan (c. 1490-1588). Though Sinan was not Muslim by birth, he was trained as a Janissary and served as the official court architect to the Sultans of Constantinople for half a century. The mosque was visibly inspired by the nearby Byzantine church of Hagia Sophia (532-537), which had been converted into a mosque after the Muslim conquest of 1453. Following its prototype, the great prayer hall of the mosque is covered by a large dome and buttressed by two lower, half-domed spaces, though Sinan's plan simplifies and streamlines that of the earlier building. Four needle-sharp minarets rise at the corners. The mosque is preceded by a large arcaded courtyard, while Suleiman is buried in an octagonal mausoleum in the cemetery behind. Sinan kept a modest residence for himself at the northern corner of the site.

60

61. **Sedefkar Mehmet Aga**, *Mosque of Sultan Ahmed*, also known as *The Blue Mosque*, Istanbul, 1609-1617 (Turkey)

62. *Sultan Qansuh al-Ghuri Caravanserai*, Cairo, 1504-1505 (Egypt)

61

62

3. **Mimar Koca Sinan ibn Abd al-Mannan**, also known as **Sinan**, *The Selimiye Mosque*, Edirne, 1568-1574 (Turkey)

64. **Mimar Koca Sinan ibn Abd al-Mannan**, also known as **Sinan**, *Shehzade Mosque*, Istanbul, 1545-1548 (Turkey)

5. *Nuruosmaniye Mosque*, Istanbul, 1748-1755 (Turkey)

66. *Shah Mosque*, Isfahan, begun in 1611 (Iran)

67

67. *Tower Houses*, Sana'a, 8th-19th century (Yemen)

68. Sir Herbert Baker, *Union Buildings*, Pretoria, 1910-1913 (South Africa)

69. Hassan Fathy, *New Gourna*, near Luxor, 1948 and later (Egypt)

70. Fareed El-Shafei, *Mausoleum of the Aga Khan*, Aswan, 1959 (Egypt)

71

71. **Arthur Erickson**, *Etisalat Tower*, Dubai, 1986 (United Arab Emirates)

72

72. **Henning Larsen**, *Ministry of Foreign Affairs*, Riyadh, 1982-1984 (Saudi Arabia)

73

73. **Michel Pinseau**, *Hassan II Mosque*, Casablanca, 1986-1993 (Morocco)

74

74. **Snøhetta**, *Bibliotheca Alexandrina*, Alexandria, 1995-2002 (Egypt)

This great new library, repository of knowledge for researchers from Egypt and neighbouring Islamic countries, deliberately recalls the illustrious precedent of the Library of Alexandria, which was utterly destroyed in ancient times. In 1974, the University of Alexandria decided to build its library on a site close to where the original building once stood. An international effort spearheaded by Egyptian President Hosni Mubarek and supported by UNESCO was launched, and a design competition was held in 1988. From over 1400 entries the Norwegian firm Snøhetta was chosen to build the new library. In plan, the major building is circular, while in profile it features 11 staggered levels that cascade down to the Mediterranean. The main reading room is lit by a glass-paneled roof some 32 metres above the floor. The walls are of Aswan granite, engraved with characters from 120 languages. Though the library has shelf space for 8 million books, it is far from full, relying mainly on donations from foreign countries to build up its holdings; it houses, however, the only copy and external backup of the Internet Archive.

75

76

75. **Moshe Safdie**, *Yad Vashem Holocaust Memorial*, Jerusalem, begun in 1953 (new buildings 1993-2005) (Israel)

76. **Zvi Hecker**, *Spiral Apartment House*, Ramat Gan, 1984-1990 (Israel)

77

77. **Peter Barber**, *Villa Anbar*, Dammam, 1992 (Saudi Arabia)

78. **Norman Foster** and **Buro Happold**, *Al Faisaliyah Tower*, Riyadh, 2000 (Saudi Arabia)

79. **Ellerbe Becket, Omrania & Associates**, *Kingdom Centre*, Riyadh, 2000 (Saudi Arabia)

80. **Carlos Ott**, *National Bank of Dubai*, Dubai, 1996-1998 (United Arab Emirates)

81

81. **Skidmore, Owings & Merrill (SOM)**, *Burj Dubai*, Dubai, 2004-2009 (United Arab Emirates)

The tallest building on earth even before it was completed, the Burj Dubai skyscraper was designed by Adrian Smith, who worked with the American architectural firm SOM until 2006. The anticipated height of the tower was left vague during its construction, but it is expected to top out at over 800 metres. Containing offices, luxury residences and a hotel, it is part of the larger "Downtown Dubai" project meant to attract visitors and investors to this small but very wealthy emirate. The tower consists of a central core surrounded by three tall elements that form a series of spiraling setbacks as they rise: in this respect it generally resembles the bundled tube form of the Sears Tower in Chicago (n° 959), also by SOM, as well as Frank Lloyd Wright's proposal for a 'Mile-High' tower of the 1950s. The building's three-lobed footprint is said to be derived from floral patterning in Islamic architecture. Its lower part has a frame of special pressure-and heat-resistant reinforced concrete; during the construction process this was mixed with ice and poured at night to allow even curing. The tower's budget and construction methods have been a source of controversy, costing over 4 billion dollars.

▶82. **Tom Wright**, *Burj al Arab hotel*, Dubai, 1993-1999 (United Arab Emirates)

ASIA AND OCEANIA

India and Southeast Asia

Little is known of the cultures that produced such prehistoric Indian cities as Harappa and Mohenjo-Daro (n° 85), which flourished along the banks of the Indus from the 3rd millennium BCE. Laid out on a grid oriented to the cardinal directions, these settlements' advanced refinements—raised citadels on stepped terraces, sewers, running water for domestic use and large ritual baths—rival those of Sumerian cities of the time, though they are oddly lacking in large royal tombs or religious buildings. In general however, the architectural traditions of the Indian subcontinent—and indeed its surviving monuments—are largely religious in nature, focused on great temple complexes. Architectural style varied according to successive ruling regimes, who dictated the favoured religious system. Four major epochs can be discerned. The most ancient Indian culture, the forerunner of modern Hinduism, is sometimes termed Indo-Aryan, and lasted from about 1500 BCE until about 1200 CE. In the 3rd century BCE the great ruler Asoka imported skilled artisans from Persia to initiate a tradition of skilled stone carving. This period also saw the creation of the first Buddhist monuments, a religion that arose in the 6th century. Substantial Buddhist *stupas* (gated and domed mounds, serving as centres of pilgrimage), *chatiyas* (temples) and *viharas* (monasteries) can be found in southern India, and—as at Ajanta—often utilise natural caves or are cut into rock hillsides. The Kailasa Temple at Ellora (n° 92) (750 CE), devoted to Hinduism, Buddhism and Jainism, is part of a great complex of rock-cut architecture at the site. Excavated out of a 2-km stretch of basalt cliff, it was begun by vertical excavation: carvers cut down through the living rock, removing some 200,000 tons of material to create a complex monolithic structure featuring tall monuments and multi-storied buildings with highly ornate wall carvings.

From the 7th century the Brahman culture erected monumental, free-standing temples, many of which still survive. Though varying by region, Hindu temples generally take the form of a walled compound enclosing a tall *vimana* (shrine), a hall of columns and lesser buildings. They are notable for their very rich, indeed overwhelming, profusion of decorative and representational carving, sometimes exhibiting erotic forms. (This relates largely to a Tantric belief that sexual activity can represent an ecstatic union of the human and the divine realms.) The Kandariya Mahadeva temple at the royal city of Khajuraho (n° 109) (c. 1050), for example, was lavishly funded and ornamented. Set on a tall plinth, it features a mountain-like arrangement of multiple towers positioned in successive order of height. Its upper levels are encrusted with densely-packed relief carvings.

India's second major period of architecture, which lasted from the 12th through the 18th centuries, was precipitated by the arrival of Islamic invaders from Afghanistan, who established a new capital at Delhi. While politically turbulent, this era witnessed a boom in monumental construction, especially with the rise of the Mughal dynasty from the 16th century. The Muslims introduced several new building types to India from the Middle East, notably the mosque with its vast prayer hall and minarets. Indian mosques consequently betray strong influence from Persian prototypes, and are notable for the increasing refinement of their masonry and decorative stone carving. This trend is most famously represented by the funerary complex known as the Taj Mahal at Agra (n° 147) (c. 1630-1653), though technically this is not a mosque. At the same time, the Muslims launched an extensive and long-lived campaign to convert or destroy all Hindu temples, with the result that the north of India is largely devoid of such structures, except in the remotest regions. The third and fourth major periods of Indian architecture, as discussed below, began with the British Raj, and saw widespread importation of Western styles and typologies into the subcontinent.

Moving further east, we see that Hinduism and Buddhism soon reached more southerly parts of Asia, including Burma, Indonesia and Indo-China, producing extraordinary temple complexes of unprecedented form and scale. The great 9th-century shrine at Borobodur (n° 104), Indonesia, for example, is the largest Buddhist temple in the world. Its huge, symmetrical plan is oriented to the cardinal directions, while its profile consists of a series of superimposed terraces that symbolically represents the successive stages of enlightenment of a Buddhist pilgrim. Another great temple, the 12th-century complex of Angkor Wat in Cambodia (n° 111), again manifests a seemingly endless sequence of platforms, galleries, porches and towers, and is representative of the achievements of the Khmer civilisation.

China

Chinese civilisation arose along the valley of the Yellow River in the 2nd millennium BCE. Monumental architecture first began to appear in the 3rd century BCE under the Ch'ing dynasty, which united the country for the first time. Its greatest built legacy of this period is, of course, the Great Wall (n° 83), which guards the northern border of the kingdom, though in the centuries since it has been rebuilt many times. In later periods Chinese cities were among the most advanced in the world. Yet little Chinese architecture dating from before the Ming period (1368-1644) survives. This is largely because most honorific buildings above the level of the stone foundations were constructed of pine or cedar wood, which has since decomposed. Stone vaulting was generally reserved for tomb structures or, later, city walls and gateways. Pagodas provide occasional exceptions: the Great Wild Goose Pagoda (n° 94), for example, a very tall building erected during the Tang Dynasty (in the 7th century) as part of a monastery, was first built of rammed earth with a stone facing and later rebuilt in brick.

It was nevertheless China's innovations in timber construction that proved most influential throughout Asia, and its traditions changed little over the centuries. Simple trabeated constructions in wood can be found as early as prehistoric times in China, and it might be said that the column (rather than the solid wall) remained the basic unit of building over the centuries. Timber was nevertheless scarce in the central part of the country, and early wooden structures made use of relatively thin columns, wide bays and walls of light infill. Most Chinese utilitarian structures—houses, fortifications and military structures—were built of rammed earth or brick, while wood was used largely for honorific buildings. The repetitive bays of this framed wooden architecture necessarily relied on a simple modular grid system, and a set of standard proportions came to be codified for Imperial use in Li Chieh's Sung-era treatise *Methods and Designs in Architecture* (1103). The characteristic curving roof of the Chinese temple, with its wide eaves, terracotta tiling and increasingly complex systems of bracketing, became the focus of carpentry skill and decorative attention. A characteristic example might be the Temple of Heaven in Beijing (n° 131) (1406-1420 and later), whose circular superstructures of timber rest on a tall marble base. Chinese palaces were generally of one storey, and like temples, were rarely freestanding but incorporated into larger compounds of buildings and courtyards. Here one must look at the 15th-century Forbidden City in Beijing (n° 128), a succession of vast halls and courtyards linked by marble balustrades. This was for almost five centuries the residence of the Chinese emperors. Based on a strict axial symmetry, its plan takes the form of a vast rectangle surrounded by a wide moat and a high wall. Its numberless buildings offer some of the best examples of Chinese palatial architecture, and it now constitutes the largest collection of ancient wooden structures in the world. Entering from Tiananmen Square, foreign ambassadors would have to pass through an intimidating sequence of huge gates and courts before arriving at the Hall of Supreme Harmony; this served as an audience hall for the emperor who received visitors while sitting on a tall dais.

Buddhist temples in China tended to follow the lead of Han dynasty palaces, but introduced a new architectural form of Indian origin: the pagoda. (Extensive underground sanctuaries also follow Indian precedent.) The oldest extant Chinese example dates from the 6th century, and—as noted above—tall and impressive structures in wood and brick from the Tang dynasty (618-906) and later are among China's oldest surviving monuments. Starting from a square or hexagonal base, the pagoda is formed of superimposed stories of diminishing width with decorative treatment of bracketing and roofs. Elaborate and colourful pagodas of this type continued to be built through the 19th century.

Japan and Korea

Some of Japan's oldest architectural monuments are its great Shinto shrines, notably those at Ise (n° 89) and Isumo. Chinese building practises, particularly the knowledge of timber construction, were carried with Buddhist missionaries to Korea and Japan in the 6th century. Many of the early temples at the capital city of Nara reflect such Chinese influence, and the complex at Horyu-ji (n° 93) is one of the oldest. The capital moved to Kyoto in 794, and the city is full of temples erected due to the patronage of the Emperor and his court. Among the other antiquities of Japan are the so-called 'keyhole tombs,' or tumuli (*kofun*), the most notable of

which is that of the Emperor Nintoku (5th century). Located near Osaka, this monumental burial mound is 486 metres long and 35 metres high, consisting of a keyhole-shaped island in which one end is round and the other trapezoidal. Equally impressive is the later Japanese tradition of feudal castle construction, which was precipitated by the turbulent political situation of the 16th century: at Osaka, Himeji (n° 137) and other locations, tall multi-gabled towers set atop moated stone foundations dominate the landscape.

The 19th and 20th Centuries

The linked rise of imperialism and industrialism radically altered the architectures of Asia and Australasia, largely supplanting native traditions with Western styles and techniques. In India the British Raj of 1858-1947 saw the importation of European traditions for churches, railway stations and the offices and homes of colonial administrators in Madras, Calcutta and elsewhere. Towards the end of this period we need only look at the monumental governmental complex at New Delhi, designed by Sir Herbert Baker and Sir Edwin Lutyens in a Classical style inflected by Mughal traditions, to see the imperial machine in operation. A new period of Indian architecture opens up with independence and nationhood for India, Pakistan and Bangladesh, one that has witnessed attempts to come to terms both with the technical and aesthetic innovations of Western modernism as well as such pressing social realities as overpopulation and poverty. Even after independence, however, India has tended to look to the West for inspiration, and in the 1950s and 1960s it was the French-Swiss architect Le Corbusier who was chosen to design the new capital city of Chandigarh in the Punjab (n° 165), and the American Louis Kahn who took charge of the government buildings of Dhaka, Bangladesh (n° 166). In recent years, Indian architects such as Charles Correa and Balkrishna Doshi, though clearly influenced by their Western mentors, have worked to generate an appropriately hybrid modernism for their native country, one that can reflect both new approaches and traditional regional concerns.

With the exception of a brief incursion of the Italian Baroque through Jesuit influence in the early 18th century, China remained closed to foreign architectural trends until the early 20th century. Contrary to what happened in Japan, a subsequent period of hybrid Western-Asian building later gave way to an implicit adoption of modernist principles, and in recent years the opening of Chinese markets to the West has led to an extraordinary boom in highrise architecture in Beijing and other economic zones. Japan, after its opening to the West in the mid-19th century, has gradually assumed its position in the forefront of contemporary architecture. Foremost among 20th century Japanese architects was Kenzo Tange, who began his career by designing the Peace Centre in Hiroshima. Tange's primary influence—as was that of his teacher Kunio Maekawa (who worked in the master's Paris atelier) and many other later Japanese architects, including Tadao Ando—is that of Le Corbusier. Following Le Corbusier's Brutalist deployment of raw concrete in bold and striking forms, Japan continues to set the world benchmark of skilful and elegant concrete construction. Towards the end of the 20th century, the increasingly futuristic approach of some Japanese architects led to a kind of modernist 'Baroque' that has produced formally complex and expressive results.

A typically forward-looking monument of the present era in Asian architecture is represented by C.Y. Lee and Partners' Taipei 101 tower in Taiwan (n° 190) (1999-2004), a centre for international finance. Its 101 stories embody a fusion of Western technology and modernist aesthetics with Asian economic might and traditional iconography. Innovative engineering— including a huge steel pendulum suspended between the 92nd to the 88th floors as a giant tuned mass damper to offset deflection of the building in high winds—

makes it an extremely stable structure, able to withstand earthquakes and typhoons. At the same time, an elaborate cosmological and numerological symbolism has been claimed for the tower, and the repeated segmentation of its envelope suggests a pagoda form.

Australia and Oceania

Over millennia the indigenous peoples of Australia and the South Sea islands developed timeless building traditions suited to local ecological conditions that nevertheless did not match Western expectations of what formal architecture should look like; their cultural productions were largely ignored by the first Western colonists. The first Western-style monumental architecture in Australia, dating from the early 19th century, evinced a late version of English Georgian Classicism when it aspired to formal elegance. Much building was necessarily utilitarian in character, though military and penal constructions could nevertheless assume a severe grandeur, and ornamental ironwork, as applied to balconies, came to characterise more upscale domestic architecture. Fuelled by the wealth generated by the Gold Rush, Australian cities soon came to display impressive examples of High Victorian-style architecture based on contemporary British modes and models. Foreign influence remained decisive through much of the 20th century, whether in the new capital city of Canberra (designed by Walter Burley Griffin, a onetime partner of Frank Lloyd Wright), or the famous Sydney Opera House (n° 163) (by the Danish architect Jørn Utzon, finished by others). Of native Australian architects, the late Harry Seidler remains the most prominent, though the buildings of Glenn Murcutt have recently aroused global interest among architectural professionals for their sensitive response to site and climate.

▶84. Mahabodi Temple, Bodh Gaya, Bihar, 250 BCE with later reconstructions (India)

84

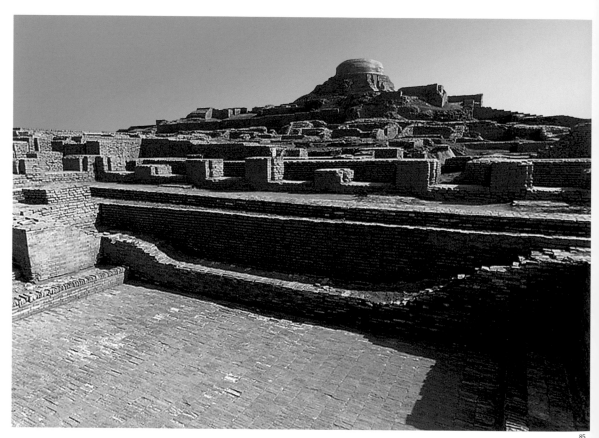

85. Ruins at Mohenhjo-Daro, Mohenjo-Daro, c. 2600-1900 BCE (Pakistan)

86

86. *Great Stupa*, Sanchi, Madhya Pradesh, begun in the 3rd century BCE (India)

The Buddhist stupa *typology evolved from domical earth mounds over the tombs of holy men, which were the focus of pilgrimages. Its form was standardised by the emperor Asoka, the first Indian ruler to be converted to Buddhism. The domical form of the building is often said to represent the vault of heaven. As here, a balustraded fence (*harmika) *typically encloses the* stupa, *symbolising the enclosed garden where the Buddha achieved enlightenment. This is further referenced by the stylised bodhi* tree (a three-tiered, umbrella-like motif known as a chatra) *on top of the mound, which at the same time emphasises the symbolic role of the* stupa *as an axis mundi, or vertical route of ascension to the heavenly realm. Four doorways, aligned roughly to the cardinal directions, represent the four winds. Monumental gateways, or* toranas, *covered with low-relief carvings of Buddhist imagery, provide access points. A short stairway on the south side leads to the circular walkway used by circumambulating priests. Like many other stupas, this important early example was attached to a monastery, of which only vestiges now remain.*

87. *Ajanta caves,* Maharashtra, 2nd century BCE and later (India)

88. *Chaitya Hall,* Karli, Maharashtra, c. 150 BCE (India)

89

89. *Ise shrine*, Uji-Yamada, early 1st century CE with later periodic rebuildings (Japan)

Part of a larger complex with housing for pilgrims and priests, the Ise shrine is a major focus of Shinto worship in Japan. The inner shrine, dedicated to the sun goddess, is situated some kilometres from the outer shrine, which is dedicated to the goddess of agriculture and the earth. Built on a domestic scale, the inner shrine is regularly duplicated every 20 years on an immediately adjacent site in order to maintain it in a state of perfect preservation and cleanliness; the older building is then demolished. The central post of each reincarnation, however, is always retained in situ to provide a sense of continuity. The present building manifests forms and building techniques dating from the 7th century and earlier, thus preserving many archaic forms of timber construction that would otherwise have disappeared, notably the crossed wooden members (chigi) of the gable ends and the stubby wooden billets (katsuogi) ranged along the roof ridge. Its form in fact seems to derive from early designs for raised granaries. Reflecting Shinto views on ritual purity, visitors are not allowed near the innermost precinct, where priests prepare a daily offering of food for the deity.

90

90. *Mỹ Sơn*, Quảng Nam province, 4th-13th century (Vietnam)

91. *Yungang caves*, Datong, late 5th century (China)

92. *Kailasa Temple*, Ellora, Maharashtra, 750 (India)

93. *Horyu-ji temple complex*, Nara Prefecture, 7th century (Japan)

Horyu-ji is the oldest surviving Buddhist temple in Japan, and one of the oldest extant wooden buildings in the world. This monastic complex dates from near the time of the introduction of Buddhism into Japan in the 6th century. It was built by Shotoku Taishi, an early convert to the new religion. All the buildings are contained within an enclosed courtyard, though the colonnaded outer walls were added some time later. The plan, while essentially regular, evidences a subtle asymmetry in the placement and size of the buildings, giving a living, dynamic quality to the composition. The trabeated mode of building, upward curve of the roof eaves and complex system of bracketing are all essentially Chinese in origin. Typical of many later Buddhist temples in Japan, Horyu-ji features a multi-tiered pagoda housing symbolic relics of the Buddha, a monumental gateway, a lecture hall (kodo) and an image hall (kondo). A single wooden post serves as the 'heart' of the pagoda, rising from the floor to the uppermost finial, while its elegantly flared eaves are supported on 'cloud-pattern' bracketing.

94. *Great Wild Goose Pagoda*, Ci'en Temple, Xi'an, Shanxi Province, 652 with later rebuildings (China)

The Chinese pagoda typology visibly derives from that of the Indian stupa, and it remains one of the chief vehicles of Buddhist ritual throughout the Far East. One of the most ancient of such structures surviving in China, the Great Wild Goose Pagoda was erected during the Tang Dynasty as part of a monastery. It originally had five stories and was about 54 metres tall. This early version, built of rammed earth with a stone facing, collapsed within a few decades, but was rebuilt in 704. The second version, in brick, was damaged by a huge earthquake in 1556, which removed three of its ten stories, leaving it with the current seven. Now 64 metres tall, the pagoda was completely renovated in the Ming Dynasty and again in 1964. The exterior is simple and blocky in appearance, the sheer brick façades relieved only by decorative banding between levels and an articulation of shallow pilasters and small arched openings. The pagoda contains sutras and statuettes of the Buddha brought to China from India. It is related to the Small Wild Goose Pagoda, also in Xi'an.

▼95. *Pancha Ratha (The Five Ratha)*, Mamallapuram, Tamil Nadu,
    c. mid-7th century (India)

94

96. *Cave-temples at Longmen*, Luoyang City, Henan Province, 672-675 (China)

97. *Elephanta Island*, also known as *Gharapuri Island*, Mumbai harbour, Maharashtra, 9th century and later (India)

98. *Daibutsuden (Great Buddha Hall), Todai-ji*, Nara, 738 with later rebuildings (Japan)

99. *Great Kyz Kala*, Merv, 651 (Turkmenistan)

100. *Jotab-dong Pagoda*, Gyenongsangbuk-do, 750 (South Korea)

101

101. *Foguang Temple*, Yingxian, Shanxi Province, 1056 (China)

102. *Somapura Mahavihara,* also known as *Paharpur,* Naogaon, c. 800 and later (Bangladesh)

103. *Temple complex at Bagan,* Bagan, 10th-13th century (Myanmar)

105

104

104. *Borobudur*, Java, c. 800-850 (Indonesia)

Illustrative of the spread of Buddhism from India to Southeast Asia through the initiative of traveling merchants, the great complex at Borobodur is said to be the largest Buddhist temple in the world. With its roughly square base, the shrine's plan is symmetrical and oriented to the cardinal directions. There are access stairs at the centre of each side. The construction is of dark volcanic stone, built over a low natural hill to reach a height of 31.5 metres. In profile, the shrine comprises a series of terraces that symbolically represent the stages of enlightenment of a Buddhist pilgrim who moves from ignorance to illumination (nirvana). Visitors would walk for several kilometres around the perimeters of the first four tiers in succession. Along the way they would encounter a continuous sequence of low-relief stone friezes illustrating many aspects of Buddhist iconography. The three concentric circular tiers that crown the complex feature 72 small stupas in the form of perforated, bell-shaped domes, each containing a statue of the Buddha. The pinnacle is occupied by the Great Stupa shrine. Once in a neglected state, the entire site was thoroughly restored from 1972 under the auspices of UNESCO.

105. *Yunyan Pagoda*, also known as *Huqiu Tower*, Suzhou, 10th century (China)

106. *Prambanan temple compound*, Java, 850 with later reconstructions (Indonesia)

107. *Tomb of the Samanids*, Bukhara, c. 940 (Uzbekistan)

108. *Brihadishwara Temple*, Thanjavur, Tamil Nadu, 11th century (India)

109. *Kandariya Mahadeva Temple*, Khajuraho, Madhya Pradesh, c. 1050 (India)

110. *Lingaraj Temple*, Bhubaneswar, Orissa, 1000 (India)

111. *Angkor Wat temple complex, Angkor, c. 1120 and later (Cambodia)*

One of the largest religious monuments in existence, the temple at Angkor Wat is a source of great national pride—it has appeared on the Cambodian flag since 1863. A great mountain-like assemblage of stone originally dedicated to the Hindu god Vishnu, its order and layout are comparable to the earlier Great Stupa at Borobodur. Angkor Wat was begun by King Suryavarman II, who was later buried there. When completed, it became the royal shrine of the Khmer dynasty, though it was eventually converted to Buddhist uses. Like Borobodur, the temple is largely sculptural rather than spatial in conception. On their quest to reach the top, dedicated visitors would cover many kilometres in circumambulating the multiple terraces. After being attacked in 1431, the complex was largely abandoned except by a colony of monks. Few Western visitors made their way to Angkor Wat before its existence was advertised by the French naturalist Henri Mouhot, who came across it in 1860. Astonished by its size and grandeur, Mouhot wrote that Angkor Wat rivalled the Temple of Solomon and was greater than any ruin left by the Greek and Roman civilisations. The complex was cleared and partly reconstructed in the 20th century.

▶113. *Ho-odo (Phoenix Hall), Byodo-in temple, Uji, c. 1053 (Japan)*

This famous monument of Japanese Buddhism, located just south of Kyoto, exemplifies the otherworldly sect of Pure Land Buddhism that became popular with the Japanese nobility from the 10th century. It was originally constructed by the wealthy Fujiwara clan as part of a rural villa, but was changed to a private temple in 1052 by Fujiwara no Yorimichi. The Phoenix Hall, or Amida Hall, is the only surviving building from this complex. In plan the layout of the Hall is symmetrical, with extensive L-shaped wings in the form of corridors connecting to pavilions on either side; a third corridor extends to the rear. From above, this configuration suggests a bird in flight, an image further echoed in the upward sweep of its eaves. The major external impression of the Ho-odo is of a huge sheltering roof upheld by a complex system of bracketing. The red and gold colourscheme suggests Chinese prototypes. The magnificent interior of the Hall is focused on a large cult image of Amida Buddha in gilded cypress wood, which was created by the famed sculptor Jocho. The inside of the roof displays statues of Chinese phoenixes. Such opulence was intended to suggest the Pure Land paradise of Buddhist teachings.

112. *Ananda Temple, Bagan, 1091-1105 (Myanmar)*

114

115

116

117

114. *Beisi Pagoda*, Suzhou, 1131-1162 (China)

115. *Qutb Minar*, Delhi, 1190s and later (India)

116. *Great South Gate (Nan-daimon) of Todai-ji*, Nara, 1199 (Japan)

This huge wooden gateway serves as the entrance to the monastic complex of Todai-ji, or Eastern Great Temple. One of the most important religious foundations in the old capital city of Nara, Todai-ji was established by the Emperor Shomu in the 8th century as part of his efforts to involve the Japanese people more directly in Buddhist ritual; this was undertaken in the hope that the resultant display of piety would protect the nation from further disaster. The dominant architectural presence at Todai-ji is the Great Buddha Hall, or Daibutsuden, reputedly the largest wooden building in the world; it houses a colossal bronze image of the Buddha that is 16 metres tall. The roof structure of the Great South Gate, exemplary of the 'Great Buddha style,' reflects an evident knowledge of contemporary building practises in Song-dynasty China. Its lower roof is supported by eight tiers of cantilevered brackets, and its upper roof by seven. These brackets are inserted directly into the supporting columns, which are linked by tie-beams. Since the gateway has no ceilings, the complexity of the entire roof structure is visible from inside. Like the other remarkable buildings at Todai-ji, the Nan-daimon has been designated a National Treasure of Japan.

117. **Ali ibn Ibrahim of Nishapur**, *Minaret of Jam*, Firuzkuh, c. 1195 (Afghanistan)

118. *Keshava Temple*, Somnathpur, Karnataka, 13th century (India)

119. *Wat Buddai Svarya Temple*, Ayutthaya, 13th century (Thailand)

120

120. *Swayambhunath Stupa*, Kathmandu Valley, c. 1372 (renovations) (Nepal)

121

121. *Ancient city of Pingyao*, Shanxi Province, 14th century and later (China)

122

122. *Old Sukhothai city*, Sukhothai, 13th-14th century (Thailand)

123

123. *Old town of Lijiang*, Lijiang, c. 1200 and later (China)

124. *Kinkaku-ji*, also known as the *Golden Pavilion*, Kyoto, 1397 (rebuilt in 1955) (Japan)

125. *Mosque city of Bagerhat*, Bagerhat, 15th century and later (Bangladesh)

126. *Great Mosque*, Xi'an, 8th century, 1328-1398 (important renovations) (China)

127. *Jongmyo Shrine*, Jongmyo, 1394 (South Korea)

128. *Forbidden City*, Beijing, 1406-1420 (China)

129. *Changdeok palace*, Seoul, 1405-1412 (South Korea)

130. *Imcheonggak Estate buildings*, Beopheungdong, Andong, Gyeongsangbukdo, 1515 (South Korea)

131. *Temple of Heaven*, Beijing, 1406-1420 and later (China)

Part of a complex of Taoist buildings in Beijing, this great walled temple was erected in the early 15th century by the Yongle Emperor, who also built the Forbidden City. As the Son of Heaven, the Emperor of China was expected to make regular and public sacrifices, and through the Ming and Qing dynasties successive rulers made twice yearly visits to the Temple to pray for a good harvest. Such rituals followed a rigid order, and their details remained highly secret. The temple complex consists of three major buildings. The central Hall of Prayer for Good Harvests, 38 metres tall, is a three-tiered circular building set on a marble base. Its construction is entirely of wood, using no nails. Opposite, to the south, is the smaller Imperial Vault of Heaven, also built on a circular plan. Even further south, accessed by a long stone causeway, is the Altar of Heaven, a three-level circular platform where the Emperor would pray for favourable weather. The complex manifests an elaborate cosmological symbolism in which the juxtaposition of circles and squares represents the unity of Heaven and Earth. Much augmented in the 16th century, the Temple of Heaven was renovated in the 18th century and again for the 2008 Olympics. It was declared a UNESCO World Heritage Site in 1998.

132. *Agra Fort Mosque*, Agra, Uttar Pradesh, 1573 (India)

133. *Isa Khan Niyazi's tomb*, Delhi, 1562-1571 (India)

134. *Lahore Fort*, Lahore, 1566 (Pakistan)

135. *Madrasa of Mir-i Arab*, Bukhara, 1535 (Uzbekistan)

136. *Friday Mosque at Fatehpur Sikri*, Fatehpur Sikri, Uttar Pradesh, c. 1571-1574 (India)

137. *White Heron Castle*, Himeji, begun in 1333 (Japan)

The great fortress at Himeji is of the most spectacular of all Japanese castles, which differ in many respects from their European counterparts. The earliest structure on this site, erected by the warlord Sadanori Akamatusu, is said to date from 1333. From 1601 this was extensively rebuilt by Ikeda Terumasu. Set on a natural outcrop, the castle dominates the city of Himeji, west of Osaka, which grew up around its base. Set on a tall stone podium and surrounded by a moat, the castle is extremely well defended: any attacker would soon become lost in a labyrinthine system of concentric walls, terraces, passages, ramps and fortified gates, all the while coming under attack from galleries above. In fact, Himeji was never besieged or damaged by hostile action. Like all Japanese castles, the central keep is built of wood, though this was made fireproof by a coating of thick plaster. The interiors are remarkably comfortable and elegant for a military building. It is known as the 'white heron' or 'egret' castle because its dramatic composition of flared roofs and white gables suggests a bird about to take flight.

138. *Panch Mahal*, Fatehpur Sikri, Uttar Pradesh c.1570-1585 (India)

139. *Golden Temple*, Amritsar, Punjab, 1585-1604 (India)

140

140. *Charminar Gate*, Hyderabad, Andhra Pradesh, 1591 (India)

141

141. *Katsura Imperial Villa*, Kyoto, c. 1616-1660 (Japan)

This sprawling villa was built as a domestically-scaled palace for the Japanese Imperial family. It was intended mainly as a temporary or seasonal retreat for meditation and relaxation, and especially for viewing the natural world at various times of day and in different seasons. The buildings of Katsura offer an exquisitely refined manifestation of the traditional Japanese aesthetic, particularly the rustic sukiye *style, as evidenced in the five teahouses on the grounds. Its deliberate restraint, or self-conscious austerity, is characteristic of Zen philosophy. The overall plan of the Katsura complex is irregular and additive, but within each building the floor plan is strictly determined by repetition of the standardised module of the* tatami *mat. The cedar framing of the palace is left unfinished, allowing an appreciation of the natural qualities of the material as well as its weathering with time and use. The interiors can be transformed through the opening and closing of sliding rice-paper partitions; along with an abundance of terraces and porches, this helps to break down the interior/exterior dichotomy, a characteristic much admired by visiting modern architects like Walter Gropius.*

2

142. *Potala Palace*, Lhasa, Tibet, 1645 and later (China)

Rising 300 metres above the valley floor, this immense hilltop palace served as the winter residence of the Dalai Lama until 1959, when the fourteenth reincarnation of the Tibetan spiritual leader was forced to flee to India. Begun under Lozang Gyatso, the fifth Dalai Lama, the Palace also served as a seat of government. Copper was poured into its foundations to assist with earthquake stability. Impressively fortress-like in appearance, the Palace's thirteen stories are set on a tall base of canted stone walls with an average thickness of 3 metres. The central portion, with its puce colouration and golden roofs, is known as the Red Palace, and is devoted solely to prayer and study. In plan the Palace forms a giant rectangle of 350 by 400 metres. It contains over a thousand richly ornamented rooms that house countless shrines and statues. The Potala Palace is named after a hill on a cape at the southern tip of India, which was seen as the abode of a revered Bodhisattva. It is now a museum, but the flow of visitors is strictly regulated. It was placed on the UNESCO World Heritage List in 1994.

143. *Gol Gumbaz* (*Dome*, or *Mausoleum of Sultan Muhammad Adil Shah*),
     Bijapur, Karnataka, mid-17th century (India)

144. *Red Fort of Delhi*, Delhi, 1639 (India)

145. *Shir Dor Madrassa*, Samarkand, 1636 (Uzbekistan)

146. *Tomb of Jahangir*, Shahdara, Lahore, 1637 (Pakistan)

147. *Taj Mahal*, Agra, Uttar Pradesh, c. 1630-1653 (India)

This most famous of all Indian monuments superficially resembles a mosque, but its function is in fact funerary and commemorative: it was built as a magnificent tomb for Mumtaz Mahal, the beloved wife of the Mongol emperor Shah Jahan; it now shelters both of their remains. Since the Taj Mahal was intended to be the most beautiful building imaginable, no expense was spared: the most famous architects of the time were hired, as were some 20,000 labourers and skilled artisans from India and neighbouring regions of Central Asia. A monumental gateway to the south guides the visitor into a huge square garden, originally planted with fragrant trees, which is divided into four quadrants by a cruciform arrangement of reflecting canals. Strongly influenced by Persian prototypes, the tomb itself sits on a tall square platform; a slender minaret, as for a mosque, is sited on each of the four corners. This graceful composition is topped by a bulbous onion dome. The tomb is clad in polished white marble, creating a dazzling effect of purity. Since Muslim tradition generally allows no human images to be represented, the carved and inlaid ornamentation is entirely floral, abstract or calligraphic in nature.

147

148. *Labrang Monastery*, southwest of Lanzhou, 1709 (China)

149. *Jantar Mantar astronomical observatory*, Jaipur, Rajasthan, 1727-1734 (India)

Comprising an extraordinary assemblage of large-scale geometrical forms, the Jantar Mantar (or "instrument for calculation") served as an astronomical observatory. It is one of five such sites in west central India which were constructed by Maharaja Jai Singh II of Jaipur, a regional king in the Mughal Empire, between 1724 and 1735; the others were located at Delhi, Ujjain, Varanasi, and Mathura (the only one no longer standing). Each of the observatory's stone devices is of unique configuration and specialised function. Informed by the principles of Islamic astronomy, these were the most advanced astronomical tools in the world at the time of their construction. The great sundial, with its huge triangular gnomon, was calibrated to measure the time of day down to the second, as well as to chart the position of the sun and other heavenly bodies. The Jantar Mantar was part of the new city of Jaipur, whose construction was begun at the same time. Remarkably modern in appearance, the observatory's forms seem to have influenced Le Corbusier in his 20th-century government buildings at Chandigarh.

150. *Badshahi Mosque*, Lahore, 1671-1673 (Pakistan)

151. *Summer Palace and gardens*, Beijing, 1750 and later (China)

152. *Batak Toba houses*, Lake Toba, Sumatra, 1800 (Indonesia)

153. *Hwaseong Fortress*, Suwon, 1794-1796 (South Korea)

154

154. **Frederick William Stevens**, *Chhatrapati Shivaji Terminus*, better known as *Victoria Terminus*, Mumbai, Maharashtra, 1887-1888 (India)

155. *Đình Cẩm Phố Communal House*, Hội An, 1818 (Vietnam)

156. **Lal Chand Ustad**, *Hawa Mahal*, Jaipur, Rajasthan, 1799 (India)

155

156

157

158. Frank Lloyd Wright, *Imperial Hotel*, Tokyo, 1916-1923 (demolished in 1968) (Japan)

Once ranked among the world's most prestigious hotels, Frank Lloyd Wright's Japanese masterwork survives only as a fragment. During his extended stays in Japan, Wright produced a design for a great symmetrical complex that would replace the original wooden building of 1890. In plan, the hotel consisted of two long parallel ranges of rooms enclosing an axial sequence of lobby and courtyard spaces. A large reflecting pool also provided water for fire-fighting. The hotel's unique and even bizarre styling, which juxtaposed dense layerings of horizontal elements with zigzag decoration, owed more to Wright's largely unacknowledged interest in Pre-Columbian architecture than to any Asian precedent. Construction was of poured concrete and concrete blocks, with cladding of red brick and volcanic stone. The Imperial Hotel famously survived the 7.9 magnitude Great Kanto earthquake of 1923 by virtue of its seismic separation joints as well as a broad and shallow foundation, which was designed to float on the muddy subsoil. Though it was demolished in 1968, reassembled portions of the façade and pool can be seen at an outdoor architectural museum near Nagoya.

157. Arthur Benison Hubback, *Kuala Lumpur Railway Station*, Kuala Lumpur, 1910 (Malaysia)

159. Sir Edwin Lutyens, *Viceroy's house, Rashtrapati Bhavan*, New Delhi, 1912-1931 (India)

158

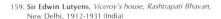

159

160. *Hiroshima Peace Memorial Park* (remains of the *Genbaku Dome*, **Jan Letzel**, 1915), Hiroshima, 1949-2002 (Japan)

161. **Harry Seidler**, *Rose Seidler House*, Turramurra, New South Wales, 1948-1950 (Australia)

162. **Le Corbusier**, *Shodan House*, Ahmedabad, Gujarat, 1956 (India)

163

163. **Jørn Utzon**, *Sydney Opera House*, Sydney, 1957-1973 (Australia)

165. Le Corbusier, *Assembly*, Chandigarh, Punjab, 1952-1959 (India)

Capital of the state of Punjab, Chandigarh was the first modern planned city in Asia. Nehru took a great interest in it, for he hoped it might represent a new India, free from the shackles of an imperialist past. Nevertheless, a team of Western planners was brought in to lay out the new city and its government buildings, and it was the Swiss-French architect Le Corbusier who dominated the project. Manifesting a typically modern approach to urbanism based on Le Corbusier's earlier theoretical model of a 'Radiant City,' Chandigarh was laid out on a grid plan and divided into sectors with zoned areas for work, living and leisure. Le Corbusier also took charge of the design of the High Court, Secretariat, National Assembly and several other buildings. Widely spaced across a broad plain and executed by local artisans in rough-faced reinforced concrete, these appear as powerfully sculptural presences against the distant Himalayas. Much of the unique character of the government buildings derives from the desire for passive heat control, as provided by various shading devices, wind catchers and cooling bodies of water. Le Corbusier's personal trademark, the Open Hand, is now the logo of the city, and is to be found everywhere within it.

166. **Louis Kahn,** *National Assembly,* Dhaka, 1962-1974 (Bangladesh)

164. **Kenzo Tange,** *Olympic Stadium,* Tokyo, 1961-1964 (Japan)

Originally trained in the tradition of Beaux-Arts classicism, Kahn spent many years as an urban planner in his native Philadelphia before emerging as one of the most original and visionary of modern architects. The scale and deceptive simplicity of his buildings has meant that he has sometimes been classified as a Brutalist, but Kahn's ambition was in fact to reconcile contemporary technology, modernist abstraction and traditional monumentality. His success in this difficult task can be judged nowhere better than in his government buildings for the capital city of Bangladesh. Following the precedent of Le Corbusier's Chandigarh, Kahn's great National Assembly, also known as the Jatiya Shangshad Bhaban complex, deploys sculptural forms on a colossal scale. Fortress-like in appearance, the Assembly's rounded volumes are constructed of load-bearing brick walls with reinforced concrete inserts; pierced by huge geometric openings, these constitute a series of hollow shells sheltering a second, internal set of forms, a design strategy which was adopted both for climatic reasons and to suggest associations with great ruins of the past. Construction on the project began in earnest in 1973, only a year before Kahn's death, and it was officially inaugurated only in 1982.

167. *Great Hall of the People,* Beijing, 1959 (China)

166

167

168. **Kenzo Tange**, *Shizuoka Press and Broadcasting Centre, Headquarters Building*, Tokyo, 1967 (Japan)

169. **Kisho Kurokawa**, *Nakagin Capsule Tower*, Tokyo, 1970-1972 (Japan)

170. **Norman Foster**, *Hong Kong and Shanghai Bank*, Hong Kong, 1979-1986 (China)

Rumoured at the time to be the most expensive building per square metre ever constructed, Norman Foster's 47-storey headquarters for the Hong Kong and Shanghai Bank was built on the site of its predecessor of 1935, which was at one time the tallest and most sophisticated building in Asia. As the machine-like articulation of the building suggests, Foster makes little distinction between architecture and engineering: here his team sourced prefabricated elements from all over the world, and the exactitude of the building's technical specifications approached that of aircraft construction. Inspired by bridge design, he divided the skyscraper into five horizontal zones: each is suspended from a steel 'coat hanger' truss to form a series of vertically stacked communities. The main structural piers are pushed out to the corners to maximise stability in typhoons. There is thus no need for a concrete central core: each floor can be completely open. Foster is also keen to foreground human concerns: daylight is channeled into the 10-storey entrance atrium through a system of computer-controlled mirrors that track the progress of the sun. The positioning of the escalators, and much else, was determined by local Feng Shui masters.

171. **Louis Kahn**, *Institute of Public Administration*, Ahmedabad, Gujarat, 1963 (India)

▶172. **Ieoh Ming Pei**, *Bank of China Tower*, Hong Kong, 1982-1990 (China)

171

173

173. **Tadao Ando**, *Rokko Housing One*, Kobe, 1983 (Japan)

Ando, a onetime boxer, truck driver and carpenter, has a direct and pugnacious approach to modern architecture that stresses the simple, the authentic and the elemental. This housing complex, built to cascade down a steep cliff face, allows unobstructed views for all residents. It forms a hillside warren of terraces, walls and balconies, linked by the vertical element of outdoor staircases. As with most of his buildings, Ando employs only cast-in-place concrete, beautifully crafted and finished. The deliberately spartan results reflect a traditional Japanese admiration for simplicity and starkness. Ando's uncompromising geometry, allowing a clear appreciation of the interplay between solid and void, light and shade, further demonstrates his belief that art and nature should be juxtaposed but kept visibly separate. The massively material character of Ando's concrete landmarks grant their inhabitants a needed sense of privacy, shelter and existential grounding, and in this respect are intended to offer a fierce resistance to the placelessness, chaos and superficiality of modern life. A second and larger development, Rokko II, was added in 1993. The complex survived the Great Hanshin Earthquake of 1995 unscathed.

174

174. **Geoffrey Bawa**, *Sri Lankan Parliament, Kotte*, Colombo, 1979-1982 (Sri Lanka)

175. **Fariborz Sahba**, *Baha'i House of Worship,* also known as *The Lotus of Bahapur,* New Delhi, 1986 (India)

176. **Philip Cox, Richardson and Taylor**, *Sydney Maritime Museum,* Sydney, 1986-1988 (Australia)

177. **Aldo Rossi**, *Hotel Il Palazzo*, Fukuoka, 1987 (Japan)

178. **Rafael Viñoly**, *Tokyo International Forum*, Tokyo, 1989-1996 (Japan)

180

181

181. **Christian de Portzamparc**, *Nexus II, Residential Block*, Fukuoka, 1989-1991 (Japan)

182

182. **Kenzo Tange**, *Fuji Television Building*, Tokyo, 1996 (Japan)

180. **Ken Yeang**, *Menara Mesiniaga office tower*, Selangor, 1991-1993 (Malaysia)

◄179. **Renzo Piano**, *Kansai Airport Terminal*, Osaka, 1987-1994 (Japan)

At 1.7 km in length, KIX is the longest airport terminal in the world. Even more remarkably, it is built on the world's largest artificial island, 4 km long, which rises 30 metres from the sea bed in Osaka Bay. One million piers and 69 huge concrete caissons give it a firm foundation, while some 48,000 sunken concrete blocks act as a barrier against typhoons. The island is far from the mainland, accessed by a single bridge 3 km long. The terminal itself was designed by the Renzo Piano Building Workshop with Noriaki Okabe. Its roof is shaped like a huge airfoil: ducts on one side of the building blow air across the curve of the ceiling and collect it on the other side, thus promoting healthy ventilation. Visitors move along the building's immense length on a driverless train system known as the Wing Shuttle. The total construction cost was around 20 billion dollars. Though the weight of fill and buildings means that the island is slowly sinking, its integrity is guaranteed by the use of hydraulic pumps and extensible columns. Kansai Terminal performed well in the Kobe earthquake of 1995, partly because of its use of sliding joints.

183

183. **Norman Foster**, *Hong Kong International Airport*, Chek Lap Kok, Hong Kong, 1992-1998 (China)

185. **Baikdoosan Architects & Engineers**, *Ryugyong Hotel*, Pyongyang, 1992 (North Korea)

186. **Renzo Piano**, *Jean-Marie Tjibaou Cultural Centre*, Nouméa, 1991-1998 (New Caledonia)

◄184. **Cesar Pelli**, *Petronas Towers*, Kuala Lumpur, 1992-1998 (Malaysia)

These 88-storey office towers, built for Malaysia's national oil company, held the world record for height from 1998 to 2004, when they were surpassed by the Taipei 101 tower. Constructed on the site of the city's old racetrack, the twin towers are 451.9 metres in height, slightly taller than the Sears Tower in Chicago (n° 959). Massive foundations, some 200 metres deep, were required to support the weight of the super-high-strength reinforced concrete used for the towers' framework. They are linked between the 41st and 42nd floors by a sky bridge soaring 170 metres above the ground; this unique feature was intended partly as a safety measure, offering an extra route of escape in emergency evacuations. The roughly circular plan of each tower is inflected by multiple protrusions; this was intended to reference an Islamic symbol known as a Rub El Hizb, consisting of two rotated squares around a circle. In the towers' base is a shopping mall and philharmonic hall. The Argentinean-American architect Cesar Pelli has been responsible for some of the most impressive skyscrapers in the world, notably at 1 Canada Place in London's Docklands, Britain's tallest building.

187

188

187. **Denton Corker Marshall**, *Sheep Farm House*, Kyneton, Victoria, 1997 (Australia)

188. **Paul Andreu**, *Shanghai Oriental Arts Centre*, Shanghai, 2000-2004 (China)

189

189. **Tadao Ando**, *Naoshima Contemporary Art Museum*, Gotanji Naoshima-cho, 1992 (Japan)

▶190. **C. Y. Lee and Partners**, *Taipei 101 tower*, Taipei, 1999-2004 (Taiwan)

EUROPE (INCLUDING RUSSIA AND TURKEY)

Since history began to be written at different times in different places, there can be no clear-cut chronology of prehistoric architecture in Europe, but one can trace similarities in form and function among funerary and ritual structures in a number of regions, notably the great stone circles of England (n° 191) and northern France (n° 194), and the remarkable tomb structures of Malta (n° 193). Some of the first inhabitable works of monumental architecture in Europe appear in the Aegean, and first of all on the island of Crete. Minoan buildings, interestingly, were not primarily religious in nature, but residential: the great unfortified Palace at Knossos (n° 192), built from the beginning of the 2nd millennium BCE, comprised a large number of storage spaces and residential chambers densely packed around a central courtyard. Serviced by running water and drainage, the palace rooms featured brilliantly coloured frescoes. The exact usage of many spaces at Knossos is unknown, but its labyrinthine and asymmetrical plan may well have suggested later legends of the Minotaur. Rising in places to three stories in height, the palace apparently made use of sturdy wooden columns that swelled towards the top. All such palaces in Crete were destroyed by a great natural cataclysm around 1400 BCE, only to be discovered, excavated and partly reconstructed by Sir Arthur Evans in the 19th century.

The other great archaeologist of bronze-age Aegean cultures, Heinrich Schliemann, made his sensational discoveries further north, when he unearthed the legendary cities of Troy and Mycenae (n° 197) in the 1870s. Flourishing in the 14th century BCE, the more militaristic Mycenaean civilisation focused on the erection of fortified hilltop residences, such as Tiryns and Mycenae, which were at the same time the headquarters of sophisticated administrations. The royal palaces were planned around a large rectangular audience hall, known as a *megaron*, which later proved to be the ancestor of the *naos*, or enclosed sanctuary, of Greek temples. These citadels were defended by massive walls of irregular masonry, the great size of the individual boulders earning this structural method the epithet of "cyclopean." Associated with these citadels was the distinctive typology of the *tholos*, or "beehive" tomb. Approached by a long stone-lined corridor (*dromos*) cut into the earth, the *tholos* utilised a simple method of corbelling to create a surprisingly tall conical dome of finely-cut stone over the anteroom to the burial chamber.

Following the lead of the Egyptians, the Greeks developed a monumental religious architecture in stone that set the precedent for Western building down to the present day. Excavations have confirmed that the first Greek temples appear to have been of timber and mud construction, though over time these came to be replaced by more durable versions in stone. This meant, however, that structural and decorative forms first deployed in wood were thus duplicated in limestone, setting into motion the development of the Greek Orders—the essential language of the Classical system of architecture. The basic principle of column, capital and entablature was likely picked up from Egypt, but the Greeks, having once established the basic *parti* of their temple, began a long process of experimentation and refinement until a perfected or standardised set of forms and proportions, felt to be the most beautiful, were delineated. The Doric, simplest and most masculine of the Orders, had minimal ornamentation, but its proportions became increasingly

◀191. *Stonehenge*, Wiltshire, c. 2900-1400 BCE (United Kingdom)

This famous circle of standing stones was the focus of successive rebuildings and ritual activities over two millennia, though its original and later purposes have remained obscure. It has at one time or another been suggested that Stonehenge may have served as a place of ritual sacrifice, an observatory, a calendar, a prestigious place of burial and even as a hospital. In its original form it consisted only of a circular ditch with earthworks and simple timber constructions. It is most famous, however, for its circle of roughly dressed megaliths topped with stone lintels, which seem to have been erected at some point between 2900 and 1400 BCE. The lintels are fitted onto the uprights by means of simple ball and socket joints. The central stones are thought to have been an altar of some sort. The significance of Stonehenge is partly astronomical or calendrical, since it seems to be aligned to certain solar events, notably the summer solstice; for a pre-literate people this would have been useful for both ritual and agricultural purposes. Some of the stones weigh up to 50 tonnes. Stonehenge was put on UNESCO's World Heritage list in 1986.

fine-tuned over the centuries, culminating in the extraordinary achievement of the Parthenon in Athens (n° 208). Developed at about the same time was the more feminine Ionic Order, recognisable for its slender proportions and the spiral volutes of its capital. The Corinthian Order, which appeared infrequently on later Greek buildings, is more elaborate and showy, the capital being wrapped with stylised acanthus leaves. In all cases the Greeks relied on a simple system of trabeation, and it might be said that their major achievement was one of supreme aesthetic refinement rather than technical innovation. Another important Greek typology was that of the open-air theatre: the remarkably well-preserved example at Epidauros (n° 212) (c. 350 BCE) was built into a natural hollow in the land and designed to seat 14,000 spectators. Its concentric stone seating once focused on a large *orchestra* area for dancers, an architectural backdrop known as the *skene*, and a raised platform, or *proskenion* (proscenium), where the actors would play their roles.

The Etruscan civilisation, reaching its height on the Italian peninsula in the 6th century BCE, laid the foundations for many later Roman building practises. The Etruscans had already developed a knack for laying out well-planned, serviced and defended city-states like Perugia and Volterra. They focused their decorative impulses on tomb structures: in some cases these constitute remarkable stone replicas of domestic interiors of the time, complete with carved utensils hanging on the walls. The necropolis at Tarquinia (n° 201) (c. 700 BCE), chief of the twelve cities of the Etruscan League, includes some 6000 tombs, many of which have vividly frescoed walls depicting everyday life.

The conquering Romans, then beginning their rise to imperial power, took over the Etruscan model of the temple, which featured a deep columnar porch fronting a dark sanctuary. This local influence was almost immediately overshadowed by the Roman love for everything Greek: the sprawling empire established by Alexander the Great had already spread Hellenic modes of building throughout the eastern Mediterranean, and the three Greek Orders—Doric, Ionic and Corinthian—were then imported wholesale into Italy. If the Romans were not especially original with regard to architectural style, which tended largely towards ever more elaborate and ostentatious versions of Greek forms, they are certainly notable for their engineering prowess, which was not to be equaled for many centuries. The extensive use of the round arch allowed aqueducts of tremendous length to be constructed, and large buildings such as baths and markets could be made durable and fireproof through stone vaulting. The Romans soon broadened their use of the arch into the creation of barrel vaults and domes, allowing monumental architecture to achieve hitherto unsuspected effects of capacious internal space. In this connection, it has often been said that Greek architecture is primarily sculptural (i.e., external) in nature, whereas Roman architecture is spatial. Though masters of stone and brick masonry, it was the Romans' increasing expertise with concrete—made possible by the easy availability of volcanic rock suitable for the mixing of cement—that allowed them to build quickly and on a colossal scale, as witnessed by the coffered dome of the Roman Pantheon (n° 239) or the great vaulted spaces of many of their public buildings. Apart from the round temple, represented in its fullest form by the Pantheon, the Romans developed a variety of new building typologies associated with the administration of large populations of imperial citizens. These included the forum (a religious and civic complex), the basilica (an administrative and legal meeting hall), the amphitheatre for athletic or gladiatorial entertainments, the multi-level apartment block (*insulae*), the public baths (*thermae*) and the triumphal arch. In line with their love of decoration, the Romans preferred to clad their concrete walls with facings of stucco, travertine or multicoloured stone, just as their domestic floors were often covered with mosaics and their walls with fresco paintings. In the same vein, the Greek Orders, though frequently invoked, soon came to assume the character of decorative appendages—half-columns or pilasters—rather than structural units.

The chaotic centuries after the fall of the Roman Empire, which entailed the substantial loss of much architectural and engineering expertise, nevertheless witnessed a slow but determined effort to recapture the forgotten art of stone vaulting. This was applied primarily to the foremost monumental structures of the time: large churches, monasteries and related buildings of a religious character. The earliest dedicated churches in Christendom, as established by the Emperor Constantine, made use of the Roman basilica typology as best suited to the needs of officially sanctioned Christian worship; i.e., the provision of a large gathering space for congregations, circulation routes for pilgrims and visitors, and an increasingly sacred hierarchy of spaces laid out along an axis culminating in an apse or sanctuary, the latter housing the altar as the focus of Christian mystery and sacramental ritual. The old basilica of St. Peter in Rome (324-354), with its *atrium* (forecourt), *narthex* (porch), double aisles, transept and terminal apse, established an important prototype, as did the Church of the Holy Sepulchre in Jerusalem (n° 24) (begun c. 325). Round churches, usually serving as martyria, again derived much of their form and structure from Roman precedent; Santa Costanza in Rome (n° 247) (324) provided the model.

The Byzantine tradition, which emerged from the eastern Roman Empire with its capital at Constantinople, emphasised the sacred symbolism of the dome. Various experiments were made as to how a round dome could be fitted onto a square base by the use of squinches or pendentives. Here the supreme achievement is the great church of Hagia Sophia in Istanbul (n° 254) (523-537), whose plan combines both axial (or basilican) and centralised qualities to focus attention on the great dome, the largest since the Pantheon (n° 239). Its exterior demanded heavy buttressing, partly provided by half-domed chapels. Inside, the resulting effect was one of otherworldly lightness as the shallow dome, springing from a continuous sequence of clerestorey windows, seemed to contemporary chroniclers to be suspended weightlessly from heaven. This essentially anti-tectonic appearance was further heightened by sunbeams picking out details of the dazzling gold mosaics that lined the walls. A contemporary basilican church in Ravenna, Sant'Apollinare in Classe (532-549), which was again built under the patronage of the Emperor Justinian, epitomises the Byzantine preference for a plain exterior and an elaborate interior: the nave arcading rests on marble columns of Classical inspiration, while the great rounded apse, vaulted with a half-dome, glows with vivid mosaics. Such striking and dramatic effects remain the hallmark of the Byzantine tradition to the present day in the domed Orthodox churches of Greece, Russia and other regions.

As Western Europe entered the Dark Ages, most Classical learning was lost or forgotten. Tribal cultures in the north evolved a tradition of large-scale timber construction for halls and similar structures, a tradition that was to persist until the advent of industrialisation. A high point in the recovery of masonry building technique was reached in the early 9th century under the Frankish leader Charlemagne, whose court at Aachen was a deliberate emulation of half-remembered Roman imperial precedent as filtered through Byzantine culture. The centralised chapel of Charlemagne's palace, covered by a dome-shaped vault, drew inspiration from San Vitale in Ravenna (n° 253), and its marble columns, mosaics and bronze fittings were brought from Italy. Larger churches of the Carolingian and succeeding Ottonian periods adopted the basilican plan, which remained a standard feature of church design through the rest of the Middle Ages. After the year 1000, monumental church building exploded throughout the continent. Drawing inspiration from Roman masonry technique (particularly the round arch), the major problem of the builders of the so-called Romanesque period (c. 1000-1200) was to roof large expanses in stone rather than the more expedient but fire-prone timber. An innovation came in the form of the ribbed cross vault, as at Durham Cathedral (n° 284) or St.-Etienne at Caen (n° 295), while other experiments included naves covered by barrel vaults or a succession of domes. Along the well-trodden route to Santiago di Compostela a series of new churches accommodated a constant stream of religious pilgrims by the provision of double aisles and ambulatories around the apse, thus allowing the easy circulation of crowds along the inner perimeter of the entire church, behind the altar, and past a variety of chapels, relics and shrines. Because of the weight of the stone vaulting, Romanesque walls remained thick and heavy, with small window openings. Externally, the dominant appearance of Romanesque architecture was thus closed and fortress-like, relieved by the occasional application of round arches in decorative arcades, monastic cloisters or telescoping entrance portals. The same massively conservative building technique and severe appearance also mark the many fortified castles of this era, particularly in England, France and Crusader outposts in the Holy Land.

The 12th century witnessed an increasing amount of trade between European cities and the near East, as funneled through Venice. This new prosperity soon found material expression in both religious and secular architecture. In Paris and the nearby cities of northern France, churches and cathedrals came to assume unprecedented qualities of height, openness and splendour. This was made possible by the structural innovations of the so-called Gothic mode of building: these comprise the pointed arch (most likely borrowed from Islamic buildings that had been seen during the Crusades), rib vaulting and flying buttresses. As first manifested on a modest scale in the ambulatory of the Basilica of Saint-Denis (n° 302), near Paris (1137 and later), the Gothic system constituted a structurally robust if spatially daring system of skeletal framing which needed only minimal masonry infill for walls and vaulting. Window openings could now occupy entire wall planes, and were often filled with vast expanses of stained glass that flooded church interiors with an otherworldly spectrum of colours. Using only simple geometry and a conservative process of trial and error (which not infrequently ended in disaster), the Gothic master masons succeeded in erecting a series of monumental churches of increasing height and complexity, a line that can be traced through the cathedrals of Laon (n° 305), Notre-Dame of Paris (n° 306), Chartres (n° 315), Reims (n° 327), Amiens (n° 328) and Beauvais (n° 329). Apart from these crucial structural considerations, the Gothic should at the same time be read as a highly symbolic mode of expression in which each element of the building contributes to the overriding notion of the church as a model of the heavenly Jerusalem: the soaring vertical lines of its piers, windows and spires point unequivocally to heaven, while its entrance portals served as a public locus for the most complex and manifold sculptural representations of Christian iconography, especially the Last Judgment. The employment of itinerant master masons soon brought the Gothic style to all regions of the continent, and it developed notably idiosyncratic local inflections in England, Italy, Spain and the regions of Eastern Europe. Although it held sway for some three centuries, Gothic building did not become more technically innovative in its later phases; rather, an increasing love of elaborate decoration took hold, whether in the French *Flamboyant* and *Rayonnant* styles, or the English Decorated and Perpendicular styles. In this period many secular buildings also became more architecturally ambitious and splendidly finished: the great town and guild halls of northern Europe, such as those at Ypres and Bruges, proclaim the sources of much of the new wealth, and even individual houses, like that of Jacques Coeur at Bourges (n° 376) (1443-1451) or the waterfront mansions along Venice's Grand Canal, manifested a new courtly elegance.

Following the lead of Humanist scholars who began to refocus attention on the Classical legacy in literature, architects of the Italian Renaissance (literally, 'rebirth') made concerted efforts to reestablish the Classical tradition in architecture. By the early 15th century, architects like Brunelleschi were visiting the half-buried remains of Roman edifices in an attempt to determine the proportions, details and structural techniques of the ancient builders. In many cases the Roman ruins had lost much of their decorative veneer, ostensibly suggesting to Renaissance architects the primacy and beauty of simple geometry and harmonic proportions. In the churches and palaces of Brunelleschi, Alberti, Bramante, Michelozzo and Sangallo, a convincing—and increasingly sculptural—Classicism began to emerge, a style that slowly came to supplant older Gothic traditions throughout Italy. Apart from the reappearance of such familiar Classical motifs as columns, capitals, round arches and entablature mouldings, the keynote of this new-old architecture was its geometric clarity and additive—or modular—quality. This can be sensed in the fascination on the part of Leonardo da Vinci and other architects for circular or central-plan churches, as put into practise at Cola da Caprarola's Santa Maria della Consolazione (n° 402) at Todi (1508), as well as the repetitive bays of many nave elevations and palace façades; in Florence, Brunelleschi's church of San Lorenzo (n° 369) (begun 1424) and Alberti's Palazzo Rucellai (n° 382) (1446-1451) are typical. Perhaps the crowning moment of the High Renaissance was the rebuilding of St. Peter's Basilica (n° 401) itself, planned by Bramante as a geometrically perfect centralised building on an unprecedentedly colossal scale. As partly executed by Michelangelo in the mid-16th century, the great crossing and dome of St. Peter's, evincing a creative and muscular approach to Classical design, set the tone for the Baroque monuments of Europe in the following century.

Baroque architecture is generally defined as exhibiting characteristics of ornamental flamboyance, sculptural plasticity, curving motion, building climaxes, theatrical illusion in the use of light and shade, and impressive scale. Perhaps most importantly, the Baroque constitutes a language of propaganda, either religious or secular, and in this capacity made use of the emotional effectiveness of its grand gestures to convince visitors to churches and palaces of the legitimacy and majesty of the ruling powers. The Baroque impulse necessarily

flowed from Rome, where St. Peter's manifested Papal authority on the greatest possible scale. Through the 17th century, smaller churches in Rome by Bernini and Borromini began to experiment with unusual and complex geometries in plan and elevation; in combination with the careful stage management of directed light, this was calculated to produce an effect of astonishment and spiritual exhilaration in the religious visitor. In the next century such unabashedly theatrical effects would be taken to even greater extremes in the churches of the Catholic regions of southern Germany—the Asam brothers' church of St. Johann Nepomuk in Munich (n° 515) (1733-1746) is a good example—though they were largely resisted in both France and England. Mansart's church of the Invalides in Paris (n° 476) (1670-1708), with its wonderfully sculptural façade and soaring gilded dome, certainly has much in common with St. Peter's and other Baroque churches in Rome, but ultimately it evinces a well-balanced grandeur rather than restless movement. And Versailles (n° 468), the vast court of Louis XIV near Paris, is deemed to be Baroque largely by virtue of its unprecedented scale and lavishness, but a closer inspection of its seemingly endless façades reveals an articulation that is both conservative and impeccably professional, indicative of the increasing formalisation of doctrinaire Classical principles in the French academic tradition. English Baroque, as represented largely by the monumental and stylistically innovative churches and palaces of Wren, Vanbrugh and Hawksmoor, developed at some remove from continental practise, and is more often than not restrained by the more sedate domestic traditions of Dutch building. Eastern Europe took more whole-heartedly to Baroque aesthetics, and a late and colourful version flourished in Russia in the 18th century thanks to Imperial patronage of architects brought in from Italy: the Russian Orthodox church of Rastrelli's Smolny Convent, St. Petersburg (n° 519) (1748-1764), built for the Empress Elizabeth, has a dizzyingly vertical façade with angled twin towers topped by slender onion domes.

A short-lived coda to the Baroque is represented by the Rococo, largely a style of interior decoration. Developed in the salons of Louis XV-era France and subsequently exported to the German courts, the Rococo miniaturised, lightened and multiplied the more robust curves of the Baroque to achieve elegant and frothy decorative effects. These often move beyond any lingering respect for Classical order to evince the barely controlled chaos of vegetative growth. In its carefree and fanciful tone, the Rococo provided the perfect domestic setting for the witty conversation, ornate costume and endless court intrigues of the period, though these same qualities would soon come to be rebuked by a rising generation of architects as decadent and licentious.

In the mid-18th century, the rediscovery of the ancient cities of Pompeii (n° 232; n° 233) and Herculaneum, which had been buried by the eruption of Mt. Vesuvius in 79 CE, gave new impetus to the search for an authentic Classicism in architecture. Since visitors could now stroll along the streets of an actual Roman city and examine the interiors of ancient houses, shops and public buildings, aristocratic patrons of architecture began to demand a new archaeological correctness in terms of typology and style, one that had not been quite so pressing in the earlier Renaissance period. Neoclassicism was in fact conceived as a deliberate reproach to the perceived lapse in taste represented by the preceding Baroque and Rococo periods: instead of irregular curves and ornamental bombast, Neoclassicism prescribed simple rectilinear geometries; instead of religious ecstasy and melodrama, Neoclassicism—as an essential part of the Enlightenment project—proposed a sober dignity that spoke of man's innate rationality. In the domestic sphere, designers like Robert Adam used Roman motifs to produce interiors of an opulent Classicism that was well suited to patrons who saw themselves, through their education and social position, as the heirs to ancient Roman virtue. For large public buildings like houses of government, banks and even churches, Neoclassicism lent an air of timelessness and grave dignity to European cities that no other style could offer.

By 1800 the Neoclassical urge seemed to reign supreme, but a new restlessness with the fixed certainties of the Classical system had already begun to appear. In general, this new Romantic trend reacted against Neoclassical restraint by proposing a return to emotionality and feeling. This took on a number of architectural manifestations. On the one hand, French architects like Ledoux and Boullée could force the simple forms of Neoclassicism to a megalomaniac extreme through a process of ruthless simplification and colossal enlargement, resulting in an architecture of massive gloom that was intended to evoke a sense of awe—a manifestation, in fact, of the aesthetic category of the 'Sublime', which was more frequently invoked by theorists of the period to describe vast and frightening natural phenomena such as storms, waterfalls or mountain scenery. On the other hand, some architects now began to take a more serious look at the previously maligned heritage of medieval Europe, and the features of Gothic churches and monasteries were studied seriously with an eye to using them in the design of contemporary houses, churches and public buildings. The rise and institutional acceptance of the neo-Gothic is best symbolised by the erection of the new Houses of Parliament in London (n° 566) (begun 1836), whose Classically regular façades by Sir Charles Barry were covered in acres of convincingly medieval ornaments designed by the untiring A.W.N. Pugin, one of the few architects in Europe to have a firm grasp of Gothic style and principles at this date. Eventually inspiring a group of like-minded reformers, Pugin's active campaigning for the more widespread adoption of the Gothic style in England was primarily motivated by religious impulses. The choice of style, it appeared, was rapidly assuming the character of a moral rather than an aesthetic debate in the 19th century, and indeed the period as a whole has aptly been characterised as a 'battle of the styles'. In another direction, the great expansion of Europe's colonial frontiers had opened the eyes of travelers and architects to a whole range of stylistic possibilities beyond the European heritage, and experiments in the so-called 'exotic' styles began to appear here and there. The Prince Regent's entertainment pavilion at Brighton (n° 556) (1815-1823), with its eclectic mixture of Islamic, Indian and Chinese motifs, is characteristic of this trend. Perhaps just as importantly, a new notion of relativity in stylistic matters insinuated itself into the architectural discourse, and just as inevitably architects now began asking themselves not only which style was best, but why the accepted historical styles—and most particularly Classicism—should have any monopoly on current practise. Taking the issue further, some even began to wonder what a contemporary style for the 19th century might look like, and the search for a 'modern' architecture was on.

With the rise of the Industrial Revolution the question of style soon became conflated with the question of technology: architects undertook a troubled consideration of how the new advances in materials and structures—most notably the introduction of metallic building elements—could profitably be employed to architectural ends. A radical but popularly successful example, which served to propel the debate, came in the form of the Crystal Palace, the great structure of iron, glass and wood that housed the World's Fair of 1851 in London. Paxton's huge transparent greenhouse thrilled its many visitors but perplexed architectural commentators, who looked in vain for any vestige of recognised style, articulation, ornament or typology. This lack of architectural pedigree was seen as a crucial impediment to the acceptance of the Crystal Palace as 'architecture'. One important school of architectural thought, that of the Arts-and-Crafts movement, then began to promote a revival of traditional handicrafts as a way by which human value could be re-infused into the apparently rote and mechanistic practise of building—here John Ruskin and William Morris were the prophets, and the sympathetic but ostensibly retrograde search for a route back to an idealised Middle Ages continued to hold sway in some sectors of European

architecture—notably domestic buildings—long into the new century.

A cautious approach to technological innovation on the part of some Victorian architects was to apply new materials to old forms, so that, for example, it was not uncommon to find Renaissance columns and Gothic arches reproduced in cast iron—the interiors of Henri Labrouste's Bibliothèque Sainte-Geneviève, Paris (n° 571) (1843-1851) or Deane and Woodward's University Museum, Oxford (n° 581) (1853-1860) are characteristic in this respect. For progressive thinkers, however, this eclecticism came to represent a failure of nerve, and a more thoroughgoing effort to achieve an approach that was new in both form *and* technique became the nucleus of the modern movement. The Art Nouveau movement of the 1890s, spearheaded by Horta and Guimard, provided an early answer, reproducing the a-historic forms of plants, leaves and tendrils in wrought iron and other materials. As manifested in the work of Walter Gropius, Le Corbusier and other architects of the 'heroic' 1920s, however, the new style was less a matter of surface decoration and aesthetics than of a radically new approach to design, which aimed to pose questions of function, use and economy—rather than nostalgia or ostentation—as the starting point of any modern building. These ideas were the hallmark of the Russian Constructivist school, who positioned the abstract forms of architectural modernism as the herald of a new phase of human social and political organisation. As markers of a new 'machine aesthetic' appropriate to the industrial age, materials such as concrete, iron, steel and glass were now pressed into service for houses and more formal public buildings. At the same time, under the influence of abstract art, the formal vocabulary of architecture was radically simplified to the most basic geometric volumes, even to the extent that such features as discrete window openings and pitched roofs could commonly be regarded as outmoded. Instead, broad planar surfaces, stripped of all decoration and colour, gave an elegant, if stark, appearance to many modern buildings. Roofs became flat, and windows were grouped into long horizontal strips. Spatial planning, too, became looser and less symmetrical, geared to the effective housing of spaces of different function rather than attempting to impose a falsely hierarchical order onto façades, as had often been the case in the Classical tradition. A point of crystallisation was reached with Ludwig Mies van der Rohe's masterplanning of the Weissenhof model housing estate in Stuttgart (n° 655) (1927), which revealed the remarkable uniformity of aesthetic approach then prevailing among many progressive architects from across Europe. Ultimately, however, modernism painted itself into a corner: having reduced the architectural vocabulary to an absolute minimum—the mythical 'glass box'—it was forced to confront the fact that subjectivity, expressivity and formal experimentation had in many cases been removed from the equation, and that it was consequently difficult to imagine any radically new futures for architecture. After the Second World War there would be a reaction to orthodox modernism in the form of greater sculptural and expressive form, as spearheaded by Le Corbusier's great Unité d'Habitation (n° 685), an apartment complex at Marseilles (1945-1952), and his pilgrimage church at Ronchamp (n° 688) (1950-55). At the same time, increasing attention began to be paid to Scandinavian achievements in modernism, and the example of the Finnish architect Alvar Aalto was held out for its humanism, warmth and formal variety.

Modernism, as its name implies, was expressly predicated on a certain cultural amnesia, rejecting the legacy of past centuries as irrelevant to contemporary cultural conditions. In postwar Europe, this ideology served the appropriate political goal of creating a progressive cultural identity, one based largely on science and commerce and free of the taint of the abhorrent ideological regimes and mass destruction of the 1940s. The UNESCO Headquarters (n° 694) (1953-1958), for example, clearly introduced the clean lines of modernism into the still somewhat suspicious milieu of Paris as a politically neutral mode of building that spoke of internationalism, technological rationalism and optimistic reconstruction as the leitmotivs of postwar Europe. At this time the first skyscrapers began to rise in European cities, some—like Ponti and Nervi's Pirelli building in Milan (n° 696) (1956-1959) or Jacobsen's SAS Royal Hotel in Copenhagen (1959-60)—achieving a uniquely urbane and elegant articulation. From the 1970s, however, European architects began to recognise the need for a renewed engagement with the past, if not a full-blown revival. Italy, as represented by Carlo Scarpa and Aldo Rossi, again showed the way, proposing an abstracted but sometimes eerie re-imagining of Classical motifs and typologies. The Venice Biennale of 1980, which for the first time proposed an architectural section, seemed to encapsulate the moment in an exhibition entitled 'The Presence of the Past': here a number of prominent architects exhibited designs for building façades, many making creative use of Classical motifs. In England, the Postmodern recapitulation of architectural history was then taken a step further by such architects as Leon Krier and Quinlan Terry, who, with the support of Prince Charles, launched a crusade to restore traditional materials and methods of building, if not a wholesale Classical revival. For the most part, however, European architects have continued to work in a modernist vein, validating abstract forms, unprecedented typologies and the newest building technologies. The most successful European architects in recent years, as represented by Richard Rogers, Renzo Piano, Norman Foster, Santiago Calatrava, Jean Nouvel and Rem Koolhaas, embrace many of the lessons of postwar modernism, and if their latest work has become increasingly large-scale, even to the point of a potential dehumanisation, this is perhaps the inevitable result of population growth and the need to rationally accommodate the flow of very large and highly mobile volumes of people in public and commercial buildings that are multi-purpose and mega-structural in character.

192

192. *Palace at Knossos*, Crete, c. 1700-1380 BCE (Greece)

Once the centre of Minoan culture, this great building complex features a loose and aggregative plan focused around an extensive rectangular courtyard. Its complexity may well have given rise to the later myth of the Minotaur and its labyrinth. The palace was excavated and partly reconstructed by Sir Arthur Evans from 1900, though his work has since been criticised as somewhat fanciful. Because only the stone foundations survived, the form and layout of the upper levels—which seem to have consisted of timber framing with rubble infill—remain hypothetical. These upper stories were supported on wooden columns of unique form, which tapered downward from a large cushion capital. Evans' hypothesis that he had discovered the palace of the fabled King Minos has largely been discarded and recent archaeology has instead suggested that the complex had a ritual or religious function throughout much of its history. It appears to have been unfortified. Along with the rest of Minoan civilisation on Crete, the palace was almost completely obliterated by a huge natural cataclysm in about 1450 BCE. The town that must once have risen by the palace has yet to be excavated.

193

193. *Megalithic temples of Malta*, Tarxien, c. 2800 BCE (Malta)

194

194. *Standing stones at Carnac*, Carnac, 3rd millennium BCE (France)

195. *Newgrange passage tomb*, County Meath, c. 3000-2500 BCE (Ireland)

195

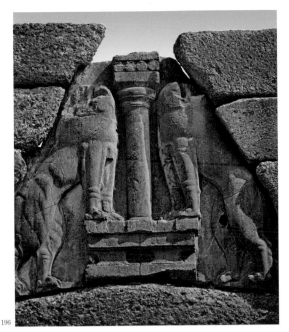

197. *Fortified citadel at Mycenae*, Mycenae, occupied c. 1600 BCE (Greece)

196. *Lion Gate*, Mycenae, c. 1250 BCE (Greece)

198. *Treasury of Atreus*, Mycenae, c. 1300 BCE (Greece)

200. *Etruscan tombs at Cerveteri*, Cerveteri, c. 9th-3rd century BCE (Italy)

201. *Etruscan tombs at Tarquinia (now Corneto)*, Corneto, c. 700 BCE (Italy)

◄199. *The Heraion*, Olympia, c. 640 BCE (Greece)

202. *Temple of Ceres*, also known as *Temple of Athena*, Paestum, c. 500 BCE (Italy)

203-204

203 and 204. *Temple of Hera I (The Basilica)*, and *Temple of Hera II (Temple of Poseidon)*, Paestum, c. 550 BCE and c. 450 BCE (Italy)

The Doric, simplest of the Classical Orders, derives directly from early timber prototypes, and many of its features, notably the triglyphs and metopes of its entablature, are petrified representations of wooden construction. Paestum was a major Greco-Roman city in the south of Italy, and its second Temple of Hera is one of the best-preserved Doric temples of the old Greek colonies of Campania. It shows the Greek temple typology in its standardised form, with a continuous peristyle of identical columns set around a rectangular plan. This is one of three major Doric temples on the site; the first, also dedicated to Hera (but often known erroneously as 'The Basilica'), is one of the earliest surviving examples of the Doric Order. Paestum thus reveals the Doric in the process of refinement, but it should be remembered that we are here also dealing with a local or provincial version of the style. At Hera II the proportions are still massive, giving the temple a heavy, earthbound feeling. Archaeology suggests that the temple may have been jointly dedicated to Hera and Zeus; the connection to the sea god Poseidon, or Neptune, is an 18th century misattribution. The remains of a large Greek altar are still visible on the east side.

205. *Treasury of the Athenians*, Delphi, 490 BCE (Greece)

206. *Temple of Olympian Zeus*, Athens, begun in the 6th century BCE (Greece)

▶207. **Mnesikles**, *The Erechtheion, Acropolis*, Athens, c. 420 BCE (Greece)

209. *Temple of Hephaestus,* also known as the *Theseion,* Athens, 449-415 BCE (Greece)

208. **Iktinos** and **Kallikrates,** *The Parthenon,* Acropolis, Athens, 448-432 BCE (Greece)

The apotheosis of the Doric Order, and perhaps the finest Greek temple of all, the Parthenon has traditionally been seen as one of the key buildings of the Western tradition. It sits atop the Acropolis (literally "high city"), a rocky outcrop in the centre of Athens, whose function was originally defensive; it later served as a royal residence and then as the city's chief religious precinct. The sacred enclosure, which occupies the top surface of the rock, also included the Propylaea, the Temple of Athena Nike and the Erechtheion. A great octastyle temple with a continuous peristyle, the Parthenon has Doric columns that exhibit a subtle entasis, or swelling curvature, giving a sense of life and elasticity to the ostensibly rectilinear forms. The temple was built to house the colossal cult image of Athena, sculpted by Phidias. Like all Greek temples, the inside of the Parthenon would have been quite dark, adding to the mystery and terror of this literal home of the city's patron goddess. The Parthenon survived in excellent condition until the 17th century, when it sustained a direct hit while serving as a powder magazine. At the start of the 19th century most of the statuary and relief carvings were taken to London by Lord Elgin, and are still to be found in the British Museum.

208

210

211

210. *Tholos at the Sanctuary of Athena Pronaia*, Delphi, 380-360 BCE (Greece)

211. *Temple of Apollo*, Didyma, late 4th century BCE (Turkey)

212. *Theatre at Epidauros*, Epidauros, c. 350 BCE and later (Greece)

212

13

213. **Kallıkrates**, *Temple of Athena Nike*, Acropolis, Athens, 427-424 BCE (Greece)

215. *The Choragic Monument of Lysicrates*, Athens, c. 335 BCE (Greece)

This tiny monument represents a rare appearance of the ornate Corinthian Order in Greek architecture, especially unusual in that it here occurs on the outer wall of a building rather than inside. Comprising a narrow cylinder set on a tall podium, the monument encloses no usable space. Its function was somewhat curious: it commemorates the victory of a citizen known as Lysicrates, who had successfully sponsored an entry in a musical drama competition dedicated to the god Dionysus. The round wall of the monument features six engaged Corinthian columns (or half-columns), thus anticipating the purely decorative use of the Orders that would become common in Hellenistic and Roman architecture. These support a delicate bas-relief frieze illustrating a mythological narrative concerning Dionysus' encounter with pirates. The diminutive size of the monument belies its later importance for Neoclassical architecture: following the carefully measured drawings published by Stuart and Revett in 1762, architects found the Choragic Monument of Lysicrates to be useful in articulating the forms of round towers and similar features.

214. *Temple of Apollo*, Delphi, 4th century BCE (Greece)

14

215

216. *Theatre at Orange*, Orange, 1st century BCE (France)

217. *Temple of Fortuna Virilis*, better known as the *Temple of Portunus*, Rome, late 2nd century BCE (Italy)

218. *Stoa of Attalus*, Athens, 159-132 BCE (reconstructed in 1952-56) (Greece)

▶219. *Great Altar of Zeus*, Pergamon, c. 180-150 BCE (now in the Pergamon Museum, Berlin, Germany) (Turkey)

220. *Porta Marzia*, Perugia, 3rd century BCE (Italy)

221. *Tower of the Winds (Horologeion of Andronicus)*, Athens, c. 50 BCE (Greece)

222. *Forum Romanum*, Rome, 1st century BCE and later (Italy)

223. *Pyramid of Cestius*, Rome, 12 BCE (Italy)

224. *Ara Pacis Augustae (Altar of Augustan Peace)*, Rome, 13-9 BCE (Italy)

225. *Pont du Gard aqueduct, Vers-Pont-du-Gard, 40-60 CE (France)*

The Roman genius for engineering is nowhere better represented than in their plumbing and hydraulics. Mastery of the round arch was put to good practical use in the construction of aqueducts, whose inclines were finely calibrated to deliver a constant flow of water over long distances purely by the force of gravity. Stretching over some 50 kilometres, this particularly elegant and well-preserved example brought fresh water into the Roman city of Nemausus and nearby settlements from *its source in a spring at Ucetia (modern-day Uzès). The water flowed along a covered channel on the uppermost level. Where the aqueduct crossed over the river Gardon it turned into a three-tiered bridge, 49 metres high, which could also accommodate wheeled and pedestrian traffic on its lowest arcade. The bridge portion of the aqueduct has a span of 273 metres. Construction is of large blocks of limestone, set in place without mortar. The projecting stones still visible here and there were used to support the wooden scaffolding that provided the framing for the arches during construction.*

226. *Maison Carrée, Nîmes, c. 10 CE (France)*

Though diminutive in comparison to many now-lost examples in Rome and its overseas colonies, the so-called Maison Carrée ("square house") in southern France is one of the best preserved of all Roman temples. In contrast to earlier religious buildings erected by the Greeks, the Roman temple was generally placed on an axis in larger urban contexts such as a courtyard or a forum, set on a tall podium, and approached by a flight of stairs. A columned porch serves as the point of entry, while *the remainder of the temple's peristyle comprises non-structural half-columns attached to the outer wall of the cella. Here the beautifully carved capitals are of the Corinthian Order. This building was later to serve as a model for the Virginia State Capitol in the United States, for Thomas Jefferson considered it stylistically and symbolically ideal for emulation by the public edifices of the new American republic. More recently, the British architect Norman Foster has borrowed the proportions of the Maison Carrée for his nearby Carré d'art, which appears as a larger but discreetly minimal recapitulation of the ancient temple typology.*

227. *Arles Amphitheatre*, Arles, c. 90 CE and later (France)

228. *Arena of Nîmes*, Nîmes, c. 50 CE and later (France)

229. *Monumental arch*, Orange, after 21 CE (France)

230. *Arch of Titus*, Rome, c. 81 CE (Italy)

151

232

233

234

◀231. *The Colosseum*, originally the *Flavian Amphitheatre*, Rome, 72-80 CE (Italy)

This immense elliptical theatre, greatest of all Roman arenas, was begun by the Emperor Vespasian and completed by Domitian. Here huge crowds of up to 50,000 people came to witness violent gladiatorial contests and cruel spectacles involving wild animals and prisoners. Its inaugural games, in 80 CE, lasted for one hundred days. In contrast to Greek theatres, the Roman typology was usually free-standing. Construction was of stone masonry and concrete, with white travertine cladding. Demonstrating the Roman genius for crowd control, seats were accessed via an efficient system of vaulted corridors or vomitoria. *For Renaissance architects, the Colosseum was exemplary for the decorative application of the Orders (from bottom to top: Doric, Ionic and two variations of the Corinthian) on its arcaded exterior. Along the uppermost level of the Colosseum can be seen the remains of stone sockets which once served to anchor wooden masts; from these were hung a huge canvas shade* (velarium) *which gave spectators partial protection from sun and rain. The nickname 'Colosseum' apparently derives from a colossal statue of Nero that once stood nearby.*

232. *City of Pompeii*, Pompeii, mostly early 1st century CE (founded in the 6th century BCE) (Italy)

233. *Villa of the Mysteries*, Pompeii, rebuilt c. 62 CE (Italy)

234. **Severus** and **Celer**, *Domus Aurea (Golden House of Nero)*, Rome, 64-68 CE (Italy)

▼235. *Aqueduct of Segovia*, Segovia, c. 100 CE (Spain)

236

236. *Library of Celsus*, Ephesus, c. 120 (Turkey)

237

237. *Column of Trajan*, Rome, 113 CE (Italy)

238

238. **Apollodorus of Damascus**, *Markets of Trajan*, Rome, c. 100-114 CE (Italy)

39

239. *Pantheon*, Rome, c. 118-128 CE (Italy)

The Pantheon, one of the most impressive and well-preserved of all Roman temples, can well claim to be the most influential building in the Western tradition. Erected in the reign of the Emperor Hadrian (who is sometimes given credit for its architectural design), the Pantheon was a place for worship of the seven planetary deities. Its hemispherical dome, covering a round-plan cella, was the largest in the ancient world. The dome's recessed coffering is both decorative and functional, as it serves to reduce *the total weight. An open oculus at the top allows light and air to penetrate. The temple's thick walls contain a series of arches and vaults for extra strength, as can be seen on the exterior. Recent research has discovered the original tracing ground for the Pantheon's building elements, which suggests that the portico is not as tall as was originally intended; this is due to the fact that the columns were quarried out of single pieces of stone. This also explains the awkward presence of a second, taller pediment partly obscured by the main portico. Later imitations of the Pantheon are numerous, and any domed building in the Classical style inevitably owes something to it.*

240. *Hadrian's Villa*, Tivoli, 117-138 CE (Italy)

241. *Baths of Caracalla*, Rome, c. 211-217 CE (Italy)

242. *Mausoleum of Hadrian*, also known as *Castel San'Angelo*, Rome, 135 CE (Italy)

243

243. *Arch of Constantine*, Rome, 312-315 CE (Italy)

The Roman invention of a freestanding arch was intended to commemorate notable military victories. Containing no interior space, the triumphal arch is really a sculptural monument rather than a building, and it is therefore not surprising to find that the columns (or rather, half-columns) on its two main façades have no structural function. This late but particularly impressive example of the Roman arch typology is located next to the Colosseum. The standing figures on the attic storey represent bound captives, while the acts of the Emperor and his legions are narrated in relief carvings;

some of these, notably the roundels, were in fact taken from earlier monuments in the city. As the Arch of Constantine was erected towards the end of the Roman Empire, the style of its newly commissioned sculptures show a retreat from naturalism, thus giving a foretaste of the artistic stylisations of the Middle Ages. Although later historical regimes—notably those of Napoleon and Hitler—resurrected the triumphal arch typology to evoke Roman imperial precedent, its architectural importance has proved to be more in the nature of a useful motif: from the Renaissance onwards the formula of triple arched openings, attached columns and attic storey was later applied to the façades of many different building types, from churches to houses.

244

244. *Diocletian's Palace*, Split, c. 300 CE (Croatia)

245

245. *Catacombs of Marcellinus and Peter*, Rome, late 3rd-early 4th century (Italy)

246

246. *Basilica of Maxentius and Constantine*, also known as *Basilica Nova*, Rome, 308-312 CE (Italy)

247

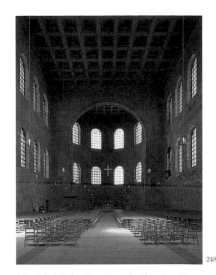

248

247. *Santa Costanza*, Rome, c. 338-350 (Italy)

248. *Cathedral of St. Peter*, Trier, early 4th century CE (Germany)

This masterpiece of late Antique architecture looks forward in many ways to the buildings of the Middle Ages. A domed, round-plan church, it originally appears to have been built in the reign of the Emperor Constantine as a mausoleum for his daughter Constantina. When the latter came to be venerated as a saint, the building was converted into a Christian place of worship. In contrast to the sumptuous interior, the exterior is of plain, arched brickwork. Its dome serves to focus attention on the central circular space of the building, 11 metres in diameter and illuminated by twelve clearstorey windows, where the sarcophagus would originally have been located. The dome rests on a tall drum, which in turn is supported on brick arches set on paired Corinthian columns of green and red marble; these serve to define a surrounding ambulatory. (An earlier outer ambulatory has disappeared.) It has been pointed out that this section is similar to that of a Roman basilica, in that it has lower aisles (i.e., the ambulatory) flanking a taller nave. The vaulting of the ambulatory space is covered in elaborate marble mosaics, foreshadowing the aesthetics of the nascent Byzantine style; a famous scene of grape harvest recalls both Bacchic mythology and early Christian iconography.

249

250

249. *Santa Maria Maggiore*, Rome, 432 and later (Italy)

250. *Baptistery of Neon*, Ravenna, 425 (Italy)

251. *Temple of Apollo*, Syracuse, Sicily, 6th century BCE (Italy)

252. *Mausoleum of Galla Placidia*, Ravenna, c. 425-426 (Italy)

253. *San Vitale*, Ravenna, 527-548 (Italy)

254

254. **Anthemius of Tralles** and **Isidorus of Miletus**, *Hagia Sophia*, Istanbul, 532-537 (Turkey)

255. *Palatine Chapel, Aachen Cathedral*, Aachen, 792-805 (Germany)

The Frankish king Charlemagne was a light in the Dark Ages, encouraging the revival of Classical culture and rebuilding religious institutions that had been destroyed by war. Seeing himself as the Roman Emperor of the West, Charlemagne modelled his court on that of the Roman rulers, and in this spirit he based the plan of his palace on that of the Lateran in Rome. His chapel, which represents a dramatic resurgence of monumental masonry technique after a lapse of centuries, is a centralised building with 16 sides. Inspired by the church of San Vitale in Ravenna, it was designed by Bishop Odo of Metz. The chapel was originally fronted by a colonnaded, open-air atrium, which could accommodate crowds gathered to hear Charlemagne speak from a second-storey balcony. The chapel was connected to the imperial throne room, known as the Basilica, by a lengthy gallery. Internally, the chapel is tall and somewhat ponderous in effect. Eight huge piers support two tiers of polychromatic arches. The stones of the chapel were likely taken from nearby Roman buildings, while the marble columns of the upper stories were imported from Ravenna. The original Carolingian building was later given a higher dome and hidden behind a large Gothic choir.

255

163

256. *Cathedral of St. Duje (St. Domnius)*, Split, c. 650 (Croatia)

257. *St. Donatus Church*, Zadar, 9th century (Croatia)

258. *The Royal Hall of Lorsch Abbey*, Lorsch, c. 830-880 (Germany)

259. *Saint-Gilles abbey church*, Saint-Gilles-du-Gard, founded in the middle of the 9th century (France)

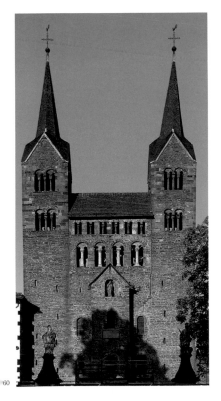

260. *Imperial Abbey of Corvey*, Corvey, 830-885 and later (Germany)

261. *Church of Saint Cyriacus*, Gernrode, begun in 961 (Germany)

165

262. *Monasteries of Mt. Athos,* founded in 963 (Greece)

263. *Saint-Philibert,* Tournus, c. 950-1120 (France)

264. *Monastery of Hosias Loukas,* near Stiris, early 11th century and later (Greece)

265

265. *St. Martin Cathedral*, Mainz, early 11th century and later (Germany)

266

266. *Monastery complex at Cluny*, Cluny, 11th century and later (founded in 909, mostly destroyed in 1790) (France)

267

267. *St. Michael's Church*, Hildesheim, 1001-1031 (Germany)

Dating from the later Ottonian period, this great church perpetuates the earlier tradition of Carolingian architecture, itself greatly indebted to ancient Roman precedent. Here, the articulation of the church as a doubled-ended basilica—having two transepts, one at each end, as well as two choirs and terminal apses, with access from the side aisles—in fact explicitly recalls a Roman secular typology. Each crossing has a square tower above it. The main altar is located in the east end, while a raised terrace for the use of the Emperor and his courtiers, another echo of Roman practise, is to be found in the western apse. Inside, polychromatic round arches rest on square piers alternating with two columns, giving a complex rhythm to the otherwise rather austere nave elevation. The beautifully carved capitals of the columns are based on Italian models. The ceiling is not vaulted, but flat, wooden and richly painted. Designed by use of a square module (as had been Charlemagne's palace at Aachen), the plan of St. Michael's was likely worked out by Bishop Bernward. Its present appearance, more closely reflecting its original state, is the result of a 20th-century restoration campaign.

268. *Abbey of Mont-Saint-Michel*, Le Mont-Saint-Michel, 11th century and later (France)

▶269. *Imperial Cathedral of Speyer*, Speyer, c. 1030 and later (Germany)

270. *Sainte-Foy abbey church*, Conques, c. 1050-1130 (France)

This small but significant masterpiece of Romanesque art is to be found in a tiny medieval village in a secluded mountain valley. Built of warm local limestone, the abbey church at Conques was a stop along on the well-travelled medieval pilgrimage route to Santiago di Compostela in northern Spain. The entrance portal is topped by a famous tympanic relief of the Last Judgment, in which Christ sternly presides over the separation of the Righteous and the Wicked. As a monastic building, Sainte-Foy had not only to accommodate an endless flow of pilgrims, but resident monks who needed to participate in the divine office seven times a day. To this end the church was designed to allow a free flow of visitors around the inner perimeter of the building: the aisles continue along both the nave and transepts to join a circular ambulatory with radiating chapels beyond the crossing. The interior is dark and cramped, featuring small, round arches set on tall piers. The crossing is crowned by a lantern of octagonal plan, somewhat resembling the inside of an umbrella, which rests on squinches. Sainte Foy (Saint Faith) was a young girl martyred in the 4th century: her remains, which are still kept here in a remarkable gold reliquary of anthropomorphic form, were a great draw for pilgrims.

271. *Saint-Martin-du-Canigou*, Casteil, 1009-1026 (France)

272. *Boyana church*, Sofia, 10th-13th century (Bulgaria)

273. *St. Sophia Cathedral*, Kiev, c. 1037-1057 (Ukraine)

274. *Cathedral of St. Sophia*, Novgorod, 1045-1050 (Russia)   ▶275. *Saint Mark's Basilica*, Venice, rebuilt in 1063-1094 (Italy)

276

277

276. *San Miniato al Monte*, Florence, 10th-12th century (Italy)

277. *Santa Maria Assunta*, Spoleto, 1198 and after (Italy)

278

278. *Piazza dei Miracoli*, Pisa, 11th century and later (Italy)

Reflecting local tradition, the baptistery and campanile (the famous "leaning tower") of Pisa's great cathedral are both free-standing in the Campo Santo. But the uniform architectural treatment of all three buildings—featuring multiple tiers of colonnaded and arcaded galleries executed in beautiful white marble—lends this religious complex a unique and impressive unity. The large cathedral is based on a basilican plan, with transepts and double aisles. A smaller oval dome covers the crossing. *Inside, the nave is memorable for its dramatic black-and-white striping. The ceilings are of trussed timber construction rather than stone vaulting. The famous "leaning tower," 55 metres high, was begun in 1173. Unfortunately, its inadequate foundations were dug into soft earth, and the three lower floors had been completed when it was discovered that the tower had already begun to lean. The subject of many unsuccessful attempts to stabilise it over the centuries, the tower remains at 5.5 degrees from vertical, and its top now overhangs its base by 5.2 metres.*

279

279. Bernard "the elder" and **Robertus Galperinus,** *Santiago de Compostela Cathedral,* Santiago de Compostela, Galicia, c. 1075-1211 and later (façade rebuilt in 1738 by Fernando de Casas y Navoa) (Spain)

280. *Basilica of St. Sernin*, Toulouse, c. 1080-1180 (France)

281. *Basilica of Sant'Ambrogio*, Milan, c. 1080-1140 (Italy)

282.

282. *Glendalough Round Tower*, Laragh, County Wicklow, c. 11th century (Ireland)

283.

283. *The White Tower (Tower of London)*, London, 1078-1080 (United Kingdom)

284.

284. *Durham Cathedral*, Durham, 1093-1133 and later (United Kingdom)

285.

285. *Maria Laach Abbey*, near Andernach, 1093-12th century (Germany)

286. *City of Carcassonne*, Carcassonne, 12th century with later restorations (France)

287. *Cathedral of St. Peter*, Worms, mainly 12th century and later (Germany)

288. *Abbey Church of Saint-Savin-sur-Gartempe*, Saint-Savin-sur-Gartempe, c. 1100 (France)

289. *Modena Cathedral*, Modena, c. 1099-1184 (Italy)

290. *Roskilde Cathedral*, Roskilde, 12th-13th century (Denmark)

291. *Parma Cathedral, campanile and baptistery*, Parma, cathedral: 1106, campanile: after 1106, baptistery: 1196-1216 (Italy)

292. *Cathedral of Saint-Front*, Périgueux, c. 1120 (France)

293. *Peterborough Cathedral*, Peterborough, Cambridgeshire, 1118-1237 (United Kingdom)

294. *St. Peter's Abbey*, Moissac, 11th-15th century (France)

295. *Benedictine Abbey of Saint-Etienne*, Abbaye-aux-Hommes, Caen, 1066-1077 (France)

296. *Vézelay Abbey*, now *Basilique Sainte-Marie-Madeleine*, Vézelay, 1120-1150 (France)

297. *Cathedral of St. Lazarus*, Autun, 1120-1146 (France)

298. *Abbey of Fontenay*, Fontenay, 1130-1147 (France)

299. *Dalmeny Church*, Dalmeny, Scotland, 1140 (United Kingdom)　　　▶300. *Urnes Stave church*, Borgund, c. 1125-1250 (Norway)

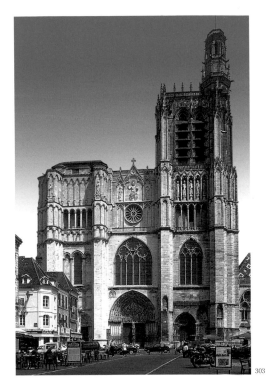

303. *St. Stephen's Cathedral*, Sens, c. 1135-1163 (France)

◀301. *Castle Hedingham*, Essex, 1140 and later (United Kingdom)

The endless warfare characteristic of life in the Middle Ages demanded new kinds of fortification that could withstand the continuing refinement of armaments and siege technique. Castle Hedingham is a fine example of a Norman motte-and-bailey (i.e., earth mound with embanked enclosure) castle with a tall stone keep. It shows many similarities to Rochester Castle, which was built at the same time. When Hedingham was granted to Aubrey de Vere in 1066, the family began the construction of the castle on an older hilltop, a site that offered sweeping, strategic views of the countryside. Although all the other original buildings have since disappeared, the four-level stone keep itself, about 35 metres tall, is very well preserved; its internal floors, originally of wood, have also been reconstructed. Built of flint rubble held together by mortar, the walls of Castle Hedingham are, unusually, faced with smooth ashlar stone, which was brought from Northamptonshire. Its most impressive interior space is the two-storey Great Hall, which features a huge Norman archway. With its large fireplace, the Hall was likely used for banqueting. The castle is still privately owned by descendants of the de Vere family.

302. *Basilica of St. Denis*, Paris, c. 1135-1144 and later (France)

Originally built to commemorate Denis, Paris's first bishop, who was martyred in the 3rd century, this church came to be the burial place of the kings and queens of France. Today St.-Denis is perhaps more famous as the birthplace of the Gothic structural system. From 1137, Abbot Suger rebuilt the church over the original Carolingian basilica, first adding a massive new west front. The new church had a compact plan with wide and shallow transepts and a large semicircular choir with a double ambulatory. The latter, of irregular plan, was ingeniously covered over by a uniform construction of rib vaults using pointed arches. Inspired by descriptions of the Temple of Solomon and early church writings on the role of visual splendour in awakening spiritual devotion, Suger illuminated each of the seven chapels of the new choir with two large stained-glass windows. Suger saw the luminous mystery of their coloured light as spiritually transformative, thus laying the aesthetic foundations for the Gothic revolution that was to follow. Now located in a drab Parisian suburb, the church is externally unimpressive, having only one tower on the entrance façade.

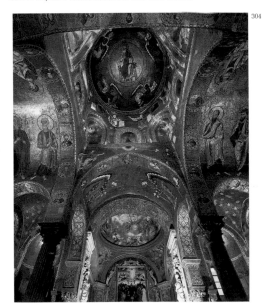

304. *Palatine Chapel*, Palermo, Sicily, 1130-1140 (Italy)

185

305

305. *Notre Dame Cathedral*, Laon, 1155-c. 1235 (France)

▶306. *Notre Dame Cathedral*, Paris, 1163-c. 1345 (France)

307. *Ratzeburg Cathedral*, Ratzeburg, 1160-1220 (Germany)

308. *Canterbury Cathedral*, Canterbury, 1174-1510 (United Kingdom)

309. *Dankwarderore Castle*, Brunswick, after 1173 (Germany)

310. *Church of Our Lady*, Kalundborg, 1170-1190 (Denmark)

310

311

312

311. *Santa María la Blanca (former synagogue)*, Toledo, 1180 (Spain)

312. *Lincoln Cathedral*, Lincoln, Lincolnshire, 1192-1280 (United Kingdom)

▶315. *Notre Dame Cathedral*, Chartres, 1194-1260 and later (France)

The great cathedral at Chartres is the first great masterpiece of the High Gothic period. The present building was erected after a major fire in 1134 destroyed most of the old building, a focus of pilgrimage. Since the cathedral's most holy relic, a piece of the Virgin's tunic, survived the disaster miraculously unscathed, it was decided to rebuild on an even grander scale. The result was a wide basilican church with prominent transepts, each terminating in a monumental porch. With the entrance portals, these contain some of the most iconographically rich sculptural cycles in all medieval architecture. Just as importantly, Chartres deployed the Gothic triumvirate of pointed arch, rib vaulting and flying buttresses to create an unprecedentedly light, skeletal structure. The breathtaking results are evident in the nave, where the arcading is tall and wide, stained-glass windows take the place of walls, and a clear vertical line can be traced from the base of the piers into the rib vaults soaring over 36 metres above. Unusual for a French cathedral, much of the medieval stained glass has survived. The famous discrepancy between the two towers of the entrance façade is due to the fact that they were built at different times, the more ornate north one being completed around 1515.

▶316. **Arnolfo di Cambio**, **Filippo Brunelleschi** and others, *Santa Maria del Fiore*, Florence, 13th century and later (dome by Filippo Brunelleschi, 15th century) (Italy)

313. *Wells Cathedral*, Wells, Somerset, 1176-1490 (United Kingdom)

314. *Salisbury Cathedral*, Salisbury, Wiltshire, 1220-1266 and later (United Kingdom)

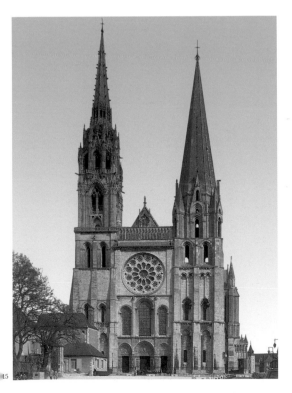

317. *Basilica of San Francesco d'Assisi*, Assisi, 13th century (Italy)

318. *City Hall*, Stralsund, 13th-15th century (Germany)

319. *Bourges Cathedral (Cathédrale Saint-Étienne de Bourges)*, Bourges, 1195-1250 (France)

320. *St. Nicholas' Church*, Tallinn, c. 1230-1275 (Estonia)

321. *Tower houses at San Gimignano*, San Gimignano, 13th-14th century (Italy)

322. *Historic centre of Tallinn*, Tallinn, 13th century (Estonia)

323. *Castle of Malbork*, Malbork, 13th century-after 1309 (Poland)

324

324. *Rila Monastery*, Rila, 13th-14th century (Bulgaria)

325

325. *Georgsdom*, Limburg, 1200-1235 (Germany)

326. *Castel del Monte*, Apulia, 1240-1250 (Italy)

327. *Notre Dame Cathedral*, Reims, begun in 1210 (France)

328. *Notre Dame Cathedral*, Amiens, begun c. 1220 (France)

329. *Saint-Pierre de Beauvais*, Beauvais, 13th-16th century (France)

330. *La Sainte-Chapelle*, Paris, 1238-1248 (France)

331

331. *León Cathedral*, León, 1205-1301 (Spain)

332

332. *St. Stephen Cathedral*, also known as *Stephansdom*, Vienna, 1137-1147 and later (Austria)

333

333. *Santi Giovanni e Paolo*, Venice, c. 1330-1430 (Italy)

▶334. *Westminster Abbey*, London, 13th-16th century (United Kingdom)

335

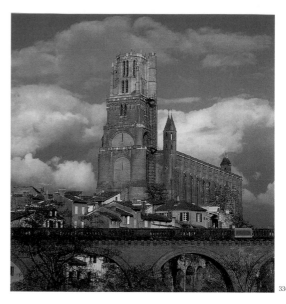

336

335. *Old New Synagogue*, Prague, c. 1270 (Czech Republic)

336. *Albi Cathedral (Cathédrale Sainte-Cécile d'Albi)*, Albi, 1282-1480 (France)

337

337. *Saint-Urbain Basilica*, Troyes, 1262 and later (France)

338

339

338. *Exeter Cathedral*, Exeter, Devon, c. 1112-1400 (United Kingdom)

339. *Harlech Castle*, Wales, 1283-1289 (United Kingdom)

340

340. *Caernarfon Castle*, Caernarfon, Wales, 1283-1327 (United Kingdom)

341. *Belfry of Bruges*, Bruges, 1280 with later additions (Belgium)

342. **Arnolfo di Cambio**, *Palazzo Vecchio*, Florence, 1299-1314 (Italy)

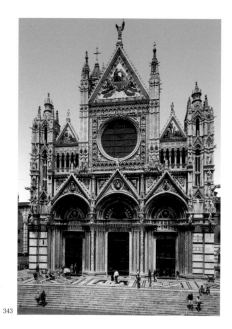

343. **Giovanni Pisano** and others, *Siena Cathedral*, Siena, 1284 and later (Italy)

344. **Fra' Bevignate**, **Lorenzo Maitani** and others, *Orvieto Cathedral*, Orvieto, begun in 1290 (Italy)

345

345. *Palazzo Pubblico*, Siena, begun in 1297 (Italy)

Reflecting the troubled times when it was erected, Siena's medieval City Hall, the Palazzo Pubblico, has an intimidating fortified appearance. Medieval city-states like Siena were not only prone to attack from neighbouring powers, but experienced frequent coups d'état from within. Seen from above, the Palazzo forms the base of a fan-shaped piazza or campo; this is where the famous horse race known as the Palio takes place each year. Civic legislation ensured that all surrounding buildings had to be articulated in a manner that complemented the Palazzo, thus creating one of the earliest scenographic treatments of a single urban space in European history. The alarmingly slender brick bell tower, one of the tallest in Italy, served as a lookout to spot approaching armies, and became a symbol of civic pride. The Palazzo's façade is Gothic in detail, as can be seen in the pointed arches of its windows, but the military-style crenellations on the skyline are more symbolic than functional. The Council Chamber contains a famous fresco cycle symbolising the effects of good and bad government; these give a vivid impression of everyday life among all social classes in medieval Siena.

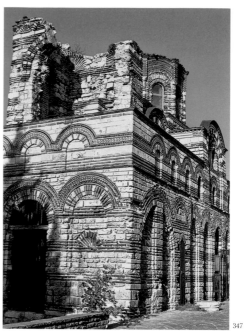

346. *Cologne Cathedral (Cathedral of St. Peter and Mary)*, Cologne, 1248-1322 and later (Germany)

347. *Church of Christ Pantocrator*, Nesebar, 13th century (Bulgaria)

348. *Akershus Fortress*, Oslo, begun in 1299 (Norway)

349. *Doge's Palace*, Venice, 1309-1438 (Italy)

The Republic of Venice owed its trading wealth to its role as middleman between Europe and the countries of the East. A key building of the city, glimpsed by visitors arriving by sea, is the magnificent lagoon-side palace that served as the official residence of the Doge, the elected ruler of Venice. This also housed the main political institutions of the Republic. Replacing an earlier fortified building, the Palace seems to have been begun by Filippo Calendario in 1309, with major additions by Giovanni and Bartolommeo Bon in the following century. It is based around a large open courtyard. The Palace's two main façades, which overlook the Adriatic and St. Mark's Square, have a simple, blocky design that might appear top-heavy were it not for the Venetian love of colour and ornament. Elements of the Gothic style are used decoratively: two levels of arcading animate the lower façades, and the upper features interlaced ogee arches that create rows of circles with open quatrefoils. Further up, delicate pink and white diaper patterning further lightens the Palace's appearance. The Venetians tended to use their decorative version of Gothic for secular buildings rather than churches, and for this reason—and because it was so famously admired by the Victorian art critic John Ruskin—the style was often emulated in 19th-century public and commercial structures in Britain.

350. **Berenguer de Montagut**, *La Seu*, Palma de Mallorca, 1229-1346 (Spain)

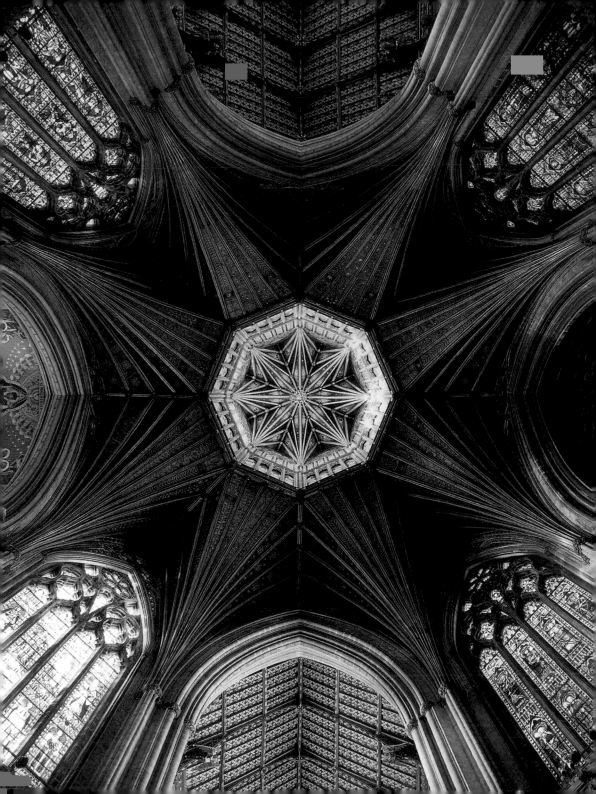

352. *Decani Monastery*, Decani, 1327-1335 (Serbia)

353. *Karlstein Castle*, Karlstein, 1348-1357 (Czech Republic)

◄351. *Ely Cathedral*, Ely, Cambridgeshire, octagonal lantern built in 1322-1347 (cathedral begun 1081) (United Kingdom)

354. **Taddeo Gaddi**, *Ponte Vecchio*, Florence, 1345 (Italy)

◀355. *Avignon Cathedral (Notre-Dame-des-Doms)* and *Palais des Papes*, Avignon, c. 14th century (France)

356. *Castelvecchio*, Verona, 1354-1356 (Italy)

357. **Francesco Di Giorgio Martini**, *The Rocca Roveresca*, Senigallia 1350-1492 (Italy)

358. **Peter Parler**, *Church of the Holy Cross*, Schwäbisch Gmünd, begun in 1351 (Germany)

359. **Johann Parler** and others, *Church of St. Barbara*, Kutná Hora, 1388-1512 (Czech Republic)

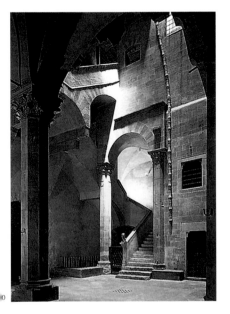

360. *Palazzo Davanzati*, Florence, late 14th century (Italy)

361. *Santa Maria Nascente Cathedral*, Milan, begun in 1386 (Italy)

362. *One of the seven painted churches of Moldavia*, Suceava County, 1487-1532 (Romania)

363. *Little Moreton Hall*, Cheshire, 15th century (United Kingdom)

364. *Church of the Pantanassa*, Mistra, 1428 (Greece)

365

65. *Piazza San Marco*, Venice, c. 1400 and later (Italy)

366

366. *St. Michael and St. Gudula Cathedral*, Brussels, 13th century (Belgium)

36

367. *Cathedral of St. James*, Sibenik, 1402-1555 (Croatia)

368

368. *Seville Cathedral (Catedral de Santa Maria de la Sede)*, Seville, 1402-1507 (Spain)

369. Filippo Brunelleschi, *Basilica of San Lorenzo*, Florence, begun in 1424 (Italy)

As one of the first Renaissance architects to have fully assimilated the Classical language of architecture, Brunelleschi conceived this monastic church as an exemplar of antique restraint, order and archaeological correctness. The building is perhaps not adventurous in a structural or typological sense, but the architect's desire to create an authentically Roman-style building is signalled, for example, by the fact that the Corinthian columns of the nave arcade support small and structurally unnecessary segments of entablature, a feature that could not be omitted without doing damage to the conventional appearance of the Order. The plan is modular in conception, as schematically indicated by marble banding on the floor. Brunelleschi's role as a re-discoverer of linear perspective also seems to be reflected in the emphatic way in which the horizontal lines of nave and ceiling recede to a vanishing point at the altar. Basic ratios prevail: the height of the nave, for example, is twice that of its width, thus setting a precedent for harmonious simplicity that came to be characteristic of much Renaissance architecture.

370. Filippo Brunelleschi, *Ospedale degli Innocenti*, Florence, 1419-1445 (Italy)

72

◀371. *The Alcazar*, Segovia, 1406-1454 (rebuilding of a castle from the 11th century) (Spain)

372. **Michelozzo di Bartolomeo**, *Palazzo Medici*, Florence, begun in 1444 (Italy)

373. **Giovanni** and **Bartolomeo Bon** with **Matteo Raverti**, *Ca' d'Oro*, Venice, 1428-1430 (Italy)

373

374. *Church of St. John of Kaneo,* Ohrid, before 1447 (Macedonia)

375. *Burgos Cathedral,* Burgos, 1221-c.1400 (Spain)

376. *House of Jacques Cœur,* Bourges, 1443-1451 (France)

377. *St. Clemens Church,* Büsum, 1434-1442 (Germany)

◀378. **Filippo Brunelleschi** and **Antonio Manetti**, *Santo Spirito*, Florence, begun in 1445 (Italy)

379. **Luciano Laurana** and others, *Palazzo Ducale*, Urbino, 15th century (Italy)

380

380. *King's College Chapel*, Cambridge, 1446-1515 (United Kingdom)

This soaring chapel is one of the great monuments of late medieval architecture. The university colleges of Oxford and Cambridge are traditionally focused around a chapel, though royal patronage made this example unusually large and lavish: originally funded by Henry VI, it was completed in the reign of Henry VIII. The chapel has a very simple plan, consisting only of an extended rectangle. The unified nature of the resulting space, acoustically suited to the hearing of sermons, is still evident despite the insertion of a large wooden choir screen and organ loft across the middle of the nave; this served to divide the congregations of students and townspeople, who were often mutually antagonistic. Stylistically, the chapel exemplifies the so-called Perpendicular period of English Gothic, evident in the insistent verticality of the wall articulation. The beautiful fan vaults, only partly structural in nature, were designed by the master mason John Wastell. King's College Chapel is comparable to the Sainte-Chapelle in Paris in that the walls have been reduced to an absolute minimum, serving only to frame large areas of stained glass.

381. **Aristotile Fioravanti (Aristotile Da Bologna)**, *Cathedral of Dormition*, Moscow, 1475-1479 (Russia)

382. **Leon Battista Alberti**, *Palazzo Rucellai*, Florence, 1446-1451 (Italy)

383. **Michelangelo Buonarroti**, also known as **Michelangelo**, *Palazzo dei Conservatori*, Rome, 1450-1568 (Italy)

384. **Filippo Brunelleschi**, *Palazzo Pitti*, Florence, begun in 1458 (courtyard by **Bartolommeo Ammanati**, 1560) (Italy)

385. *Palais de Justice*, Rouen, c. 1499-1509 with later additions (France)

386. **Bernardo Rossellino**, *Duomo*, Pienza, 1459-1462 (Italy)

387. **Leon Battista Alberti**, *Basilica di Sant'Andrea*, Mantua, 1462-1494 (Italy)

388. **Leon Battista Alberti** (façade), *Santa Maria Novella*, Florence, 1456-1470 (nave built in 1278-c. 1350) (Italy)

Alberti was not just an architect: he was the original 'Renaissance man' who wrote treatises on many subjects. Renowned as a Humanist, or Classical scholar, Alberti produced his architectural essay, the Ten Books on Architecture, in emulation of Vitruvius. His career illustrates how the architect's identity now begins to shift from craftsman to intellectual. This recasing of an older basilican structure produced the first executed church façade in the new Renaissance style. Alberti's classicising

veneer is based on his close study of Roman monuments. The upper portion, for example, suggests a Roman temple front, though here the columns have been reduced to non-structural pilasters and the overall effect is one of flat, polychromatic decoration. The design was generated by an interplay of basic geometrical figures, especially the square and the circle. Large scrolls or volutes serve to conceal the sloping roofs over the aisles, a solution much imitated by later Renaissance architects. The cheerful patterning in white and green marble in fact derives from local Romanesque traditions: the façade has much in common with that of the Florentine church of San Miniato al Monte, which dates from some three centuries earlier.

389

389. **Giuliano da Sangallo**, *Medici Villa di Poggio a Caiano*, Florence, begun in 1485 (Italy)

390

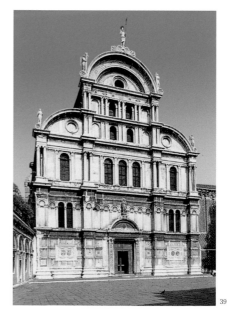

391

390. **Pietro Lombardo**, *Santa Maria dei Miracoli*, Venice, 1481-1489 (Italy)

391. **Mauro Codussi**, *San Zaccaria*, Venice, c. 1483-1515 (Italy)

392. *Knole*, Sevenoaks, 1486 (United Kingdom)

393. **Donato Bramante**, *Santa Maria delle Grazie*, Milan, 1492 (Italy)

394. *Wooden Church of Maramure*, Transylvania, c. 17th century (Romania)

395. **Benedetto da Maiano**, *Palazzo Strozzi*, Florence, 1489-1504 (Italy)

396. **Sir Reginald Bray**, *Henry VII Lady Chapel, Westminster Abbey*, London, 1503 (United Kingdom)

397. *Saint-Maclou*, Rouen, c. 1430-1521 (France)

398. *St. Anne's Church*, Vilnius, 1495-1500 (Lithuania)

399. **Donato Bramante**, *Tempietto San Pietro in Montorio*, Rome, 1502 (Italy)

400. *New Cathedral of Salamanca*, Salamanca, 1533-1733 (Spain)

402. **Cola de Caprarola**, *Santa Maria della Consolazione*, Todi, 1508-1607 (Italy)

401. **Donato Bramante**, **Michelangelo** and later architects, *St. Peter's Basilica*, Vatican, 1505-late 17th century (Vatican City)

Headquarters of the Roman Catholic Church, Vatican City is an independent state within the city of Rome. Its great basilica, St. Peter's, is built on the site of the earlier church of that name, which was founded by the Emperor Constantine. Its high altar is said to have been set over the tomb of St. Peter himself. Begun in 1505 and consecrated in 1626, the present building is the product of multiple building campaigns. The initial plan proposed by Bramante in 1505 was a centralised Greek cross topped by a massive dome. This somewhat idealistic scheme was later modified by Raphael and Sangallo, who decided to create a longer and more practical nave. As later executed by Maderno, this feature creates an unforgettable impression of a vast and magnificent space inside, but has the unfortunate effect of blocking views of the great dome as one approaches the building. Michelangelo, then in his 70s, devoted the last part of his life to the completion of St. Peter's, and his powerfully sculptural designs for the crossing, dome and east end were largely executed according to his wishes. Though the main building was complete by 1615, two final additions were Bernini's famous elliptical piazza and the ornate bronze baldacchino over the high altar.

401

403

403. *Belém Tower*, Lisbon, 1515-1520 (Portugal)

404. **Philibert de l'Orme, Jean Bullant** and others, *Château de Chenonceaux*, Chenonceaux, 1513-1521 and later (France)

405. **Colin Biart, Pietro da Cortona** and others, *Château de Blois*, Blois, 1498 and later (France)

405

406

406. **Raffaelo Sanzio**, also known as **Raphael**, *Villa Madama*, Rome, begun c. 1516 (Italy)

407. **Michelangelo Buonarroti**, also known as **Michelangelo**, *Laurentian Library*, Florence, begun in 1525 (Italy)

408. **Michelangelo Buonarroti**, also known as **Michelangelo**, *New Sacristy and Medici Chapel, Basilica of San Lorenzo*, Florence, begun in 1519 (Italy)

This remarkable funerary chapel was added to the south transept of Brunelleschi's church as a burial place for prominent members of Florence's Medici clan. In its general design it was meant to complement Brunelleschi's Old Sacristy of the 1420s, located at the extremity of San Lorenzo's other transept. But instead of emulating the clarity and simple geometry of the earlier space, Michelangelo altered the proportions and manipulated the standard language of Classicism to powerful emotional effect. In its

willful distortion of conventional elements, the chapel epitomises the nascent Mannerist style. There are many unusual and non-functional features in this vein: blank windows are given a tapered profile, niches—too shallow to contain any sculpture but too wide for their setting—are jammed between pilasters, the mouldings of pediments are segmental and broken, and so on. Michelangelo, who thought of himself primarily as a sculptor, saw the wall not as a neutral, flat plane, but as a dynamic matrix that could be composed of many layers of recession and projection. The famous monumental tombs of Lorenzo and Giulio de'Medici, also designed and sculpted by Michelangelo, feature colossal symbolic figures balanced precariously on the lids of sarcophagi.

408

409. **Jacopo Sansovino**, *National Library of St. Mark's*, Venice, 1536-1588 (Italy)

410. *Château de Chambord*, Chambord, 1519-1547 (France)

411. **Giulio Romano**, *Palazzo del Te*, Mantua, 1525-1534 (Italy)

412. **Juan Gil de Hontanon**, *Segovia Cathedral*, Segovia, 1522-1577 (Spain)

413. **Arnold van Mulken**, *Palace of the Prince Bishopric of Liège*, Liège, begun in 1526 (Belgium)

414. **Bartolomeo Berecci**, *Chapel of King Sigismund I*, Krakow, 1519-1533 (Poland)

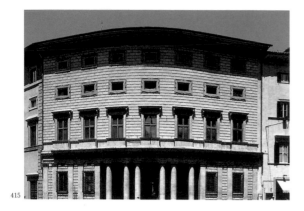

415

415. **Baldassare Peruzzi**, *Palazzo Massimo alle Colonne*, Rome, 1532-1536 (Italy)

41

416. **Jacopo Sansovino**, *Palazzo Corner della Ca' Grande*, Venice, 1537-1561 (Italy)

417

417. *Palace of Fontainebleau*, Fontainebleau, begun in 1528 (France)

418. **Antonio da Sangallo the Younger** and **Michelangelo**, *Palazzo Farnese*, Rome, c. 1517-1550 (Italy)

419. **Michelangelo Buonarroti**, also known as **Michelangelo**, *Capitoline Hill*, Rome, 1536-1546 (Italy)

420. *Cotehele House*, St. Dominick, Saltash, 1485-1539 (United Kingdom)

421. **Pierre Lescot** and **Jacques Lemercier**, *Cour Carrée of the Louvre*, Paris, begun in 1546 (France)

422. *Falkland Palace*, Cupar, Scotland, 1501-1541 (United Kingdom)

423

424

425

426

423. **Andrea Palladio**, *Basilica Palladiana*, also known as *Palazzo della Ragione*, Vicenza, 1549-1614 (Italy)

424. *Villa Garzoni*, Lucca, 1547-1550 (Italy)

425. **Robert Smythson**, *Longleat house*, Wiltshire, 1554 and later (United Kingdom)

426. **Posnik Yakovlev** (and **"Barma"**?), *Cathedral of St. Basil the Blessed*, Moscow, 1554-1563 (Russia)

◀427. **Andrea Palladio**, *Palazzo Chiericati*, Grumolo delle Abbadesse, 1550 (Italy)

428. **Andrea Palladio**, *Villa Foscari*, also known as *La Malcontenta*, near Mira, c. 1558-1560 (Italy)

429. **Andrea Palladio**, *Villa Rotonda*, Vicenza, 1556-1571 (Italy)

Most famous of all Palladio's villas, this hilltop retreat—more properly known as the Villa Almerico-Capra—was built for a retired priest, who used it for rural entertaining. Palladio famously set an identical pedimented temple front on all four façades of the main block, the better, he said, to frame the extensive views on every side. The architect was mistakenly convinced that such porticoes formed part of the Roman villas described by Cicero or Pliny, though in Antiquity their use was in fact limited largely to temples. The façades are rotated 45 degrees from the cardinal directions in order to allow some sun to each. The plan of the villa is square, with a bilaterally symmetrical distribution of rooms and a tall rotunda over the central hall. After Palladio's death the house was finished by his pupil Scamozzi; at this time the intended dome was completed as a smaller cupola. Like most of Palladio's buildings, the construction is inexpensive, mainly brick and plaster, but the precision of his proportioning outweighs such considerations. The house influenced countless architects in the following centuries, almost all of whom would have known about it only through the woodcut illustrations in Palladio's Four Books of Architecture *(1570). It is still privately owned, though open to the public.*

430. **Andrea Palladio**, *Villa Barbaro*, Maser, 1554-1560 (Italy)

431. **Giacomo da Vignola**, *Villa Farnese*, Caprarola, 1560 (Italy)

432. *Ottoheinrichsbau, Heidelberg Castle,* Heidelberg, 1556-1559 (Germany)

433. **Juan Bautista de Toledo** and **Juan de Herrera**, *El Escorial*, Madrid, 1563-1584 (Spain)

434. **Andrea Palladio**, *San Giorgio Maggiore*, Venice, begun in 1566 (Italy)

435. **Michelangelo Buonarroti**, also known as **Michelangelo**, *Porta Pia*, Rome, 1561-1565 (Italy)

436. **Giorgio Vasari**, *Uffizi*, Florence, begun in 1560 (Italy)

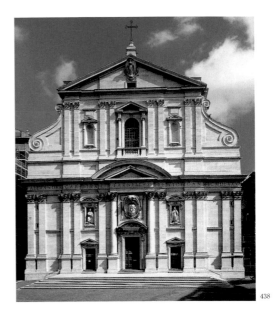

437. **Andrea Palladio**, *Il Redentore*, Venice, 1576-1591 (Italy)

438. **Giacomo da Vignola** and **Giacomo della Porta**, *Church of the Gesù*, Rome, 1568-1584 (Italy)

439. **Cornelis Floris de Vriendt**, *Stadhuis (Town Hall)*, Antwerp, 1565 (Belgium)

440. **Robert Smythson**, *Longleat Castle*, Wiltshire, 1568 (United Kingdom)

441. *Litomysl Castle*, Litomysl, 1568-1581 (Czech Republic)

442. **Andrea Palladio** and **Vincenzo Scamozzi**, *Teatro Olimpico*, Vicenza, 1579-1580 (Italy)

443. **Robert Smythson**, *Hardwick Hall*, Derbyshire, 1590-1597 (United Kingdom)

444

445

444. Giacomo della Porta, *Villa Aldobrandini*, Frascati, 1598-1603 (Italy)

445. Robert Smythson, *Wollaton Hall*, Nottingham, 1580-1588 (United Kingdom)

446

446. William Arnold, *Montacute House*, Montacute, 1601 (United Kingdom)

▶**447. Cosimo Fanzago**, *St. Martin's Charterhouse*, Naples, 1623 (Italy)

448. *Place Royale* (now *Place des Vosges*), Paris, 1605-1612 (France)

449. **Carlo Maderno**, *Santa Susanna*, Rome, 1596-1603 (Italy)

450. **Giovanni Trevano**, *Church of St. Peter and St. Paul*, Krakow, 1597-1619 (Poland)

451. **Inigo Jones**, *The Queen's House*, Greenwich, 1616-1635 (United Kingdom)

The architectural innovations of the Italian Renaissance took some two centuries to reach England. The plain but subtly elegant character of this royal retreat, begun for Anne of Denmark, the Queen of James I, would have been seen as a foreign novelty in a London whose timber and brick buildings were still constructed using medieval methods. Inigo Jones was a courtier who devised sets and costumes for royal masques, but after extensive travels in Italy with the Earl of Arundel he had become uniquely familiar with the work of Palladio; his copy of the Four Books of

Architecture, annotated during his visits to Italian buildings, reveals much of his nascent architectural philosophy. One of his earliest designs, the Queen's House was originally an adjunct to the large Tudor palace at Greenwich, which has since disappeared. It may lay claim to the title of the first truly Classical building in England. The exterior shows typically Palladian restraint: set on a lightly rusticated basement, its façades are regular and astylar, while the central portion only barely detaches itself from the main block. Later incorporated into Wren's Royal Naval Hospital, it now houses displays from the National Maritime Museum and surveys the radically rebuilt expanses of London's Docklands across the Thames.

452. **Peter Huyssens** and **Franciscus Aguilonius**, *St. Carolus Borromeus*, Antwerp, 1615-1621 (Belgium)

453. **Inigo Jones**, *Banqueting House*, London, 1619-1622 (United Kingdom)

◄454. **Gian Lorenzo Bernini**, *St. Peter's Baldachin*, Vatican, 1623-1633 (Vatican City)

455. **Gian Lorenzo Bernini** and **Francesco Borromini**, *Palazzo Barberini*, Rome, 1627-1633 (Italy)

456. **Francesco Borromini**, *Church of St. Charles at the Four Fountains*, Rome, begun in 1634 (Italy)

Built on a restricted urban site as part of a monastic foundation, this small church is highly sculptural and ornate, both inside and out. The sinuous convex and concave curves of the façade (built from 1665-67) seem to undulate, creating a dramatic sense of movement that is typical of Italian Baroque architecture. Borromini was a student of Bernini, and later his chief architectural rival in Rome. But while Bernini was outgoing and socially successful, Borromini was bitter, introverted and depressive, and he eventually committed suicide. The church's ostensibly amoeboid plan was in fact derived from an interplay of geometric forms, and can be read as a modified Greek cross. The interior has many unconventional features, notably a dense interplay of octagons, hexagons and crosses in the coffering of the small oval dome. Later critics of the Baroque, like the French sculptor Falconet, could see only "disorders of the imagination" in Borromini's idiosyncratic buildings. But here the overall result, while visually complicated and perhaps perverse, forms a complete spatial unity in which all parts are indissolubly fused rather than additive.

455

457. **Baldassare Longhena**, *Santa Maria della Salute*, Venice, 1631 and later (Italy)

56

457

458

458. **Jacob van Campen** and **Pieter Post**, *Mauritshuis*, The Hague, 1636-1641 (Netherlands)

459

46

459. **Inigo Jones**, *St. Paul's, Covent Garden*, London, 1630-1635 (United Kingdom)

460. **Bertel Lange**, **Hans van Steenwinckel**, **King Christian IV**, *Rosenborg Castle*, Copenhagen, 1624 and later (Denmark)

51. **Gian Lorenzo Bernini** and **Francesco Borromini**, *Piazza Navona*, Rome, begun in 1644 (*Church of Sant'Agnese in Agone* by **Carlo Rinaldi** and **Francesco Borromini**, begun in 1652) (Italy)

462. **Gian Lorenzo Bernini**, *St. Peter's Square (Piazza San Pietro)*, Rome, 1656-1667 (Italy)

463

463. **Francesco Borromini**, *Sant'Ivo della Sapienza*, Rome, 1642-1650 (Italy)

464

464. **François Mansart** and others, *Church of Val-de-Grâce*, Paris, 1644-1646 and later (France)

465

465. **Pietro da Cortona**, *Santa Maria della Pace*, Rome, 1656-1667 (Italy)

466

466. **Gian Lorenzo Bernini**, *Sant'Andrea al Quirinale*, Rome, 1658-1678 (Italy)

468. **Louis Le Vau, André Le Nôtre** and **Jules-Hardouin Mansart**,
Palace of Versailles, Versailles, begun in 1661 (France)

468

467

467. **Louis Le Vau**, **Charles Le Brun** and **André Le Nôtre**, *Château de Vaux-le-Vicomte, Maincy, 1658-1661 (France)*

This great country house was built for Nicolas Fouquet, who managed the finances of Louis XIV, France's all-powerful 'Sun King.' As the descendant of an earlier French typology of fortified houses, Vaux-le-Vicomte features steep slate roofs and moats on three sides. The plan of the château is compact and symmetrical, with all elements tightly integrated. Breaking with tradition, the central block forms a semicircular projection; an oval salon under an oval dome is housed inside. In typical French manner, the end pavilions are salient. The axis of the house extends across a bridge, through a forecourt and out into the garden. The latter, manifesting a rigidly ordered sense of geometry in its deployment of decorative parterres, water basins, canals, fountains, and graveled walks, typifies the grand manner of French gardening at this period. For a few years Vaux-le-Vicomte was a great centre of artistic patronage; it was inaugurated with a play by Molière. After a great fête in 1661, a jealous Louis XIV had Fouquet arrested and his estate confiscated. The King would then go on to employ the same trio of designers in the massive redevelopment of the hunting lodge at Versailles as his new palace and centre of government.

469

469. **Louis Le Vau**, *Collège des Quatre Nations*, now the *Institut de France*, Paris, 1662-1688 (France)

▶472. **Gian Lorenzo Bernini**, *Scala Regia*, Vatican, 1663-1666 (Vatican City)

470

471

470. **Baldassare Longhena** and **Gian Antonio Gaspari**, *Ca' Pesaro*, Venice, before 1663-1710 (Italy)

471. **Agostino Barelli**, *Nymphenburg*, Munich, c. 1664 (Germany)

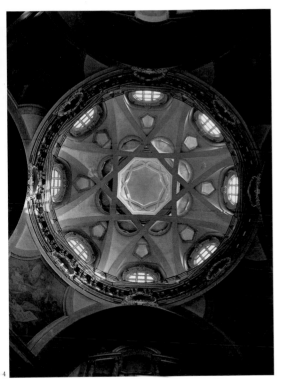

475

◄473. **Sir Christopher Wren**, *St. Paul's Cathedral*, London, 1675-1709
(United Kingdom)

Wren, the greatest architect of the English Baroque, was a mathematician and astronomer by profession, and derived almost all his knowledge of architecture from books; a brief trip to France to examine the work of Bernini at the Louvre gave him his only direct experience of European buildings. This Classical cathedral at the heart of London was built following the Great Fire of 1666, which destroyed much of its great medieval predecessor. After attempts at reconstruction, it was decided to demolish the ruins and begin anew. Wren produced a sequence of designs, some centralised in plan, the last of which was built in modified form as the present building. Some of Wren's inventive engineering strategies are not immediately evident: the great dome is partly held in place by hidden chains that counteract lateral thrust, for example, while the side façades have an upper storey that conceals flying buttresses, a Gothic feature that could not visibly be accommodated by the Classical style. The doubled columns of the west façade may be a reminiscence of Wren's visit to the Louvre, while the west towers have a Baroque flamboyance that recalls Borromini. The interior, as Wren intended, was largely plain and undecorated to allow the harmonious rhythm of the great bays to be appreciated, though this has to some extent been obscured by Victorian monuments and mosaic work.

474. **Camillo-Guarino Guarini**, *San Lorenzo*, Turin, 1666-1679 (Italy)

475. **Camillo-Guarino Guarini**, *Cappella della Sacra Sindone*, Turin, 1667-1694
(Italy)

476. **Jules-Hardouin Mansart**, *Church of St. Louis des Invalides*, Paris,
1670-1708 (France)

476

477. **Louis Le Vau, Charles Le Brun** and **Claude Perrault**, *East façade of the Louvre*, Paris, 1667-1670 (France)

478. **Jean-Baptiste Mathey** and **Johann Joseph Wirch**, *Palace of the Archbishop at Hradcany*, Prague, 1694 (Czech Republic)

479. **Sir Christopher Wren**, *Wren Library, Trinity College*, Cambridge, 1676-1695 (United Kingdom)

480. Sir Christopher Wren, *Rebuilding of Hampton Court Palace*, Surrey, 1689 (United Kingdom)

481. Camillo-Guarino Guarini, *Palazzo Carignano*, Turin, begun in 1679 (Italy)

482. **Johann Bernhard Fischer von Erlach**, *Schönbrunn Palace*, Vienna, 1696 and later (Austria)

483. **Sir Christopher Wren** and **Nicholas Hawksmoor**, *Royal Naval Hospital*, Greenwich, 1696-1716 (United Kingdom)

484. **Sir John Vanbrugh** and **Nicholas Hawksmoor**, *Castle Howard*, Yorkshire, 1699-1712 (United Kingdom)

485. Nicodemus Tessin the Elder and Nicodemus Tessin the Younger, *Royal Domain of Drottningholm*, 1662 and later (Sweden)

486. Jules Hardouin-Mansart, *Place Vendôme*, Paris, 1699 (France)

487

487. Sir John Vanbrugh and **Nicholas Hawksmoor**, *Blenheim Palace*, Woodstock, Oxfordshire, 1705-1722 (United Kingdom)

Blenheim Palace is England's greatest country house, built for John Churchill, the 1st Duke of Marlborough, in recognition of his leadership in military victories over the French. It was co-designed by Vanbrugh, erstwhile playwright and spy, who gave the building an appropriately theatrical character. Built on the site of Woodstock, a royal hunting ground, Blenheim's scale and grandeur were meant as a symbolic challenge to Versailles. Approached through a Great Court with curving wings, Blenheim's entrance façade presents the visitor with a powerfully dynamic and sculptural articulation, amply demonstrating its identity as a pre-eminent manifestation of the short-lived English Baroque. The house was enjoyed by the Duke for only a short time, as political infighting led to his exile. Vanbrugh's exuberant approach was not approved by the Duchess, Sarah, who constantly hindered his plans by insisting—not without reason—on domesticity and frugality; she eventually banned the architect from the grounds. Blenheim's martial origins ensured that it features much political iconography, including a colossal trophy bust of Louis XIV and sculptures of a British lion mauling a French rooster. Later birthplace and ancestral home of Winston Churchill, Blenheim remains the seat of the Dukes of Marlborough.

488

488. Matthaus Pöppelman and **Balthasar Permoser**, *Zwinger Pavilion*, Dresden, 1710-1728 (Germany)

▶**489. Jakob Prandtauer**, *Melk Abbey*, Melk, 1702-1736 and later (Austria)

490. **Enrico Zuccalli**, *Ettal Abbey*, Ettal, 1709 (Germany)

491. **Johann Friedrich Nette** and **Donato Giuseppe Frisoni**, *Ludwigsburg Palace*, Ludwigsburg, 1704-1733 (Germany)

492. **Johann Bernhard Fischer von Erlach** and **J. E. Fischer von Erlach**, *Karlskirche*,
also known as the *Church of St. Charles Borromeo*, Vienna, 1716-1737 (Austria)

493. *Church of the Transfiguration*, Kizhi, 1714 (Russia)

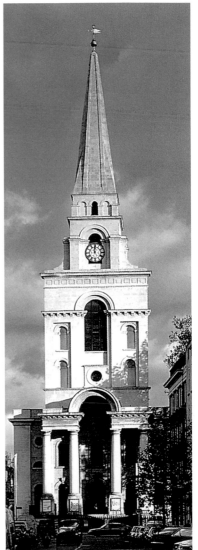

494. **Nicholas Hawksmoor**, *Christ Church, Spitalfields*,
London, 1714-1729 (United Kingdom)

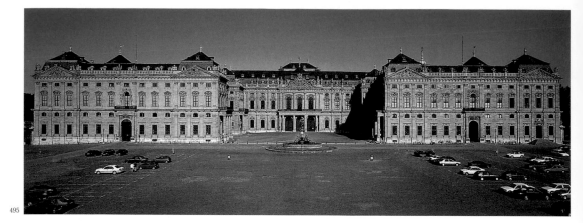

495

495. Johann Balthasar Neumann, *Residenz*, Würzburg, 1720 and later (Germany)

The magnificence of Louis XIV's court at Versailles set the precedent for many local rulers in the German-speaking countries. One of the grandest and most unified of all later Baroque palaces, the Residenz at Würzburg is built within a fortified town. It was the seat of the powerful Prince-Bishops of the Schönborn family. Their court architect was Balthasar Neumann, greatest master of the German Baroque: his buildings are noted for their ornate richness and spatial complexity. Consisting of three major wings, the Residenz has almost 400 rooms.

The great rounded element of its central block recalls the château at Vaux-le-Vicomte. The palace is equally famed for its extensive frescoes, carried out from 1750-1753 by Giambattista Tiepolo and his son. The grand staircase, typically used as a place of reception, has a huge painted composition depicting the four continents on its vaulted ceiling: at 677 square metres in area, this is said to be the largest ceiling fresco in the world. The Hall is also decorated with ornate stucco work and a frescoed dome by Tiepolo showing scenes from the history of Würzburg. Much damaged in World War II, the Residenz has since been in a constant state of restoration.

496

496. Johann Lukas von Hildebrandt, *Upper Belvedere*, Vienna, 1720-1723 (Austria)

497. **Filippo Juvarra**, *Basilica of Superga*, Superga, near Turin, 1717-1731 (Italy)

498. **James Gibbs**, *St. Martin-in-the-Fields*, London, 1721-1726 (United Kingdom)

499. *St. Michael's Golden-Domed Monastery*, Kiev, finished in 1720 (Ukraine)

500. **Jan Blazej Santini-Aichel**, *Pilgrimage Church of St. John Nepomuk*, Žd'ár nad Sázavou, 1720-1727 (Czech Republic)

501

502

501. **Pedro de Ribera**, *Portal of the Hospicio de San Fernando*, Madrid, 1722-1726 (Spain)

502. **J. F. Modlhammer** and **Melchior Hefele**, *Esterhaza*, Fertöd, 1720-1784 (Hungary)

503

503. **Kaspar Moosbrugger**, *Einsiedeln Abbey Church*, Einsiedeln, 1719-1735 (Switzerland)

504. **Francesco de Sanctis** and **Alessandro Specchi**, *The Spanish Steps*, Rome, 1723 1726 (Italy)

505. *Sacred Way Staircase, Bom Jesus do Monte Church*, Braga, begun in 1722 (Portugal)

506. **Johann Bernhard Fischer von Erlach**, *Imperial Library*, Vienna, 1721-1723 (Austria)

507. **Filippo Juvarra,** *Palazzina di caccia (hunting residence),* Stupinigi, 1729-1733 (Italy)

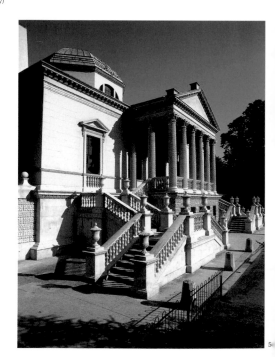

508. **Rosario Gagliardi,** *San Domenico,* Noto, 1727 (Italy)

◀509. **Lord Burlington** and **William Kent**, *Chiswick House*, near London, 1725-1729 (United Kingdom)

This small but finely detailed pavilion represents a seminal step in the formation of English Neo-Palladianism. The 3rd Earl of Burlington, inspired by a grand tour of Italy, decided to give a practical demonstration of his architectural allegiances by the construction of an extension to his (now-demolished) suburban retreat at Chiswick. Now standing alone, this tiny domed building shows a decisive rejection of Baroque experimentation in favour of a return to Classical restraint and order. It is largely modelled on Palladio's Villa Rotonda, with details taken from the works of the Venetian master's assistants. Its small scale, in conjunction with the richly

ornamental carving of its capitals and mouldings, gives the building a slightly miniaturised feel. Burlington's villa was not intended for occupation, and it contains neither bedrooms nor kitchen; rather, it was a space for leisure, entertainment and artistic display, and Handel, Pope and Swift were among its visitors. Its velvet-walled interiors are unexpectedly luxurious and colourful. The basement originally housed Burlington's personal library. The gardens at Chiswick, laid out by William Kent, represent some of the earliest impulses towards a more naturalistic approach in British landscaping. The house is open to the public.

510. **Johann Friedrich Ludwig**, also known as **João Federico Ludovice**, *Royal Palace at Mafra*, Mafra, 1730 (Portugal)

511. **Roger Morris**, *Marble Hill House*, London, 1724-1729 (United Kingdom)

512

512. **William Kent** and **Matthew Brettingham**, *Holkham Hall*, Norfolk, 1734 (United Kingdom)

513. **Nicola Salvi**, *Trevi Fountain*, Rome, 1732-1762 (Italy)

513

514. **James Gibbs**, *The Radcliffe Camera*, Oxford, 1737-1749 (United Kingdom)

515. **Cosmas Damian Asam** and **Egid Quirin Asam**, *Church of St. Johann Nepomuk*, better known as the *Asam Church*, Munich, 1733-1746 (Germany)

516. **Johann Balthasar Neumann**, *Vierzehnheiligen*, also known as the *Basilica of the Fourteen Holy Helpers*, near Bamberg, 1743-1772 (Germany)

517

517. **Henry Hoare II, Henry Flitcroft** and others, *Stourhead landscape gardens*, Wiltshire, laid out beginning in 1743 (United Kingdom)

518. **Mateus Vicente de Oliveira**, *Ceremonial façade of the Queluz National Palace*, Queluz, 1747-1752 (Portugal)

518

519. Bartolomeo Francesco Rastrelli, *Smolny Convent*, St. Petersburg, 1748-1764 (Russia)

520. Horace Walpole and others, *Strawberry Hill House*, Twickenham, 1748-1792 (United Kingdom)

521. Hans Georg Wenzeslaus von Knobelsdorff, *Sanssouci*, Potsdam, 1748 (Germany)

522. **Johann Michael Berr** and **Peter Thumb**, *Façade of the old abbey church*, now *Cathedral*, St. Gallen, 1755-1767 (Switzerland)

523. **Bartolomeo Francesco Rastrelli**, *St. Andrew's Church*, Kiev, 1747-1754 (Ukraine)

524. **Luis de Arévalo** and **F. Manuel Vasquez**, *Sacristy of the Charterhouse*, Granada, 1727-1764 (Spain)

525. *Santuário de Nossa Senhora dos Remédios*, Lamego, 1750-1760 (Portugal)

526. **Luigi Vanvitelli**, *Caserta Palace*, Naples, 1752 and later (Italy)

527. **Ange-Jacques Gabriel**, *Place de la Concorde*, Paris, 1755-1772 (France)

528. **Bartolomeo Francesco Rastrelli**, *The Catherine Palace, Tsarskoye Selo*, Pushkin, 1752-1756 (Russia)

529. **Bartolomeo Francesco Rastrelli**, *The Winter Palace*, St. Petersburg, 1754 and later (Russia)

530. **John Wood I**, *The Circus*, Bath, 1754-1758 (United Kingdom) ▶531. **Jacques-Germain Soufflot** and others, *Panthéon*, Paris, 1758-1791 (France)

532

532. **Robert Adam**, *Kedleston House*, Derbyshire, 1758-1767 (United Kingdom)

A constant preoccupation of the Neoclassical movement was the search for archaeological prototypes. As a young architect, Robert Adam travelled not only to Rome, but to the distant coast of Dalmatia, where he examined and recorded Diocletian's palace at Split; he later published his measured drawings of this great complex in the form of a book. The completion of Kedleston house, seat of the Curzon family, gave Adam an early chance to demonstrate his newly-acquired knowledge of Roman architecture and decoration. His goal, however, was not to

create slavish reconstructions of actual Roman buildings, but rather to deploy selected Roman motifs to give an authentically Classical feel. The central portion of Kedleston's south façade, with its four attached Corinthian columns supporting statues, is closely modelled on the Arch of Constantine in Rome. This composition is topped by an attic storey and a low dome, visible only at a distance. The great marble entrance hall, suggesting the atrium of a Roman villa, is adorned with 20 alabaster columns; it leads to the domed saloon lit by a glazed oculus, recalling the Pantheon. This erudite referencing of Classical precedent suited Adam's clients, who saw themselves as the heirs of ancient Roman virtue.

533

533. **Robert Adam**, *Syon House*, Middlesex, 1760-1769 (United Kingdom)

53

534. **Ange-Jacques Gabriel**, *Le Petit Trianon*, Versailles, 1762-1768 (France)

535

535. **Marie-Joseph Peyre** and **Charles de Wailly**, *The Odéon (Théâtre de l'Odéon)*, Paris, 1767-1782 (France)

536

536. **John Wood II**, *The Royal Crescent*, Bath, 1767 and later (United Kingdom)

537. **Jacques Denis Antoine**, *Hôtel des Monnaies*, Paris, 1771-1775 (France)

538. **Victor Louis**, *Grand Théâtre*, Bordeaux, 1773-1780 (France)

539. **Jacques Gondouin**, *Medical School*, Paris, 1769-1786 (France)

540

541

540. **Claude Nicolas Ledoux**, *Saltworks of Arc-et-Senans*, Arc-et-Senans, 1775-1779 (France)

Ledoux was an architectural visionary who took the language of Classicism into new realms of expression. Here a utilitarian commission for a salt manufactory became a manifestation of the Enlightenment urge to rationalise industry and society. The grandeur of the Saltworks is partly due to its royal patronage: the state maintained a strict monopoly on salt production. The high value of the commodity thus justified the severe and even fortified appearance of the complex. The semi-circular yard is entered through a massive Doric portico enclosing a cavernous hall that gives an impression of an actual salt mine. Referencing the activities taking place within, the motif of water gushing from outfalls is carved in stone on the exterior façades of the industrial blocks. Set between these is the House of the Director, with its powerful blocked columns. Despite his radically new mode of design, Ledoux was an establishment architect, notorious for his series of massive government tollhouses that once ringed Paris. He was imprisoned after the Revolution of 1789, and spent much of his time thereafter composing a treatise in which the Saltworks were enlarged into an ideal city known as Chaux.

541. **Giuseppe Piermarini**, *La Scala opera house*, Milan, 1770s and later (Italy)

542. **Antonio Rinaldi**, *Chinese Palace, Oranienbaum*, St. Petersburg, 1762-1768 (Russia)

542

543. *The Church of Mercy (Igreja da Misericórdia)*, Viseu, 18th century (Portugal)

544. **Sir William Chambers**, *Somerset House*, London, 1776-1796 (United Kingdom)

545. **James Gandon**, *The Four Courts*, Dublin, 1776-1796 (Ireland)

546. **Claude Nicolas Ledoux**, *Barrière de la Villette*, Paris, 1784-1787 (France)

547. **Sir John Soane**, *The Bank of England*, London, 1788 and later (United Kingdom)

548. *Pfaueninsel*, Berlin, 1796 (Germany)

550

◀549. **Andreyan Zakharov**, *The Admiralty*, St. Petersburg, 1806-1823 (Russia)

550. **James Wyatt**, *Castle Coole*, Enniskillen, Northern Ireland, 1789-1798 (United Kingdom)

551

552

551. **Pierre-Alexandre Vignon**, *Madeleine Church*, Paris, 1763-1842 (France)

552. **Thomas de Thomon**, *The Stock Exchange*, St. Petersburg, 1804 (Russia)

553

553. **Charles Percier** and **Pierre François Léonard Fontaine**,
Arc de Triomphe du Carrousel, Paris, 1807-1809 (France)

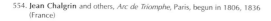

554. **Jean Chalgrin** and others, *Arc de Triomphe*, Paris, begun in 1806, 1836
    (France)

A universally known symbol of Paris, the Arc de Triomphe is also one of the most characteristic monuments of Neoclassicism, both for its fidelity to Roman prototypes and for its colossal size. Seeing himself as the inheritor of the Roman imperial tradition, Napoleon cultivated artistic and architectural references in this vein. After his victory at Austerlitz he decided to build a great monument on what were then the outskirts of Paris, a building that would reproduce the Roman triumphal arch typology on a colossal scale. At 49.5 metres in height, the Parisian arch far surpasses its relatively small prototype, the Arch of Titus in Rome (n° 230). Construction turned out to be an arduous task: the laying of the foundations alone took two years, and after Waterloo the project was left unfinished. Completed only in the 1830s, it was later made the focus of several new radiating boulevards laid out by Baron Haussmann. It now stands at the centre of the traffic-clogged Place de l'Étoile. The arch's sculptures and friezes represent French military victories, and the most famous of its high-relief groups is François Rude's Departure of the Volunteers of 1792, also known as La Marseillaise. The Tomb of the Unknown Soldier was added at its base after World War I.

554

555

555. **Sir John Soane**, *Dulwich Picture Gallery*, London, 1811-1814 (United Kingdom)

556

556. **John Nash**, *The Royal Pavilion*, Brighton, 1815-1823 (United Kingdom)

55

557. **Karl Friedrich Schinkel**, *Neue Wache (New Guardhouse)*, Berlin, 1816-1818 (Germany)

558. **John Nash**, *Crescent Park*, Regent's Park, London, 1812 and later (United Kingdom)

559. **Raffaele Stern**, *New wing of the Museo Chiaramonti*, Vatican, 1817-1822 (Vatican City)

560. **Sir John Soane**, *Sir John Soane's House and Museum*, London, 1812-1837 (United Kingdom)

561

561. **Antti Piimänen**, *Vihti Church*, Vihti, 1772-1929 (Finland)

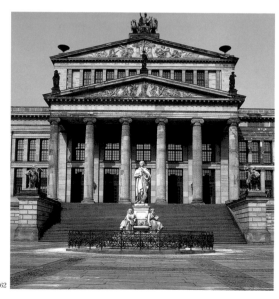

562

563

562. **Karl Friedrich Schinkel**, *Schauspielhaus*, also known as the
    Konzerthaus, Berlin, 1818-1821 (Germany)

563. **Leo von Klenze**, *Walhalla*, Donaustauf, 1831-1842 (Germany)

564. Sir Robert Smirke, *The British Museum*, London, begun in 1823 (United Kingdom)

One of the largest museums in the world, the British Museum houses some 3.2 km of exhibition space. The somewhat severe character of the original Greek Revival building reflects the reforming zeal of the Neoclassicists, who attempted to give Classical architecture a more rigorous archaeological exactitude. The earliest part to be built was the East Wing, housing the King's Library. The famous entrance façade of the South Wing, finished in 1847, is fronted by 44 huge Ionic columns, their capitals based on those of the Temple of Athena Polias at Priene. The pediment sculptures by Sir Richard Westmacott form an allegorical composition representing The Progress of Civilisation. Appropriately but controversially, this icon of Neoclassical architecture houses the famous Elgin marbles, taken from the Parthenon in the early 19th century. In 1846 the architect's brother, Sidney Smirke, took over construction and added the famous Round Reading Room (1854-57). The latest addition is Norman Foster's Great Court, opened in 2000, built within the central open quadrangle after the departure of the British Library; it features a glass and steel roof with 1656 uniquely formed panes of glass.*

565. Karl Friedrich Schinkel, *Altes Museum*, Berlin, 1823-1828 (Germany)

566. Sir Charles Barry and **Augustus Welby Northmore Pugin**, *Palace of Westminster*, also known as *the Houses of Parliament*, London, 1836-c. 1860 (United Kingdom)

The Palace of Westminster, as this great complex is more correctly termed, is the seat of the two British Houses of Parliament. It was erected following the destruction of most of the old parliamentary buildings in a great fire in 1834. The chosen style was Perpendicular Gothic of the 15th century, meant to reflect the medieval origins of the English parliamentary system and to harmonise with surviving medieval fragments of Westminster Hall and St. Stephen's Chapel, as well as neighbouring Westminster

Abbey. Barry, a Classicist, produced façades with a regular system of bays; Pugin, a pioneering and committed Gothic Revivalist, found this too repetitive: he once remarked that the Palace was "All Grecian... Tudor details on a classic body." Indeed, only a few major elements lend the composition a calculated asymmetry: these include the 98.5 metre Victoria Tower (housing the Parliamentary archives) and the 96.3 metre Clock Tower (often mistakenly referred to as 'Big Ben,' which is actually the name of the 14-tonne bell inside it). Pugin toiled endlessly to produce authentically medieval designs for wallpapers, tiled floors, sculptures, stained glass and large-scale furnishings, including the royal thrones and canopies. Comprising about 1100 rooms, the Palace was only fully completed in 1870.

567

568

569

567. **Gottfried Semper**, *Semper Opera House*, Dresden, 1838-1841 (rebuilt in 1871) (Germany)

568. **M. G. B. Bindesbøll**, *Thorvaldsen Museum*, Copenhagen, 1839-1848 (Denmark)

569. **Augustus Welby Northmore Pugin**, *St. Giles*, Cheadle, Staffordshire, 1839-1846 (United Kingdom)

570. **Harvey Lonsdale Elmes**, *St. George's Hall*, Liverpool, 1841-1854 (United Kingdom)

▶571. **Henri Labrouste**, *Bibliothèque Sainte-Geneviève*, Paris, 1843-1851 (France)

572. **Decimus Burton** and **Richard Turner**, *The Palm House*, Kew Gardens, London, 1845-1847 (United Kingdom)

573. **Baron von Eschwege**, *Palácio Nacional da Pena*, Sintra, 1839-1885 (Portugal)

574. **William Butterfield**, *All Saints, Margaret Street church*, London, 1849-1859 (United Kingdom)

575. **Sara Losh**, *Church of St Mary*, Wreay, Cumbria, 1840-1842 (United Kingdom)

576. **Cuthbert Brodrick**, *Leeds Town Hall*, Leeds, 1853-1858 (United Kingdom)

577. **Leo von Klenze**, *Propylaea*, Munich, 1862 (Germany)

579

◄578. **Léon Vaudoyer**, *Marseille Cathedral*, Marseille, 1852-1896 (France)

579. **Heinrich von Ferstel**, *Votivkirche*, Vienna, 1856-1879 (Austria)

580. **Charles Garnier**, *The Opera*, Paris, 1861-1875 (France)

581

581. **Deane** & **Woodward**, *The University Museum*, Oxford, 1853-1860 (United Kingdom)

Oxford's University Museum was founded by Sir Henry Wentworth Acland to consolidate all the dispersed science facilities in one building, though almost all of these have since moved on to newer facilities. The Neo-Gothic edifice was designed by two Irish architects, Thomas Newenham Deane and Benjamin Woodward. It is focused around a large square court for the display of specimens of natural history; its glass roof is supported by tall pillars of cast iron, creating three aisles. Despite this unorthodox metallic construction, the use of pointed Gothic arches continues the medieval theme. The decorative elements, mainly naturalistic representations of plants, were all funded by public subscription, and are still incomplete. Following the ideas of the art critic John Ruskin, the Irish stone carvers O'Shea and Whelan were allowed a free hand to create their own designs on the window frames; this famously backfired when a dispute led to them sculpting caricatures of certain members of the University Congregation as parrots and owls.

582. **Henri Labrouste**, *Bibliothèque nationale de France*, Paris, 1862-1868 (France)

583. **Giuseppe Mengoni**, *Galleria Vittorio Emanuele*, Milan, 1867-1878 (Italy)

584. **Thomas Burgh, Thomas Deane, Benjamin Woodward**, *Long Room Library*, Dublin, 1860 (Ireland)

585

585. **Philip Webb** (for **William Morris**), *Red House*, Bexleyheath, Kent, 1859-1860 (United Kingdom)

This seminal building in the nascent Arts and Crafts Movement was designed for William Morris and his new wife, but they lived there for only five years. Intended to be the gathering place of a new brotherhood of artists, designers and craftsmen, Red House was a physical manifestation of Morris's moral dedication to the revival of craft traditions. With its steep tile roofs and asymmetrical plan it generally suggests a late

medieval building that has been added to over centuries, for many of the details—such as sash windows—borrow eclectically from different periods. Morris's colleague Dante Gabriel Rossetti remarked that it was "more of a poem than a house." Though emphasising simplicity and natural materials, the interior contains rich wall paintings and stained glass by Edward Burne-Jones. In 1904 the German architect and scholar Hermann Muthesius described Webb's building as "the first house to be conceived as a whole inside and out, the very first example in the history of the modern house." Red House was acquired by the National Trust in 2003, and is now open to the public.

586

586. **Alfred Waterhouse**, *Museum of Natural History*, London, 1860-1880 (United Kingdom)

587. **Sir George Gilbert Scott**, *Midland Grand Hotel* and *St. Pancras Railway Station*, London, 1861-1876 (train shed by W. H. Barlow and R. M. Ordish) (United Kingdom)

588. **Frigyes Feszl**, *Pesti Vidago*, Budapest, 1865 (Hungary)

589. **Sir George Gilbert Scott**, *Royal Albert Hall*, London, 1871 (United Kingdom)

590. **Eduard Riedel** and **Christian Jank**, *Neuschwanstein Castle*, near Füssen, 1869-1881 (Germany)

590

591. **William Butterfield**, *Keble College Chapel*, Oxford, 19th century (United Kingdom)

592. **Friedrich von Schmidt**, *Rathaus (Town Hall)*, Vienna, 1872-1883 (Austria)

◄593. **Alfred Waterhouse**, *Town Hall*, Manchester, 1867-1877 (United Kingdom)

A symbol of Victorian pride in industry, the Manchester Town Hall is also a tour de force of the Gothic Revival in England. Granted city status only in 1853, Manchester waited to demonstrate its new economic importance by the construction of a grand new civic centre. Waterhouse, later the architect of the Natural History Museum in London, beat out 136 other entries in a competition to design the Town Hall, which had to be built on an awkward triangular site. The style chosen was the currently fashionable 13th-century Early English Gothic, which also paid tribute to the medieval origins of Manchester's textile trade. The picturesque skyline is dominated by an 85-metre-tall Bell Tower over the main entrance. The exterior walls have an ashlar facing of sandstone and statues of important civic figures. Similarly, the central Great Hall features twelve murals by Ford Madox Brown showing scenes from city history. The entrance hall has an impressive vaulted ceiling and floor mosaics featuring bees, symbols of the city as a 'hive of industry.' One of the first buildings to be heated by forced air, the Town Hall has been cited by Norman Foster as a decisive factor in his early decision to enter the field of architecture.

594. **Paul Abadie**, *Basilica of Sacré-Cœur*, Paris, 1875-1914 (France)

595. **Alexander Pomerantsev**, *St. Alexander Nevsky Cathedral*, Sofia, 1882-1912 (Bulgaria)

596. **Marco Treves**, **Mariano Falcini** and **Vincenzo Micheli**, *Tempio Maggiore Israelitico (Great Synagogue)*, Florence, 1874-1882 (Italy)

597

597. **Antoni Gaudí**, *Expiatory Temple of the Holy Family*, known as the *Sagrada Família*, Barcelona, begun in 1882 (Spain)

One of the most popular tourist attractions in Spain, this great church dedicated to the Holy Family remains incomplete over 125 years after it was started. Gaudí, a Catalonian architect of brilliant unconventionality, was a devoted Catholic, and worked obsessively on the Sagrada Família for over 40 years. Popular support for the project waned towards the end of his life, and Gaudí was at one point reduced to going door-to-door to solicit funds. He died before he came anywhere near to realising his full plans, which in any case seem never to have

achieved a definitive form. Begun in a conventional neo-Gothic style, the façades and their immensely tall towers increasingly came to manifest a teeming organic complexity with few historical precedents. The eastern façade was the only one finished before the Spanish Civil War, and in 1936 a fire in the crypt destroyed some of Gaudí's drawings and models. Not without controversy, construction was restarted in the 1980s. Computer technology has now speeded up the work, which is scheduled to be finished in 2026; when complete, the Sagrada Família will have 18 tall towers representing New Testament figures. It receives no church or government funding, and relies solely on donations and visitors' fees.

598. **Richard Norman Shaw**, *Cragside House*, Northumberland, 1863-1870 (United Kingdom)

599. **Imre Steindl**, *Parliament*, Budapest, 1885-1904 (Hungary)

600. **Giuseppe Sacconi**, *Monument to Victor Emmanuel II*, Rome, 1885-1911 (Italy)

601. **Horace Jones**, *Tower Bridge*, London, 1886-1894 (United Kingdom)

▶602. **Gustave Eiffel**, *Eiffel Tower*, Paris, 1887-1889 (France)

One of the most recognisable buildings on the planet, the Tower was first erected as a temporary structure for the Universal Exhibition of 1889. 300 metres tall, it held the world record for height until it was overtaken by New York's Chrysler Building in 1930. Eiffel, an engineer rather than an architect, made his name designing audacious bridges and railway viaducts. Here much of the calculation and planning was in fact done by two of his assistants. Standardised cast-iron elements were used to construct a building that was strong, light and wind-resistant: it has been said that the volume of air enclosed by the Tower weighs more than the structure itself, and that if all its iron was melted down it would fill the square area of its base only to the height of about 15 cm. It rests on four great canted pylons connected by arches whose value is largely ornamental; other decorative elements have been removed over the years. While the tower has always been successful with the public, at the time of its conception it was denounced by French artists, writers and intellectuals as an ugly industrial blemish on the skyline. It now attracts some five million visitors a year.

603. **Henry van de Velde**, *Bloemenwerf House*, Brussels, 1895 (Belgium)

604. **Joseph Maria Olbrich**, *Vienna Secession Building*, Vienna, 1897-1898 (Austria)

605. **Hector Guimard**, *Castel Béranger*, Paris, 1895-1898 (France)

606. **Victor Horta**, *Tassel House*, Brussels, 1892-1893 (Belgium)

607. **Victor Horta**, *Hôtel van Eetvelde*, Brussels, 1895-1898 (Belgium)

608. **Victor Horta**, *Hôtel Solvay*, Brussels, 1895-1900 (Belgium)

609

6

609. **Hendrik P. Berlage**, *Amsterdam Stock Exchange*, Amsterdam, 1897-1909 (Netherlands)

610. **Charles Rennie Mackintosh**, *Glasgow School of Art*, Glasgow, Scotland, 1896-1909 (United Kingdom)

611

611. **Victor Horta**, *Horta House*, now *Horta Museum*, Brussels, 1898 (Belgium)

612. **Otto Wagner**, *Karlsplatz Metro Station*, Vienna, 1899 (Austria)

613. **Otto Wagner**, *Majolikahaus apartments*, Vienna, 1898-1899 (Austria)

615. **Giuseppe Brega**, *Villino Ruggeri*, Pesaro, 1907 (Italy)

616. **Henri Sauvage**, *Villa Majorelle*, Nancy, 1898-1902 (France)

◀614. **Antoni Gaudí**, *Park Güell*, Barcelona, 1900-1914 (Spain)

617. **M. H. Baillie Scott**, *Blackwell*, Bowness-on-Windermere, Cumbria, 1898-1900 (United Kingdom)

618. **Charles Rennie Mackintosh**, *Hill House*, Helensburgh, Scotland, 1902-1904 (United Kingdom)

619. **Eliel Saarinen**, *Hvittrask*, near Helsinki, 1902 (Finland)

620. **Auguste Perret**, *Rue Franklin apartments*, Paris, 1902-1904 (France)

621. **Giles Gilbert Scott**, *Cathedral Church of Christ*, Liverpool, 1904-1978 (United Kingdom)

622. **Raul Mesnier de Ponsard**, *Santa Justa Lift*, Lisbon, 1900-1902 (Portugal)

623. **Frantz Jourdain**, *La Samaritaine*, Paris, 1903-1907 (France)

624

624. **Otto Wagner**, *Church of St. Leopold am Steinhof*, Vienna, 1905-1907 (Austria)

625

625. **Antonin Balsanek** and **Osvald Polivka**, *Municipal House*, Prague, 1905-1912 (Czech Republic)

626

627

627. **Hector Guimard**, *Castel d'Orgeval*, Villemoisson-sur-Orge, 1904 (France)

626. **Otto Wagner**, *Austrian Postal Savings Bank*, Vienna, 1904-1912 (Austria)

Wagner was the elder statesman of the avant-garde Viennese cultural group known as the Secession, who attempted to find a new mode of artistic expression suited to modern life. This great office complex in a rigorously ordered and rectilinear style exemplifies Wagner's purified version of Classicism. The street façade is austerely geometric, but the upper floors are clad in white marble plaques ostensibly attached to the wall by aluminum bolts, thus lending the building a feel of both luxury and lightness. The main banking hall, seemingly inspired by railway stations or exhibition buildings, features a light steel framework supporting a glass roof. The floor is also of glass blocks, while opaque panels of white glass attached to the walls were justified by Wagner as being both durable and resistant to any off-the-cuff calculations that might be written on them by absent-minded customers. This space must have seemed distinctly modern, or perhaps incongruously industrial, at the time it was built. Theorists of architectural modernism have admired Wagner's frank exposure of mechanical services, such as the free-standing aluminum ventilation tubes of the banking hall, but the elegance and care seen in such details ensure that they are in no sense crudely industrial in character.

▶628. **Antoni Gaudí**, *Casa Batlló*, Barcelona, 1904-1906 (Spain)

629. **Antoni Gaudí**, *Casa Milà*, Barcelona, 1905-1907 (Spain)

630. **Lluís Domènech i Montaner**, *Palau de la Música Catalana*, Barcelona, 1905-1908 (Spain)

631. **Friedrich Ohmann**, *Hôtel Central*, Prague, 1902 (Czech Republic)

632. **Ragnar Östberg**, *Town Hall*, Stockholm, 1911-1923 (Sweden)

633. **Josef Hoffmann**, *Stoclet Palace*, Brussels, 1905-1911 (Belgium)

634. **Peter Behrens**, *A.E.G. Turbine Factory*, Berlin, 1909 (Germany)

635. **Walter Gropius**, *Fagus Factory*, Alfeld, 1911-1913 (Germany)

This seminal industrial building, a shoe-last factory, displays many of the features that would come to characterise modern architecture. These include flat roofs, simple rectilinear geometry, eschewal of conventional style and ornament, walls as floor-to-ceiling screens of glass, the use of new industrial materials, and an embrace of the machine in both a technical and an aesthetic sense. Gropius was at this time very interested in American factory buildings, while the idea of a modern style suited to industry was taken from his mentor, Peter Behrens. At the

same time, Gropius's evident desire to introduce light and air into the factory reflected a socialist desire to improve industrial working conditions. Flouting convention, the corners of the building are deliberately left open, clad only in steel-framed plate glass, thus emphasising the role of the wall as a transparent screen with no load-bearing function. Bauhaus designers took charge of the interior and furniture following the First World War. Recent restoration work has revealed that the internal structure is not, as was long believed, reinforced concrete. The plan of the factory was designed by the architect Eduard Werner; only the façades are by the team of Gropius & Meyer.

636. **Adolf Loos**, *Steiner House*, Vienna, 1910 (Austria)

637. **Adolf Loos**, *Goldman & Salatsch store*, Vienna, 1910 (Austria)

638. **Ferdinand Cheval**, *Ideal Palace*, Hauterives, 1879-1912 (France)

639. **Gustaf Wickman**, *Church at Kiruna*, Kiruna, 1902-1912 (Sweden)

640

640. **J. M. van der Mey**, *Scheepvaarthuis*, Amsterdam, 1912 (Netherlands)

641

641. **Hector Guimard**, *Agoudas Hakehilos Synagogue*, Paris, 1913-1914 (France)

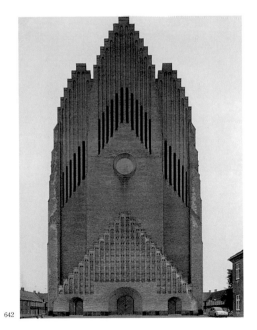

642

642. **Peder Jensen Klint**, *Grundtvig's Church*, Copenhagen, 1921-1940 (Denmark)

643

643. **Josef Chochol**, *Hodek apartments*, Prague, 1913 (Czech Republic)

644

644. **Robert van't Hoff**, *Villa at Huis ter Heide*, near Utrecht, 1916 (Netherlands)

645. **Giacomo Matté-Trucco**, *Fiat-Lingotto automobile factory*, Turin, 1916-1923 (Italy)

646. **Max Berg**, *Hala Ludowa*, Wroclaw, 1911-1913 (Poland)

647. **Erik Gunnar Asplund**, *Stockholm Central Library*, Stockholm, 1918-1927 (Sweden)

648. **Michel de Klerk** and **Piet Kramer**, *Eigen Haard Housing Estate*, Amsterdam, 1912-1921 (Netherlands)

649. **Erich Mendelsohn**, *Einstein Tower*, Potsdam, 1919-1921 (Germany)

650. **Auguste Perret**, *Church of Notre Dame du Raincy*, Le Raincy, 1922-1923 (France)

651. **Willem Dudok**, *Town Hall*, Hilversum, 1928-1931 (Netherlands)

652. **Gerrit Rietveld**, *Schroder House*, Utrecht, 1924-1925 (Netherlands)

653. **Walter Gropius**, *Bauhaus*, Dessau, 1925-1926 (Germany)

654. **Johannes Brinkman**, *Van Nelle Factory*, Rotterdam, 1926-1930 (Netherlands)

655. **Ludwig Mies van der Rohe** and other architects, *Weissenhof Estate*, Stuttgart, 1927 (Germany)

656. **Konstantin Melnikov**, *Melnikov House*, Moscow, 1927 (Russia)

657. **Konstantin Melnikov**, *Rusakov Workers' Club*, Moscow, 1927-1929 (Russia)

658. **I. P. Golosov**, *Zuyev Workers' Club*, Moscow, 1928 (Russia)

659. **Sir Edwin Lutyens**, *Thiepval Memorial to the Missing of the Somme*, Thiepval, 1928-1932 (France)

660. **Rudolf Steiner**, *Second Goetheanum*, Dornach, 1925-1928 (Switzerland)

661

661. **Bernard Bijvoet** and **Pierre Chareau**, *La Maison de Verre (House of Glass)*, Paris, 1928-1931 (France)

662. **Alvar Aalto**, *Municipal Library*, Viipuri, 1927-1935 (Russia)

662

663. **Jože Plečnik**, *Church of the Sacred Heart*, Prague, 1921-1932 (Czech Republic)

664. **Alvar Aalto**, *Paimio Tuberculosis Sanatorium*, Paimio, 1929-1933 (Finland)

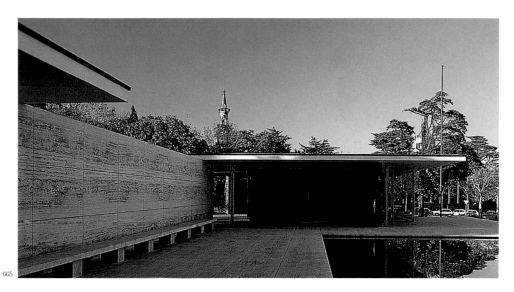

665. **Ludwig Mies van der Rohe**, *German Pavilion*, Barcelona, 1929 (reconstructed in 1986) (Spain)

666. **Le Corbusier**, *Villa Savoye*, Poissy, 1928-1931 (France)

This small weekend villa outside Paris is perhaps the greatest manifestation of Le Corbusier's famous notion of the modern house as a "machine for living in." Its stark geometric forms and complete eschewal of traditional house typologies signal a radical rethinking of the 20th-century domestic environment. Seen from a distance, it appears as if a spaceship has landed on a grassy field. The main floor of the villa is raised above the ground on piers, or pilotis, which provide a firm internal skeleton for the building; consequently, the plans of the three floors are free to be articulated in any way desired. A shallow ramp serves as a central spine, rising from the glazed entrance hall on the ground floor through the main living space and open patio to a rooftop sunbathing area. Continuous strip windows flood the interior with light, stressing the conceptual identity of the house as an open frame by which the natural world may be appreciated rather than a dark, enclosed shelter. Built as a weekend pied-à-terre for a Parisian businessman, the Villa Savoye was inhabited only for a few years before the Second World War; it subsequently served as a military outpost and even a stable before it was taken over by the French government and opened to the public as a museum.

667. **Eileen Gray**, *E-1027*, Roquebrune-Cap Martin, 1924-1929 (France)

668. **Adolf Loos**, *Moller House*, Vienna, 1930 (Austria)

669. **Ludwig Mies van der Rohe**, *Villa Tugendhat*, Brno, 1930 (Czech Republic)

670. **Jacobus Johannes Pieter Oud**, *Kiefhoek Housing Development*, Rotterdam, 1925-1929 (Netherlands)

671. **Amyas Douglas Connell**, *High and Over country house*, Amersham, Buckinghamshire, 1929-1931 (United Kingdom)

672. **Giuseppe Terragni**, *Casa del Fascio*, Como, 1932-1936 (Italy)

673. **Alexey Shchusev**, *The Lenin Mausoleum* (and the walls of the Kremlin, 1485-1495), Moscow, 1929-1930 (Russia)

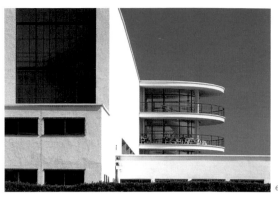

675

674. **P. Dreimanis, Riga Market Construction Office**, *Central Market Halls*, Riga, 1928-1930 (Latvia)

675. **Erich Mendelsohn**, *De La Warr Pavilion*, Bexhill-on-Sea, East Sussex, 1935 (United Kingdom)

677

676. **Wells Coates**, *Isokon Building*, London, 1934 (United Kingdom)

677. **Erik Gunnar Asplund**, *Woodland Crematorium*, Stockholm, 1935-1940 (Sweden)

679

678. **Frits P. J. Peutz**, *Glaspaleis*, Heerlen, 1935 (Netherlands)

679. **Le Corbusier**, *Tsentrosoyuz Building*, Moscow, 1929-1936 (Russia)

680. **Alvar Aalto**, *Villa Mairea*, Noormarkku, 1937-1939 (Finland)

681. **Albert Speer**, *Zeppelin Field Tribune*, Nuremberg, 1937 (Germany)

682. **Virgil Bierbauer** and **Laszlo Kralik**, *Budapest Airport*, Budapest, 1935-1937 (Hungary)

683. **Arne Jacobsen**, *Aarhus Town Hall*, Aarhus, 1937 (Denmark)

684. **Jože Plečnik**, *Church of St. Michael*, Ljubljana, 1937-1940 (Slovenia)

685

685. Le Corbusier, *Unité d'Habitation (Cité Radieuse)*, Marseille, 1945-1952 (France)

Drawing on the inspiration of ocean liners, Le Corbusier conceived his giant housing complex as a self-sufficient city in the sky. As such, it represents a long-delayed manifestation of his theoretical 'La Cité Radieuse', which he had been elaborating through the previous decades. The colossal block, which seems to sail through the surrounding vegetation like a great ship, contains over three hundred apartments and an internal street with shops, post office and hotel; on the roof are a running track, gymnasium and nursery. Le Corbusier's pioneering use of rough-surfaced reinforced concrete as the primary building material was in fact necessitated by a post-war steel shortage, but the architect later claimed that the crudeness and irregularities of this material gave the building character, like the lines and wrinkles in a face. The Unité was extremely influential, spawning imitation housing blocks of varying degrees of social success all over Europe and North America through the following decades. Its brash aesthetic also gave rise to the so-called Brutalist movement, which championed bold form and honest exposure of industrial materials over genteel or superficial conventions of architectural beauty.

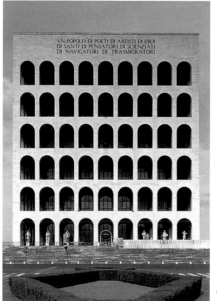

686

686. Giovanni Guerrini, Ernesto Lapadula and **Mario Romano**, *Palazzo della Civiltà Italiana*, Rome, 1938-1940 (Italy)

687. **Peter** and **Alison Smithson**, *Smithdon High School*, Hunstanton, Norfolk, 1949-1954 (United Kingdom)

688. **Le Corbusier**, *Notre-Dame-du-Haut*, Ronchamp, 1950-1955 (France)

689. **Alvar Aalto**, *Town Hall*, Säynätsalo, 1950-1952 (Finland)

690. **Alvar Aalto**, *Helsinki University of Technology*, Otaniemi, completed in 1949-1966 (Finland)

691. Alvar Aalto, *Aalto Studio*, Helsinki, 1954-1956 (Finland)

692. Alvar Aalto, *House of Culture*, Helsinki, 1955-1958 (Finland)

693. Le Corbusier, *Jaoul houses*, Neuilly-sur-Seine, 1954-1956 (France)

694. **Marcel Breuer**, **Pier Luigi Nervi** and **Bernard Zehrfuss**, *UNESCO Headquarters*, Paris, 1953-1958 (France)

695. **Alvar Aalto**, *Vouksenniska Church*, Imatra, 1956-1958 (Finland)

696. **Gio Ponti** and **Pier Luigi Nervi**, *Pirelli Building*, Milan, 1956-1959 (Italy)

697. **Le Corbusier**, *Monastery of Sainte-Marie de la Tourette*, Éveux, 1956-1960 (France)

698. **Banfi, Belgiojoso, Peresutti** and **Rogers**, *Torre Velasca*, Milan, 1956-1958 (Italy)

698

699. **Pier Luigi Nervi**, *Palazzetto dello Sport*, Rome, 1957-1960 (Italy)

700. **Hans Scharoun**, *Berlin Philharmonic Hall*, Berlin, 1956-1963 (Germany)

701. **Pier Luigi Nervi**, *Palazzo del Lavoro*, Turin, 1959-1961 (Italy)

702. **André Waterkeyn**, *The Atomium*, Brussels, 1958 (Belgium)

◀703. **Stirling and Gowan**, *Engineering School, University of Leicester*, Leicester, Leicestershire, 1959-1963 (United Kingdom)

704. **Aldo van Eyck**, *Amsterdam Orphanage*, Amsterdam, 1960-1961 (Netherlands)

705. **Gottfried Böhm**, *Pilgrimage Church*, Velbert, 1963-1972 (Germany)

706. **Alvar Aalto**, *Seinajoki Library*, Seinajoki, 1963-1965 (Finland)

707. **Le Corbusier**, *Church of Saint-Pierre*, Firminy, designed in 1963, built in 1970-2006 (France)

708

708. **Bengt Larsson**, *Church at Haparanda*, Haparanda, 1967 (Sweden)

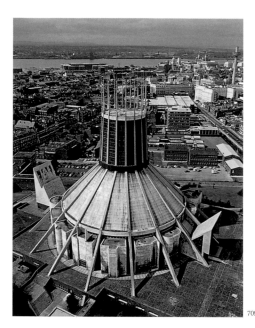

709

709. **Frederick Gibberd**, *Liverpool Metropolitan Cathedral*, Liverpool, 1967 (United Kingdom)

710

710. **Ralph Erskine**, *Byker Redevelopment*, Newcastle-upon-Tyne, 1973-1978 (United Kingdom)

711

711. **Hermann Hertzberger**, *Central Beheer office complex*, Apeldoorn, 1967-1972 (Netherlands)

712. **Richard Rogers** and **Su Rogers**, *Dr. Rogers' House*, London, 1967 (United Kingdom)

713. **Arne Jacobsen**, *St. Catherine's College*, Oxford, 1963 (United Kingdom)

714. **Carlo Scarpa**, *Brion-Vega Cemetery*, San Vito d'Altivole, 1970-1972 (Italy)

715. **Mario Botta**, *Family house at Riva San Vitale*, Riva San Vitale, Ticino, 1972-1973 (Switzerland)

716. **Renzo Piano** and **Richard Rogers**, *Centre Georges Pompidou*, Paris, 1971-1977 (France)

717. **Norman Foster**, *Willis Faber & Dumas Headquarters*, Ipswich, Suffolk, 1971-1975 (United Kingdom)

718. **Jørn Utzon**, *Bagsværd Church*, Bagsværd, 1974-1976 (Denmark)

719. **Rafael Moneo**, *National Museum of Roman Art*, Mérida, 1980-1985 (Spain)

720. **Ricardo Bofill**, *Walden7 apartments*, Barcelona, 1974 (Spain)

721. **James Stirling**, *Neue Staatsgalerie*, Stuttgart, 1977-1984 (Germany)

722. **Richard Rogers Partnership**, *Lloyd's of London*, London, 1978-1986 (United Kingdom)

723. **Mario Botta**, *House in Stabio*, Stabio, Ticino, 1981-1982 (Switzerland)

723

724. **Norman Foster**, *Sainsbury Centre for the Visual Arts*, Norwich, Norfolk, 1974-1978 (United Kingdom)

725. **Gae Aulenti** and **ACT Architecture**, *Musée d'Orsay*, Paris, 1980-1986
(rehabilitation of **Victor Laloux**'s *Gare d'Orsay*, 1900) (France)

726. **Christian de Portzamparc**, *Cité de la Musique*, Paris, 1984-1990 (France)

727. Johann Otto von Spreckelsen and **Paul Andreu**, *La Grande Arche de La Défense*, Puteaux, 1989 (France)

728. **Piet Blom**, *Cubic House*, Rotterdam, 1984 (Netherlands)

729. **Friedensreich Hundertwasser**, *Hundertwasser House*, Vienna, 1983-1986 (Austria)

730. **Anton Alberts** and **Max van Huut**, *NMB* (now *ING*) *Bank Headquarters*, Amsterdam, 1983-1987 (Netherlands)

728

729

730

731.

731. **Jean Nouvel**, *Arab World Institute*, Paris, 1981-1987 (France)

732.

732. **Rem Koolhaas**, *Netherlands Dance Theatre*, The Hague, 1984-1988 (Netherlands)

733. **Venturi, Scott Brown and Associates**, *Sainsbury Wing of the National Gallery*, London, 1986-1991 (United Kingdom)

734. **Gudjon Samúelsson**, *Hallgrímskirkja (Church of Hallgrímur)*, Reykjavik, 1945-1986 (Iceland)

735. **Günther Domenig**, *Steinhaus*, Steindorf, 1986-2008 (Austria)

736. **Dominique Perrault**, *ESIEE University for Engineering*, Marne-la-Vallée, 1984-1987 (France)

737. **John Outram**, *Storm Water Pumping Station, Isle of Dogs*, London, 1988 (United Kingdom)

738. **Piers Gough**, *Street-Porter House*, London, 1988 (United Kingdom)

738

739

739. **Santiago Calatrava**, *Gare de Saint-Exupéry TGV* (formerly *Gare de Satolas*), Lyon, 1989-1994 (France)

740. **Nicholas Grimshaw and Partners**, *International Terminal Waterloo*, London, 1993 (closed in 2007) (United Kingdom)

740

741. **Ieoh Ming Pei**, *Louvre Pyramids*, Paris, 1981-1999 (France)

742

742. **Dominique Perrault**, *Bibliothèque nationale de France*, Paris, 1989-1995 (France)

743. **Alvar Aalto** and **Elissa Aalto**, *Aalto Theatre*, Essen, 1983-1988 (Germany)

744. **Ralph Erskine**, *The London Ark office building*, London, 1989-1992 (United Kingdom)

745. **Santiago Calatrava**, *The Zubizuri*, also called the *Campo Volantin Bridge*, Bilbao, 1990-1997 (Spain)

746

747

746. **Michael Hopkins and Partners**, *Glyndebourne Opera House*, near Lewes, East Sussex, 1990-1994 (United Kingdom)

747. **Daniel Libeskind**, *Jewish Museum*, Berlin, 1999 (Germany)

748

748. **Hans Hollein**, *Haas House*, Vienna, 1990 (Austria)

749. **Mario Botta**, *Cathedral of the Resurrection*, Évry, 1992-1995 (France)

750. **Mario Botta**, *Santa Maria degli Angeli*, Monte Tamaro, Ticino, 1990-1996 (Switzerland)

752

◀751. **Norman Foster**, *Reichstag building, for the new German Parliament*, Berlin, 1992-1999 (Germany)

752. **Frank Gehry**, *Nationale-Nederlanden building*, called *The Dancing House*, Prague, 1994-1996 (Czech Republic)

753. **Herzog & de Meuron**, *Goetz Collection*, Munich, 1991-1992 (Germany)

754. **Zaha Hadid**, *Vitra Fire Station*, now *Vitra Chair Museum*, Weil am Rhein, 1993-1994 (Germany)

755. **Studio Granda**, *House Aktion Poliphile*, Taunus, Wiesbaden, 1992 (Germany)

756. **Peter Zumthor**, *Vals Spa*, Vals, 1993-1996 (Switzerland)

757. **Santiago Calatrava**, *Montjuic Communications Tower*, Barcelona, 1989-1992 (Spain)

758

758. **Terry Farrell & Partners**, *Vauxhall Cross*, also known as the *MI6 Building*, London, 1993-1998 (United Kingdom)

759

76

759. **Alsop and Störmer**, *Le Grand Bleu (municipal centre of the Bouches-du-Rhône department)*, Marseille, 1994 (France)

760. **Jean Nouvel**, *Fondation Cartier*, Paris, 1991-1994 (France)

761. **Foster and Partners**, *Carré d'Art*, Nîmes, 1984-1993 (France)

762. **Tadao Ando**, *Vitra Conference Pavilion*, Weil am Rhein, 1993 (Germany)

763

764

763. **Herzog & de Meuron**, *Signal Box*, Basel, 1994-1999 (Switzerland)

764. **Peter Zumthor**, *Kunsthaus*, Bregenz, 1997 (Austria)

765

765. **Frank Gehry**, *Guggenheim Museum*, Bilbao, 1997 (Spain)

▶766. **Norman Foster**, *Commerzbank headquarters*, Frankfurt, 1991-1997 (Germany)

768

◀767. **Norman Foster**, *City Hall*, London, 1998-2002 (United Kingdom)

Located near Tower Bridge, London's new City Hall—actually the headquarters of the Greater London Authority—has given the capital a bold new landmark that speaks about the pressing need to respond to environmental concerns. Displaying no discrete façades, only a continuous rounded surface clad in glass, the form of the building was designed to reduce surface area and thus to improve energy efficiency. The modified sphere, 45 metres tall, leans back toward the south, thus minimising its exposure to direct sunlight. By means of 'green' technology the building is said to consume only a quarter of the energy of a conventional office building: roof vents are controlled by weather sensors, solar panels are used to generate energy, and it is naturally ventilated by operable windows in all offices. The heat produced by computers and lights is recycled. Inside, a 500-metre-long helical walkway rises the full height of the building; recalling the ramp of the Guggenheim Museum, it is more closely related to a similar feature in Foster's Berlin Reichstag. At the base of the spiral is a multi-use debating chamber with viewing gallery. Security concerns have unfortunately precluded access to the interior for regular visitors.

768. **MVRDV**, *WoZoCo*, Amsterdam, 1997 (Netherlands)

769. **Enric Miralles**, *Scottish Parliament Building*, Edinburgh, Scotland, 1998-2004 (United Kingdom)

769

770. **Richard Rogers Partnership**, *O₂, New Millenium Experience*, known as the *Millennium Dome*, London, 1996-1999 (United Kingdom)

771. **Santiago Calatrava**, *City of Arts and Sciences*, Valencia, 1991-2004 (Spain)

▶772. **Nicholas Grimshaw and Partners**, *The Eden Project*, Cornwall, 1998-2001 (United Kingdom)

773. **Future Systems**, *Lord's Media Centre*, London, 1994-1999 (United Kingdom)

774. **Alvaro Siza**, *Pavilion of Portugal*, Lisbon, 1998 (Portugal)

775. **Santiago Calatrava**, *Gare do Oriente*, Lisbon, 1993-1998 (Portugal)

776. **Alsop and Störmer**, *Peckham Library*, London, 2000 (United Kingdom)

777. **Lunde & Lovseth Arkitekter**, *Norwegian Petroleum Museum*, Stavanger, 1999 (Norway)

778. **Friedensreich Hundertwasser**, *Waldspirale apartments*, Darmstadt, 2000 (Germany)

779. **Richard Meier**, *Jubilee Church*, Rome, 1996-2003 (Italy)

780. **Foster and Partners**, *Great Glass House*, Llanarthney, Wales, 1995-2000 (United Kingdom)

781. **Michael Wilford & Partners**, *British Embassy in Berlin*, Berlin, 2000 (Germany)

782. **Zaha Hadid**, *Phaeno Science Centre*, Wolfsburg, 2000-2005 (Germany)

783. **Herzog & de Meuron**, *Tate Modern*, London, 2000 (rehabilitation of **Sir Giles Gilbert Scott**'s *Bankside Power Station*, 1947-1963) (United Kingdom)

The Swiss architectural firm of Herzog & de Meuron has given London a great new cultural landmark, by converting the shell of an obsolete power station into a massive new modern art museum. Externally, this change of function is evident by the addition of a new glass attic atop the stark brick façades of the older building. Inside, escalators move visitors through five levels of galleries and other facilities. The interior spaces retain an industrial feel, with large areas of glass and concrete, austere white walls, and rough, unvarnished wooden floors. The 3400 square metres of floor space of the Great Turbine Hall, which once housed huge generators, are used for the exhibition of large, specially commissioned works from contemporary artists. A dramatically angular extension to Tate Modern by the same architects is due to open in 2012.

784. **Henn Architekten**, *Autostadt Wolfsburg*, Wolfsburg, 2000 (Germany)

785. **Norman Foster**, *Swiss Re building*, *30 St Mary Axe*, London, 1997-2004 (United Kingdom)

786. **Michael Wilford & Partners**, *Lowry Centre*, Salford, Greater Manchester, 1992-2000 (United Kingdom)

787. **Norman Foster**, *Millau Viaduct*, Millau, 1993-2004 (France)

788. **Morger-Degelo** and **Christian Kerez**, *Kunstmuseum Liechtenstein*, Vaduz, 2000 (Liechtenstein)

789. **Carlos Ferrater**, *International JCDecaux headquarters*, Madrid, 1998-2001 (Spain)

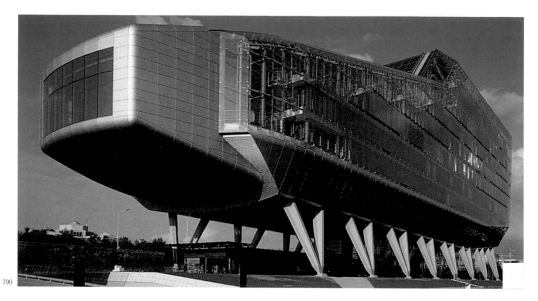

790. **Meyer and Van Schooten,** *ING House,* Amsterdam, 1998-2002 (Netherlands)

791. **Micha de Haas,** *Aluminum Centre,* Houten, 2001 (Netherlands)

792. **MVRDV**, *Silodam*, Amsterdam, 1995-2003 (Netherlands)

793. **SWECO FFNS Architects**, *Ekonologia House*, Malmö, 2002 (Sweden)

794. **David Adjaye**, *Dirty House*, London, 2002 (United Kingdom)

795. **Robbrecht en Daem**, *Bruges Concert Hall*, Bruges, 1999-2002 (Belgium)

796. **Szotynscy Zaleski Architekci**, *Crooked House*, Sopot, 2003 (Poland)

797. **Future Systems**, *Selfridges*, Birmingham, 1999-2003 (United Kingdom)

798. **Peter Cook** and **Colin Fournier**, *Kunsthaus*, Graz, 2001-2002 (Austria)

799. **Santiago Calatrava**, *Auditorium of Tenerife*, Tenerife, Canary Islands, 1991-2003 (Spain)

800. **Sarah Wigglesworth Architects**, *9 Stock Orchard Street*, London, 2004 (United Kingdom)

801. **Abalos & Herreros**, *Usera Library*, Madrid, 2003 (Spain)

802. **Bernard Tschumi**, *Vacheron Constantin Watch Factory*, Geneva, 2001-2003 (Switzerland)

803. **Nio Architects**, *The Amazing Whale Jaw bus station*, Hoofddorp, 1999-2003 (Netherlands)

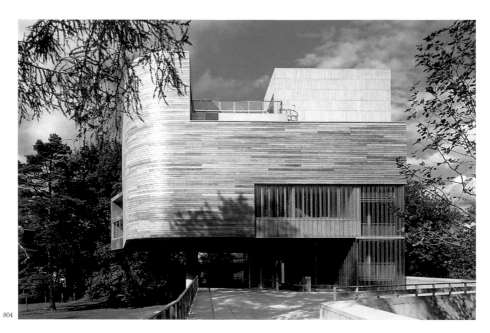

804

804. **Sheila O'Donnell** and **John Tuomey**, *Lewis Glucksman Gallery*, Cork, 1999-2004 (Ireland)

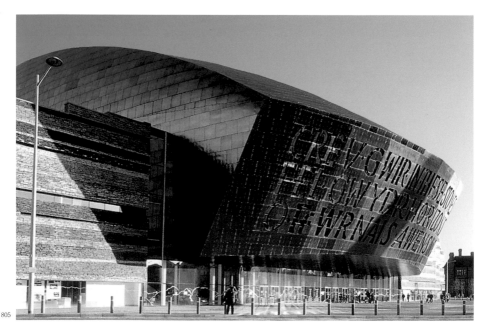

805

805. **Capita Percy Thomas**, *Wales Millenium Centre*, Cardiff, Wales, 2001-2004 (United Kingdom)

806

806. **MVRDV**, *Mirador*, Madrid, 2001-2005 (Spain)

807. **Tadao Ando**, *Langen Foundation*, Neuss, 2004 (Germany)

808. **Rem Koolhaas and Ellen van Loon – Office for Metropolitan Architecture**, *Casa de Música*, Porto, 2005 (Portugal)

809. **UN Studio**, *Mercedes Benz Museum*, Stuttgart, 2001-2006 (Germany)

810. **Herzog & de Meuron**, *Allianz Arena*, Munich, 2002-2005 (Germany)

811

811. **Santiago Calatrava**, *Turning Torso*, Malmö, 1999-2005 (Sweden)

812. **Terry Farrell & Partners**, *Green Building*, Manchester, 2000-2005 (United Kingdom)

813

813. **SGA Architecture** and others, *Hotel Puerta América*, Madrid, 2005 (Spain)
[Level -1 designed by **Teresa Sapey**,
Level 0 by **John Pawson**,
Level 1 by **Zaha Hadid**,
Level 2 by **Norman Foster**,
Level 3 by **David Chipperfield**,
Level 4 by **Plasma Studio**,
Level 5 by **Victorio & Lucchino**,
Level 6 by **Marc Newson**,
Level 7 by **Ron Arad**,
Level 8 by **Kathryn Kindlay**,
Level 9 by **Richard Gluckman**,
Level 10 by **Arato Isozaki**,
Level 11 by **Mariscal & Salas**,
Level 12 by **Jean Nouvel**]

814. *Pyramid of the Sun*, Teotihuacán, begun c. 100 BCE (Mexico)

THE AMERICAS

efore the arrival of Columbus and the Spanish conquistadors, the architecture of the ancient Americas bears witness to a diverse set of cultures, each of which evolved—entirely independently of events in the rest of the world—a distinctive but related set of building traditions. The spectacular achievements of the Pre-Columbian civilisations, with their colossal pyramids, palaces and temples, is even more impressive when we consider that they did not make use of the wheel, animal transport of building materials, measures, weights or iron utensils. Their construction techniques, though often characterised by exquisite precision in the field of stonemasonry, were indeed of the most basic sort, and did not engage the use of the true arch. An interesting but largely speculative task would be to compare the phases of architectural development in Pre-Columbian America with the achievements of the ancient Middle East, and intriguing parallels with the typologies of Mesopotamia and Egypt—the great tradition of pyramid and temple construction, for example—would not be difficult to find.

With the exception of some impressive prehistoric earthworks in the American South and Midwest and the remarkable abandoned pueblos of the American Southwest, almost all of the monumental architecture in the Pre-Columbian Americas is to be found in Central and South America. Here the most proficient builders were the Aztecs and their predecessors, the Mayas on the Yucatan peninsula, and, far to the south, the Incas. There are also more isolated but intriguing manifestations of the monumental urge, notably the mysterious ground drawings on the Nazca Plain in Peru (ca. 200 BCE-200 CE), a huge network of lines formed by the removal of rocks and earth to create geometric forms and images of plants and animals; these are only legible, strangely enough, from an aerial perspective. Teotihuacán, or "place of the gods," was the largest metropolis of Mesoamerica, and its conspicuous ruins are still to be found northeast of modern-day Mexico City. Roughly contemporary with Rome, Teotihuacán was once home to some 200,000 people. Its pyramids, temples and palaces assumed awesome proportions—the Pyramid of the Sun (n° 814), for example, is about 66 metres high and 230 metres long on each side of its square base. Smaller but more decorative, the Temple of the Feathered Serpent at Teotihuacán (n° 815) was ornamented with sculptures of fierce serpent heads and masks of the rain god Tlaloc. Teotihuacán, however, had already been abandoned for half a millennium by the time the conquering Aztecs arrived in the region in the 12th century.

Smaller but equally impressive are the surviving temples of the Maya, who inhabited the dense rainforests of southern Mexico, Honduras and Guatemala from the 4th through the 10th centuries. Mayan temples, built at the behest of dynastic rulers and a priestly caste, were intended to overawe the observer. They consist of earth mounds covered with stone cladding, giving them a characteristically steep profile with a diminutive temple set on top. Since the use of the round arch was unknown, the dark and cramped interior spaces of the Maya builders could only be spanned by simple corbelling, usually of triangular section.

It has been speculated that these unwelcoming stone chambers might have been used for storage rather than habitation. Apart from the temples, other large structures tended to be horizontal, set on long earth terraces. Notable here are the courts for the Mayan ball game, which was ritualistic and religious in nature rather than recreational. The temple building tradition was continued in the capitals of the Zapotec and Toltec cultures at Monte Alban and Tula, respectively. These structures, in turn, served as prototypes for the warlike Aztecs. Most Aztec work survives only in fragments, since their capital city, Tenochtitlán, was thoroughly destroyed by Cortés and his conquistadors, and its remains were deliberately buried beneath the colonial capital of Mexico City; recent archaeology has nevertheless uncovered the foundations of the colossal Templo Mayor, the onetime focus of many bloodthirsty Aztec rituals. Much further south, in the Andes mountains of Peru, the Incas set a new standard for mortarless stonemasonry: without the use of iron tools, huge stones were laboriously shaped into rectangular or smoothly polygonal forms, and so closely set together that the blade of a knife cannot be inserted into the joints between them. The massively fortified structures of the Incas, while beautifully crafted, were largely undecorated, notwithstanding early conquistador records that described several buildings as being clad in plates of pure gold. The fortified city of Machu Picchu (n° 826) (15th-16th centuries), only discovered in 1911, was largely protected by its inaccessibility. Set precariously on a mountaintop, it was originally surrounded by huge areas of terraced agricultural land, allowing it to be self-sufficient. While Machu Picchu was fortified, it also served as a centre for Incan religious and astronomical practises.

The next phase of architecture in the Americas came with the arrival of colonial conquerors from Spain and Portugal in the south and from France, England and the Netherlands in the north. All imported their own building traditions, though these were to some extent inflected by available building materials, lack of funds, a dearth of skilled builders, and disparities in climate with the homeland. Colonial churches in Central and South America were in this respect simplified and retardataire versions of Hispanic Baroque models, though the size and elaboration of many larger cathedrals, especially in Mexico and Brazil, often came to rival their Old World models. French-Canadian settlements like Montreal and Quebec tended to reproduce the building patterns of provincial France. In the United States, British colonial buildings of the 18th century, notably the Virginia state capitol at Williamsburg, emulated the more sedate Classicism of the Wren school or the Neo-Palladians back in England, and the Revolution of 1776 saw no dramatic departure from the current versions of Neoclassicism then popular over the Atlantic. It is telling that Charles Bulfinch's Massachusetts State House in Boston (1795-1797), built in the epicenter of Revolutionary activity, was modelled in part on a British government building in London, William Chambers' Somerset House (n° 544) (1776-1796). Thomas Jefferson, statesman and amateur architect, built his own country house, Monticello (n° 836) (1769-1809), in a style that accords with English Neo-Palladian precedent, and the sources of many details can be traced to treatises by Palladio or other architectural authorities represented in Jefferson's personal library. For Jefferson, the form of the Roman temple was appropriate both stylistically and politically for the new Virginia state capitol that he designed (n° 841) (1785), for to him it embodied the most noble mode of architecture known to history while evincing appropriate associations with Roman republicanism. As a long series of American state capitols, churches, banks and government buildings attest, the Neoclassical urge was persistent in the formal architecture of the United States. The 19th century even concluded with a renewed push towards Classical grandeur: this was sparked by the great white pavilions and colonnades of the 1893 World's Fair in Chicago, thus setting into motion an American 'Renaissance' that found more permanent expression in such monuments as McKim, Mead & White's Boston Public Library (n° 865) (1887-1895), Carrère and Hastings' New York Public Library (n° 866) (1897-1911), and New York's much-lamented Pennsylvania Station (1910).

North America closely followed the newer trends in European—and more particularly British—architecture throughout the 19th century, and when successive phases of the Gothic Revival were fashionable in London they also made an appearance in the great churches and public buildings of New York, Washington, Ottawa and Montreal. By the end of the century, however, several American architects, tiring of the inveterate stylistic dependence on older European models, began to take steps towards the achievement of a more distinctively native expression. A pioneer in this regard was the formidable figure of Henry Hobson Richardson, whose Trinity Church in Boston (n° 854) (1872-1877) introduced a radical new style into American architecture: its bold, massy and polychromatic appearance embodies what has since come to be called the Richardsonian Romanesque style, a free and eclectic interpretation of medieval French and Spanish motifs that seems to epitomise the robust and energetic spirit of post-Civil War America. Shortly afterwards, Louis Sullivan, and in turn his pupil Frank Lloyd Wright, proposed that American architecture had to be rooted in both a political ideology of democratic individualism and an acknowledgement of regional nature and topography. The result, a so-called 'organic' architecture, revitalised the American tradition but failed to establish a long-lasting school. Most importantly, Sullivan had begun the search for an appropriate relationship with modern technology, the most striking result of which was the birth of the skyscraper. This new and unprecedented building type first appeared in Chicago and then New York in the 1870s and 1880s, prompted by simple economics but made possible by technical advances in steel construction and the invention of the passenger elevator. No inhabitable buildings of this height had yet been attempted in Europe, nor were they to be until after the Second World War. The spiritual apotheosis of the skyscraper typology was attained with the erection of William van Alen's Chrysler Building in New York City (n° 886) (1928-1930), whose cubistic Art Deco stylings make it the symbol of Jazz Age New York. The construction of Lamb & Harmon's nearby Empire State Building (n° 891) (1930-1931) took only 410 days, but it held the title of world's tallest building for some 40 years. Its crowning mast, which in its final form gives the tower a total height of 443 metres, was originally conceived as a mooring point for airships. Though framed in steel, the Empire State Building was nevertheless clad in stone, thus obscuring the crucial technical innovation at its heart.

Constant innovation was the hallmark of the prodigious output of Frank Lloyd Wright from the late 19th century through the 1950s. His innovative 'Prairie House' typology of the 1890s, which proposed a new emphasis on horizontality and freedom of internal space, found late but characteristic expression in the Robie house in Chicago (n° 873) (1909). His second great period of creative achievement came in the 1930s, when he produced a series of masterpieces including Fallingwater house in Pennsylvania (n° 896) (1936-1939), the Johnson Wax Headquarters in Racine, Wisconsin (n° 894) (1936), and the innovative and affordable 'Usonian' house as represented by the first Herbert Jacobs house, Madison, Wisconsin (1936). Wright's spatial inventiveness never flagged, and if his last buildings, like the Guggenheim Museum in New York City (n° 925) (1956-1959) or the Marin County Civic Center in San Rafael, California (n° 932) (begun 1957), betray an obsession with geometries of striking appearance but questionable utility, he nevertheless stands for a protean creative energy and an unswervingly personal approach that characterises American architecture at its best.

The indigenous American search for a rapprochement between technology and architecture that had been pursued by Sullivan and Wright was largely overshadowed in the 1930s by the arrival of European modernist émigrés like Walter Gropius and Ludwig Mies van der Rohe, whose design method already contained this issue at its heart. Due to their great influence in commercial building and architectural pedagogy, Bauhaus-style modernism came to prevail as orthodoxy in North American architecture from the end of the Second World War through the 1970s. Modernism produced a large number of pedestrian structures as well as a handful of acknowledged masterpieces like Eero Saarinen's General Motors Technical Center in Michigan (n° 906) (1946-1955) and Mies van der Rohe's Seagram Building in New York (n° 916) (1954-1958). Modernism even made limited inroads into the more conservative field of domestic architecture, as most memorably manifested in the Los Angeles school of experimental steel-and-glass house design that was spearheaded by Richard Neutra in the 1920s and taken up again by Charles Eames and his colleagues in the 1950s. In Central and South America, the innovations of modernism were espoused by such pioneers as Lucio Costa and Oscar Niemeyer in Brazil and Juan O'Gorman and Luis Barragán in Mexico, though these immediately came to be inflected with a distinctively Latin approach manifested in terms of form, materials and vernacular references.

Drawing on the innovations of Le Corbusier and the British Brutalists, a second generation of North American modernists like Eero Saarinen, Marcel Breuer, Louis Kahn, Paul Rudolph and Arthur Erickson began to expand the language of modernism to embrace a more varied and sculpturally expressive use of shapes and textures. This sometimes heavy-handed approach came, in turn, to be superseded by a Postmodern experimentation with historical references, largely limited to pastiches of Classical elements; the work of Charles Moore, Michael Graves and Philip Johnson is exemplary of this school. More recently, a renewed interest in the forms—if not the social ideology—of modernism has come to characterise much of the monumental construction of North America, though the introduction of the computer into design and construction has allowed contemporary architects like Frank Gehry and Daniel Libeskind to achieve buildings of an extraordinary geometrical and spatial complexity that would have been unthinkable only a generation before.

815. *Temple of the Feathered Serpent*, Teotihuacán, 200-800 (Mexico)

816. *Monte Albán complex*, Monte Albán, Oaxaca, c. 100-800 (Mexico)

817. *Great Jaguar Temple and other buildings*, Tikal, 5th-7th century (Guatemala)

818. *Temple and palace complex*, Palenque, 7th-10th century (Mexico)

819. *City of Copán*, before the 10th century (Honduras)

820. *Mud city of Chan Chan*, c. 850-c. 1470 (Peru)

821. *Pyramid of the Magician*, Uxmal, c. 900 and later (Mexico)

822. *The Nunnery*, Uxmal, c. 900 and later (Mexico)

823. *El Castillo,* Chichen Itza, after 900 (Mexico)

824. *The Governor's Palace,* Uxmal, c. 900 and later (Mexico)

825. *Pueblo Bonito,* Chaco Canyon, New Mexico, c. 900-1120 (U.S.A.)

826. *Fortified city of Machu Picchu,* 15th-16th century (Peru)

826

827

827. *Cliff palace*, Mesa Verde, Colorado, c. 1100-1300 (U.S.A.)

This ancient stone pueblo in southwest Colorado is the largest alcove dwelling in North America. An entire city is located at the top of a sheer cliff face, sheltered by a massive overhang of natural rock. This unusual choice of site offered various advantages, including protection from the colder north winds and inaccessibility to invaders. Its builders were the ancestral Pueblo people, also known as the Anasazi, or 'Ancient Ones.' The settlement at Mesa Verde consists of over 200 rooms and *23 kivas; the latter are round-plan structures, developed from an earlier sunken pit house typology, that seem to have served both religious and social functions. The stonework of the Cliff Palace originally had a protective covering of plaster. Everyday life was carried out in the upper stories, while the darker areas below were likely reserved for food storage. The site was abandoned by 1300 for unknown reasons. The Anasazi also established freestanding settlements for trade in the region, notably Pueblo Bonito at Chaco Canyon in New Mexico. Mesa Verde is a US National Park and a UNESCO World Heritage Site.*

828. *Fortress of Cartagena*, Cartagena, 1533 (Colombia)

829. *Sacsayhuamán Fortress and other Inca buildings*, Cuzco, c. 1500 (Peru)

830. *Taos pueblo*, New Mexico, 1500s, rebuilt after 1700 (U.S.A.)

831. *Nueva Panama Cathedral*, Panama, 18th century (Panama)

832. *Igreja de Nossa Senhora das Neves, Capela de São Roque e Convento de São Francisco*, Olinda, 1708-1755 (Brazil)

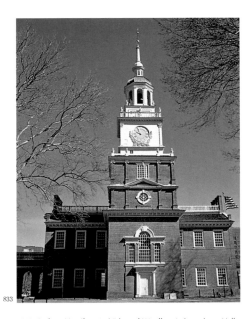

833. **Andrew Hamilton** and **Edmund Woolley**, *Independence Hall*, Philadelphia, Pennsylvania, 1732-1753 (U.S.A.)

834. *Basilica Menor de San Francisco de Asís*, Havana, 1580-1591 and 1730-1739 (Cuba)

835. *Drayton Hall*, Charleston, South Carolina, 1738-1742 (U.S.A.)

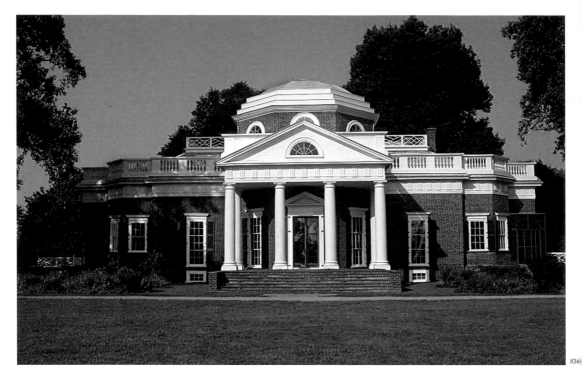

836. **Thomas Jefferson**, *Monticello*, Charlottesville, Virginia, 1769-1809 and later (U.S.A.)

Third President of the United States and chief author of the Declaration of Independence, Thomas Jefferson chose to build his house on a relatively modest scale atop a wooded hill. 'Monticello,' as he called his rural residence, reveals his indebtedness to English Neo-Palladian precedent, while the sources of many details can be traced to Palladio or other architectural authorities represented in Jefferson's library. But his idiosyncratic notions on domestic design are also patent: his bed, for example, was built into a wall alcove open on both sides, thus allowing him to enter either room upon waking. The house also has many skylights, as well as early examples of indoor privies. Built and rebuilt over a period of almost 40 years, the final building features porticoes on the east and west façades, with a parlor and entrance hall set on axis between them; the latter displays items collected by Lewis and Clark on their expedition to the West. The dome was only installed in 1809. Recent research has focused on the symbolism of Jefferson's careful concealment of the servant (i.e., slave) spaces, located both underground and in outlying pavilions, which suggests his conflicted ideas on slavery. Monticello is commemorated on the back of the American 5 cent coin.

837. **José Pereira dos Santos**, *Nossa Senhora do Rosário Dos Homens Pretos*, Ouro Preto, started in 1766 (Brazil)

▶838. *San Pedro Church*, San Pedro de Atacama, 1774 (Chile)

▶839. **Antonio Francisco Lisboa**, also known as **Aleijadinho**, *Chapel of the Third Order of St. Francis of Assisi*, Ouro Preto, 1766-1794 (Brazil)

▶840. **Antonio Francisco Lisboa**, also known as **Aleijadinho**, *Nossa Senhora do Carmo, façade*, Sabara, begun in 1770 (Brazil)

837

841. **Thomas Jefferson**, *Virginia State Capitol*, Richmond, Virginia, 1785 (U.S.A.)

842. *Santuario y Basílica de la Vírgen de Ocotlán*, Tlaxcala, 1670-1781 (Mexico)

843. **William Thornton**, **Benjamin Latrobe**, **Thomas U. Walter** and others, *United States Capitol*, Washington, D.C., begun in 1792 (U.S.A.)

▶844. **James Hoban**, *The White House*, Washington, D.C., 1793-1801 and later (U.S.A.)

845. **Thomas Jefferson**, *University of Virginia*, Charlottesville, Virginia, 1804-1826 (U.S.A.)

846. *Basilica of Our Lady of Copacabana*, Copacabana, 1601-1619 (Bolivia)

847. *Round Stone Barn*, Hancock Shaker Village, Massachusetts, 1826 (U.S.A.)

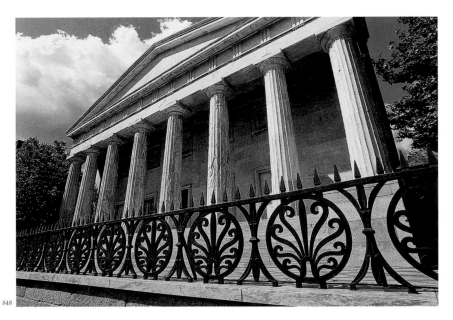

848. **William Strickland**, *Second Bank of the United States*, Philadelphia, Pennsylvania, 1818-1824 (U.S.A.)

849

849. **William Strickland**, *Merchants' Exchange*, Philadelphia, Pennsylvania, 1832-1834 (U.S.A.)

850

850. **Ithiel Town** and **A.J. Davis**, *U.S. Custom House*, now *Federal Hall*, New York, New York, 1833-1842 (U.S.A.)

851

851. **Richard Upjohn**, *Trinity Church*, New York, New York, 1839-1846 (U.S.A.)

852

852. **James Renwick**, *St. Patrick's Cathedral*, New York, New York, 1853-1878 (U.S.A.)

853

853 **Frank Furness**, *Pennsylvania Academy of the Fine Arts*, Philadelphia, Pennsylvania, 1871-1876 (U.S.A.)

854

854. **Henry Hobson Richardson**, *Trinity Church*, Boston, Massachusetts, 1872-1877 (U.S.A.)

Located on Copley Square in Boston's Back Bay area, this church introduced a radical new style into American architecture. Burly and larger than life, H.H. Richardson forged a unique architectural manner to match his persona, and Trinity is the first great manifestation of what has come to be called Richardsonian Romanesque: massive and sculptural, it embraces picturesque surface variety through polychromy and texturing. This eclectic approach derives from the Romanesque style of the 11th and 12th centuries, as particularly witnessed in the heavy round arches that Richardson so often deployed. The church is built on a compact Greek cross plan, creating a vast and unified space within. Its walls feature extensive cycles of murals and stained glass. Externally, the church is dominated by a massive square tower, 64 metres tall, with corner turrets. It is entered through a red sandstone porch with three great portals. The church influenced many public buildings across North America: at one time few towns were without a Richardsonian Romanesque building—town hall, railway station, library, courthouse or post office—of some sort. The dynamic and extroverted qualities of the new church are also said to have been well suited to the forceful and innovative preaching of its charismatic rector, Phillips Brooks.

856. **Henry Hobson Richardson**, *Allegheny County Courthouse*, Pittsburgh,
Pennsylvania, 1884-1888 (U.S.A.)

◀855. **John A.** and **Washington A. Roebling**, *The Brooklyn Bridge*, New York,
New York, 1867-1883 (U.S.A.)

857. **Henry Hobson Richardson**, *Glessner House*, Chicago, Illinois,
1885-1887 (U.S.A.)

858

859

860

861

802

863

864

858. **Adler & Sullivan**, *Auditorium Building*, Chicago, Illinois, 1887-1889 (U.S.A.)

859. **Burnham and Root**, *Monadnock Building*, Chicago, Illinois, 1889-1891 (U.S.A.)

860. **Daniel H. Burnham**, *Reliance Building*, Chicago, Illinois, 1890-1894 (U.S.A.)

861. **Louis Sullivan**, *Carson Pirie Scott department store*, Chicago, Illinois, 1899-1904 (U.S.A.)

862. **Adler & Sullivan**, *Wainwright Building*, St. Louis, Missouri, 1890-1891 (U.S.A.)

863. **Adler & Sullivan**, *Guaranty Building*, Buffalo, New York, 1894 (U.S.A.)

864. **McKim, Mead & White**, *University Club*, New York, New York, 1900 (U.S.A.)

865. **McKim, Mead & White**, *Boston Public Library*, Boston, Massachusetts, 1887-1895 (U.S.A.)

56. Carrère and Hastings, *New York Public Library*, New York, New York, 1897-1911 (U.S.A.)

867

867. **Frank Lloyd Wright**, *Ward W. Willits House*, Highland Park, Illinois, 1901-1902 (U.S.A.)

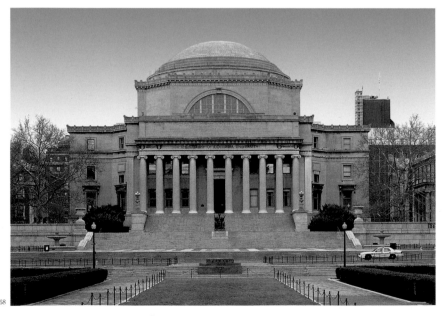

868

868. **McKim**, **Mead & White**, *Low Memorial Library*, *Columbia University*, New York, New York, 1895 (U.S.A.)

▶869. **Daniel H. Burnham**, *Flatiron Building*, New York, New York, 1902 (U.S.A.)

870. **Reed and Stem, Warren and Wetmore,** *Grand Central Terminal,* New York, New York, 1903-1913 (U.S.A.)

871. **Frank Lloyd Wright,** *Unity Temple,* Oak Park, Illinois, 1905-1908 (U.S.A.)

872. **Greene and Greene**, *Gamble House*, Pasadena, California, 1908-1909 (U.S.A.)

873. **Frank Lloyd Wright**, *Robie House*, Chicago, Illinois, 1909 (U.S.A.)

▶874. **Frank Lloyd Wright**, *Taliesin*, Spring Green, Wisconsin, 1911 with later rebuildings and additions (U.S.A.)

875. **Cass Gilbert**, *Woolworth Building*, New York, New York, 1910-1913 (U.S.A.)

876. **Willis J. Polk**, *Hallidie Building*, San Francisco, California, 1918 (U.S.A.)

877. **Henry Bacon**, *The Lincoln Memorial*, Washington, D.C., 1915-1922 (U.S.A.)

878. **Sir Ambrose Macdonald Poynter**, *Torre Monumental (Torre de los Ingleses)*, Buenos Aires, 1909-1916 (Argentina)

879

880

879. **John Mead Howells** and **Raymond Hood**, *The Chicago Tribune Tower*, Chicago, Illinois, 1922-1925 (U.S.A.)

880. **Frank Lloyd Wright**, *Millard House*, Pasadena, California, 1923 (U.S.A.)

881

881. **Rudolf Schindler**, *Schindler-Chase House*, West Hollywood, California, 1921-1922 (U.S.A.)

882

882. Julia Morgan, *Hearst Castle*, near San Simeon, California, 1919-1947 (U.S.A.)

Located on a remote stretch of California coastline halfway between San Francisco and Los Angeles, this palatial hilltop retreat for the powerful newspaper publisher William Randolph Hearst is one of the strangest and most remarkable houses ever built. Its architect, Julia Morgan, was herself a prodigy, the first woman to graduate with an architectural degree from the famed École des Beaux-Arts in Paris. Morgan, who commuted down from San Francisco on weekends to supervise construction on what Hearst called his "Cuesta Encatada," had to use all of her historical knowledge to produce a grand and eclectic design that could accommodate Hearst's extensive collection of architectural antiques; much of this material was never used and remains in warehouses. Perhaps appropriately for the region, the main house draws inspiration from 16th-century Spanish ecclesiastical architecture, while at the same time referencing the appearance of the California missions. Hearst Castle has 56 bedrooms and 61 bathrooms, indoor and outdoor swimming pools, tennis courts, a movie theatre, an airfield and a private zoo. Many Hollywood stars and prominent politicians were entertained here in the 1920s and 1930s. Left incomplete at the start of World War II, it is now a national and state historical monument open for public tours.

883

883. Bruce Price, *Château Frontenac*, Quebec, 1893-1923 (Canada)

884

884. **Rudolf Schindler**, *Lovell Beach House*, Newport Beach, California, 1926 (U.S.A.)

885

885. **Richard Neutra**, *Lovell House*, Los Angeles, California, 1927-1929 (U.S.A.)

887

886. **William van Alen**, *Chrysler Building*, New York, New York, 1928-1930 (U.S.A.)

887. **Charles Howard Crane**, *Fox Theatre*, Detroit, Michigan, 1928 (U.S.A.)

888

889

888. **Howe & Lescaze**, *Philadelphia Savings Fund Society building*, Philadelphia, Pennsylvania, 1929-1932 (U.S.A.)

889. **Reinhard & Hofmeister**, **Raymond Hood**, **Wallace K. Harrison** and others, *Rockefeller Center*, New York, New York, 1930-1939 (U.S.A.)

890. **Raymond Hood**, *McGraw-Hill Building*, New York, New York, 1930 (U.S.A.)

891. **Shreve, Lamb & Harmon**, *Empire State Building*, New York, New York, 1930-1931 (U.S.A.)

892. **Cass Gilbert**, *United States Supreme Court*, Washington, D.C., 1935 (U.S.A.)

893. **McKim, Mead & White**, *Hotel Nacional de Cuba*, Havana, 1930 (Cuba)

894. **Frank Lloyd Wright**, *Johnson Wax Headquarters*, Racine, Wisconsin, 1936 (U.S.A.)

896

896. **Frank Lloyd Wright**, *Fallingwater*, Pennsylvania, 1936-1939 (U.S.A.)

◄895. **Joseph B. Strauss** (chief engineer) and **Irving F. Morrow** (consulting architect), *Golden Gate Bridge*, San Francisco, California, 1933-1937 (U.S.A.)

One of the most stunning engineering achievements of the 20th century, the Golden Gate Bridge was for many years the tallest and longest bridge in the world. Its twin pylons rise to 227 metres. Making using of suspension cables, the bridge spans the cold and fast-flowing waters of the Golden Gate to connect San Francisco with Marin County to the north. The project was championed by the engineer Joseph Strauss through the 1920s, and he eventually overcame many powerful bureaucratic *obstacles to see it through to completion at a cost of over 26 million dollars. Apart from the unprecedented length of the span, his design needed to take into account the certainty of major earthquakes and the erosive power of the powerful currents sweeping through the narrow channel. The south pylon had to be sunk some 30 metres into the sea bed. Despite Strauss's high profile, much of the calculation seems to have been done by the engineer Charles Alton Ellis. Irving Morrow, a residential architect, created the distinctive Art Deco styling of the towers. The bridge's famous International Orange colour was originally that of the preliminary sealant, but proved popular with the public and now forms an essential part of the bridge's character.*

897. **Walter Gropius**, *Gropius house*, Lincoln, Massachusetts, 1937 (U.S.A.)

898. **Frank Lloyd Wright**, *Taliesin West*, Scottsdale, Arizona, 1937 and later (U.S.A.)

899. **George Bergstrom**, *The Pentagon*, Arlington, Virginia, 1941-1943 (U.S.A.)

900. **Gregorio Sanchez, Ernesto Lagos, Luis Maria de la Torre**, *Kavanagh apartment building*, Buenos Aires, 1936 (Argentina)

901. **Philip S. Goodwin** and **Edward D. Stone**, *The Museum of Modern Art*, New York, New York, 1938-1939 with later additions and extensions (U.S.A.)

902

902. **John Russell Pope**, *The Jefferson Memorial*, Washington, D.C., 1943 (U.S.A.)

The national memorial to Thomas Jefferson, America's third President, is a distinguished if belated example of the Neoclassical impulse that shaped the earlier monuments of the American capital. Of an exceptional purity and dignity, this domed rotunda rises by the tidal basin of the Potomac River. Begun on the initiative of Franklin Roosevelt, the Memorial was designed by John Russell Pope, also responsible for the original West building of the National Gallery of Art. Pope, sadly, died in 1937, two years before the cornerstone was laid. As a late Beaux-Arts monument, the Jefferson Memorial was criticised by the rising school of architectural modernists who saw allegiance to the Roman past as a tired irrelevancy. Its exterior features a tall Ionic colonnade fronted by a Classical portico, thus referencing both the Roman Pantheon and Jefferson's Rotunda for the University of Virginia, which he had founded and housed in buildings of his own design. The rotunda is constructed of variously coloured marbles sourced from four states. The interior walls are engraved with excerpts from the Declaration of Independence and other writings by Jefferson. Built during the Second World War at a cost of over 3 million dollars, it was dedicated on April 13, 1943, the 200th anniversary of Jefferson's birthday.

903

904

903. **Charles Eames**, *Eames House*, Pacific Palisades, California, 1945-1949 (U.S.A.)

904. **Richard Neutra**, *Kaufmann Desert House*, Palm Springs, California, 1946-1947 (U.S.A.)

905. **Luis Barragan**, *Luis Barragan House*, Mexico City, 1948 (Mexico)

906. **Eero Saarinen**, *General Motors Technical Center*, Warren, Michigan, 1946-1955 (U.S.A.)

907. **Oscar Niemeyer**, *Church of St. Francis*, Pampulha, Belo Horizonte, 1943 (Brazil)

908. **Frank Lloyd Wright**, *Unitarian Meeting House*, Madison, Wisconsin, 1947-1951 (U.S.A.)

▶909. **Harrison & Abramowitz** and consulting architects, *United Nations Headquarters*, New York, New York, 1947-1952 (U.S.A.)

The headquarters of the United Nations rises near the East River in Manhattan, on land formerly occupied by slaughterhouses. Ending months of speculation as to where the new international organisation would be based, this unlikely site was acquired from developer William Zeckendorff by the Rockefeller family, who then offered it to the UN. It is now considered as international territory. Idealistically, it was decided that the design of the UN complex would be a collaborative effort by a team of architects from various countries, overseen by Wallace Harrison, the Rockefellers' architectural advisor. The final design, however, owes most to the ideas of Oscar Niemeyer and Le Corbusier. Controversially, the headquarters was resolutely modern in style and conception, its stark and geometrical forms eschewing any national tradition while looking forward to an optimistic future based on scientific and technological progress. The 38-storey rectangular slab of the Secretariat, its main façades clad in heat-resistant glass, dominates the site, while the General Assembly is housed in a lower building with concave external walls and a diminutive dome. Badly in need of repair for many years, the seat of the UN is presently due to undergo an extensive program of improvement and restoration.

911

◀910. **Eero Saarinen**, *Gateway Arch, Jefferson National Expansion Memorial*, St. Louis, Missouri, 1963-1965 (U.S.A.)

911. **Philip Johnson**, *The Glass House*, New Canaan, Connecticut, 1947-1949 (U.S.A.)

912

912. **Ludwig Mies van der Rohe**, *Farnsworth House*, Plano, Illinois, 1951 (U.S.A.)

A diminutive masterpiece of modern architecture, this largely transparent dwelling was built as a one-room weekend retreat for Dr. Edith Farnsworth, a prominent Chicago medical doctor with artistic tastes. Using modern materials and characteristically minimal means, Mies designed an unfettered space of personal freedom that was at the same time open to nature. It is probably the architect's most widely admired building in America. Only 140 square metres in area, the house consists of a beautifully

detailed glass box raised off a flood plain on four pairs of I-beams. With walls of plate glass, it appears simply as three horizontal planes—terrace, floor and roof—floating above the ground, thus epitomising the German-American modernist's ideal of architecture as "almost nothing." The Farnsworth house has no interior dividing walls: it is zoned only by carefully chosen and sited furniture and by the presence of two freestanding wooden elements, one serving as a wardrobe and the other housing a kitchen, toilet and fireplace. Owned until recently by the British property magnate Peter Palumbo, the house is now open to the public as a museum.

913

913. **Frank Lloyd Wright**, *Price Tower*, Bartlesville, Oklahoma, 1952-1956 (U.S.A.)

914

914. **Ludwig Mies van der Rohe**, *Lake Shore Drive apartments*, Chicago, Illinois, 1948-1951 (U.S.A.)

915

915. **Gordon Bunshaft/SOM**, *Lever House*, New York, New York, 1951-1952 (U.S.A.)

916

916. **Ludwig Mies van der Rohe**, *Seagram Building*, New York, New York, 1954-1958 (U.S.A.)

917. **Louis Kahn**, *Yale University Art Gallery*, New Haven, Connecticut, 1951-1954 (U.S.A.)

918. **Juan O'Gorman**, *UNAM Library*, Mexico City, 1953 (Mexico)

919. **Frank Lloyd Wright**, *Beth Sholom Synagogue*, Elkins Park, Pennsylvania, 1953-1959 (U.S.A.)

920. **Le Corbusier**, *Curutchet House*, La Plata, 1951-1955 (Argentina)

921. **Marcel Breuer**, *St. John's Abbey*, Collegeville, Minnesota, 1953-1961 (U.S.A.)

922. **Ludwig Mies van der Rohe**, *Crown Hall, Illinois Institute of Technology*, Chicago, Illinois, 1950-1956 (U.S.A.)

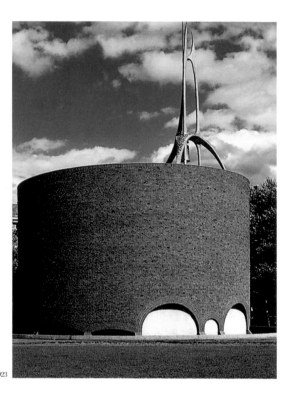

923

923. **Eero Saarinen**, *Kresge Chapel, MIT*, Cambridge, Massachusetts, 1955 (U.S.A.)

924. **Lucio Costa** and **Oscar Niemeyer**, *City of Brasilia*, Brasilia, begun in 1960 (Brazil)

▼925. **Frank Lloyd Wright**, *Guggenheim Museum*, New York, New York, 1956-1959 (U.S.A.)

One of the great landmarks of 20th-century architecture, the Guggenheim Museum was also one of Wright's last undisputed masterworks. Though Wright himself did not like modern painting (and actively despised New York City), he accepted the commission to design a new home for a famous collection of abstract, or 'non-objective,' works of art. From the outside the Guggenheim appears as a strikingly original composition, its upper portion articulated as a top-heavy helix. Its emphatic rotundity was certainly intended by Wright as a riposte to the pervasive rectilinearity of surrounding buildings and indeed of the Manhattan grid itself. The raison d'être for this unusual configuration was the conceit of a giant ramp: spiraling up around a sky-lit atrium, it would allow visitors to experience the works of art in a continuous historical sequence. A common complaint here is that the architecture overshadows the art, and some critics have seen the museum as formalistic, self-indulgent and nonfunctional; the Guggenheim did, however, establish a long-lived precedent for the commissioning of art museums of unconventional form and name-brand prestige.

924

THE SOLOMON GUGGENHEIM MUSEUM

ONE WAY

926. **Eero Saarinen**, *TWA Terminal*, John F. Kennedy International Airport, New York, New York, 1956-1962 (U.S.A.)

927. **Eero Saarinen**, *Yale Hockey Rink*, New Haven, Connecticut, 1956-1958 (U.S.A.)

928. **Louis Kahn**, *Salk Institute for Biological Studics*, La Jolla, California, 1956-1966 (U.S.A.)

929. **Eero Saarinen**, *Dulles Airport*, Chantilly, Virginia, 1958-1962 (U.S.A.)

930

930. **Louis Kahn**, *Richards Medical Research Building*, University of Pennsylvania, Philadelphia, Pennsylvania, 1957-1961 (U.S.A.)

931

931. **Bertrand Goldberg**, *Marina City apartments and offices*, Chicago, Illinois, 1959-1964 (U.S.A.)

932

932. **Frank Lloyd Wright**, *Marin County Civic Center*, San Rafael, California, 1957-1962 (U.S.A.)

933. **Louis Kahn**, *First Unitarian Church*, Rochester, New York, 1959 (U.S.A.)

934. **Louis Kahn**, *Erdman Hall dormitories*, Bryn Mawr, Pennsylvania, 1960-1965 (U.S.A.)

935. **Pierre Koenig**, *Stahl House, Case Study House No. 22*, Los Angeles, California, 1960 (U.S.A.)

936. **John Lautner**, *The Chemosphere*, Los Angeles, California, 1960 (U.S.A.)

937. **Oscar Niemeyer**, *Planalto Palace*, Brasilia, 1960 (Brazil)

938. **Craig Ellwood**, *Rosen House*, Los Angeles, California, 1961-1963 (U.S.A.)

939. **Venturi, Scott Brown and Associates**, *Vanna Venturi House*, Chestnut Hill,
Pennsylvania, 1961-1964 (U.S.A.)

This modest but perplexing suburban house may claim to be the starting point of architectural Postmodernism. Deliberately designed to be complex and contradictory, it exemplifies the theories of Philadelphia architect Robert Venturi, who was among the first designers to question modernist orthodoxies. Borrowing Pop Art's irony and deadpan embrace of mundane commercial realities, Venturi has said that this house for his mother proposes nothing heroic: the façade consists of a large gable, suggesting a symbol of a house or a house as a child might draw it, as well as being a common feature of the everyday American tract dwelling. Yet, the fact that the ridge is broken at the top seems ambiguous and perverse: the gap seems to negate the point of having a peaked roof at all. A curved strip over the door alludes to historical tradition by symbolising an arch. The interiors are similarly counterintuitive, and the fireplace and staircase form an unresolved conglomeration. Venturi has said that architecture can be seen as basic shelter with decoration applied to it, seeming to appear 'ordinary' while embodying covert references to architectural history. Many critics found the house to be coy, ugly and irrational, but its calculated provocations set the tone for over two decades of Postmodern design.

940. **Ieoh Ming Pei**, *National Center for Atmospheric Research*, Boulder, Colorado,
1961-1967 (U.S.A.)

941. **Eero Saarinen**, *John Deere headquarters*, Moline, Illinois, 1963 (U.S.A.)

942. **Marcel Breuer**, *Whitney Museum of American Art*, New York, New York, 1963-1966 (U.S.A.)

943. **Kevin Roche John Dinkeloo and Associates LLC**, *Ford Foundation Building*, New York, New York, 1963-1968 (U.S.A.)

944. **John B. Parkin Associates** and **Viljo Revell**, *Toronto City Hall*, Toronto, 1961-1965 (Canada)

945. **Charles Gwathmey**, *Gwathmey residence and studio*, Amagansett, New York, 1965-1967 (U.S.A.)

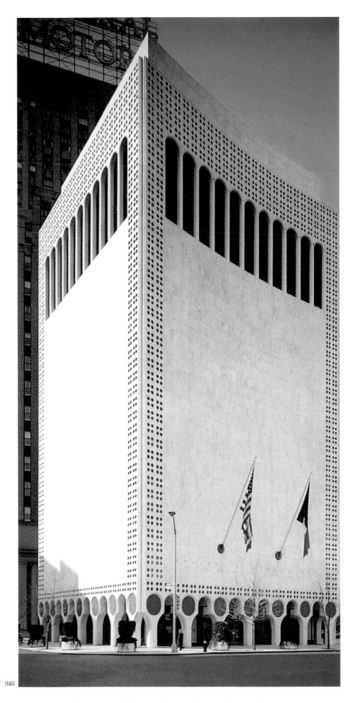

946

946. **Edward Durell Stone**, *2 Columbus Circle*, New York, New York, 1964 (U.S.A.)

Wate

r Place

◀947. **Bruce Graham/SOM**, *John Hancock Center*, Chicago, Illinois, 1965-1969 (U.S.A.)   948. **Richard Buckminster Fuller**, *U.S. Pavilion, Expo '67*, Montreal, 1967 (Canada)

949. **Louis Kahn**, *Kimbell Art Museum*, Fort Worth, Texas, 1967-1972 (U.S.A.)   950. **Moshe Safdie**, *Habitat, Expo '67*, Montreal, 1967 (Canada)

951. **Louis Kahn**, *Library of Phillips Exeter Academy*, Andover, New Hampshire, 1967-1972 (U.S.A.)

952. **Joseph Esherick**, *The Cannery*, San Francisco, California, 1968 (U.S.A.)

953. **Kevin Roche John Dinkeloo and Associates LLC**, *College Life Insurance Co.*, Indianapolis, Indiana, 1967-1971 (U.S.A.)

954

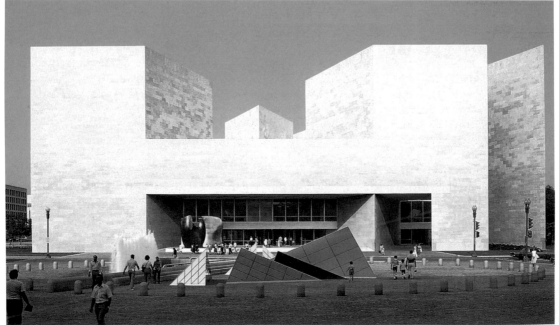

95

956

956. **John Lautner**, *Sheats Goldstein Residence*, Beverly Hills, California, 1961-1963 (U.S.A.)

◄954. **Gordon Bunshaft/SOM**, *Hirshhorn Museum*, Washington, D.C., 1974 (U.S.A.)

◄955. **Ieoh Ming Pei**, *East Wing of the National Gallery*, Washington, D.C., 1974-1978 (U.S.A.)

Many have seen Ieoh Ming Pei's extension to the National Gallery of Art as a vindication of modernist ideals even as they began to come under siege by Postmodern polemicists. Originally from China, Pei studied under Gropius and Breuer at Harvard, thus absorbing a modernist dedication to simplicity, abstraction and functionalism. Here he was presented with a difficult commission, having to make use of an awkward trapezoidal site adjacent to the earlier West Wing of the National Gallery, which had been built by John Russell Pope in a traditional Neoclassical idiom. Cannily selecting the triangle as his basic motif, Pei created a successful fusion of Classical monumentality and modernist abstraction. The resulting building has stark façades and unusually sharp angles. But its white marble cladding, sourced from the original quarries, relates the East Wing closely to older monuments in the capital. It features a huge central court covered by an immense skylight, and is connected to the West Wing by a long underground corridor.

957. **Ieoh Ming Pei** and **Henry N. Cobb**, *Hancock Place*, Boston, Massachusetts, 1977 (U.S.A.)

▼958. **William Pereira & Associates**, *Transamerica Pyramid*, San Francisco, California, 1969-1972 (U.S.A.)

957

959. **Bruce Graham/SOM**, *Sears Tower*, Chicago, Illinois, 1970-1973 (U.S.A.)

960. **Hugh Stubbins**, *Citigroup Center*, New York, New York, 1974-1977 (U.S.A.)

961. **Arthur Erickson**, *Museum of Anthropology, University of British Columbia*, Vancouver, 1971-1976 (Canada)

962. **Louis Kahn**, *Yale Center for British Art*, New Haven, Connecticut, 1969-1977 (U.S.A.)

963. **Gio Ponti**, *Denver Art Museum, north building*, Denver, Colorado, 1971 (U.S.A.)

964. **Richard Meier**, *Douglas House*, Harbor Springs, Michigan, 1973 (U.S.A.)

965. **Frank Gehry**, *Gehry House*, Santa Monica, California, 1977-1978 (modified in 1991-1994) (U.S.A.)

966. **Philip Johnson** and **John Burgee**, *Garden Grove Church*, better known as *The Crystal Cathedral*, Garden Grove, California, 1977-1990 (U.S.A.)

967

967. Richard Meier, *The Athoneum*, New Harmony, Indiana, 1975-1979 (U.S.A.)

Richard Meier began as one of the New York Five, a group of architects informed by linguistic theory who saw design as a complex language of form, with rules that often bypassed the mere accommodation of function. Their pure, abstract approach earned them the nickname of 'the Whites,' though this could equally refer to the usual colour of their buildings. Meier and the Five appropriated the formal vocabulary of the early modernists—notably Le Corbusier—but often bracketed out the older architects' preoccupation with functionalism, industry and social value.

This breathtakingly sculptural visitor centre on the site of an early 19th-century utopian colony manifests Meier's trademark whiteness and complex play with abstract geometries. Since the building is clad in steel panels coated with baked enamel, as a stove or a refrigerator might be, it is easy to maintain in a state of pristine cleanliness. The plan is based around an angled circulation ramp leading to an observation platform on the upper floor. Much of the conception and detailing is patently Corbusian, and Meier has been frank in admitting his debt to the master. Meier has since gone on to design many more cultural institutions of a similar character, notably the High Museum in Atlanta, Georgia (1980-84).

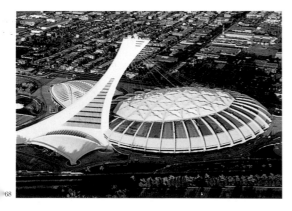

68

969

968. Roger Taillibert, *Olympic Stadium*, Montreal, 1973-1976 with later renovations (Canada)

969. Charles Moore, *Piazza d'Italia*, New Orleans, Louisiana, 1976-1979 (U.S.A.)

970. **Arthur Erickson**, *Fire Island house*, Fire Island, New York, 1977 (U.S.A.)

971. **Renzo Piano**, *Menil Collection*, Houston, Texas, 1982-1986 (U.S.A.)

972. **Philip Johnson** and **John Burgee**, *AT&T* (now *Sony*) *Building*, New York, New York, 1978-1984 (U.S.A.)

973. **Michael Graves**, *Humana Building*, Louisville, Kentucky, 1982-1985 (U.S.A.)

974. **Ieoh Ming Pei**, *Javits Convention Center*, New York, New York, 1979-1986 (U.S.A.)

975. **Richard Meier**, *High Museum of Art*, Atlanta, Georgia, 1980-1983 (U.S.A.)

976. **Venturi, Scott Brown and Associates**, *Gordon Wu Hall*, Princeton University, New Jersey, 1983 (U.S.A.)

977. **Douglas Cardinal** and others, *Canadian Museum of Civilisation*, Gatineau, 1982-1989 (Canada)

978. **Richard Meier**, *Getty Center*, Los Angeles, California, 1984-1997 (U.S.A.)

A once-in-a-lifetime commission for architect Richard Meier, this impressive cultural acropolis overlooking a Los Angeles freeway seems to have been built on a nearly unlimited budget. Set on a series of marble terraces with fountains and gardens, the Getty comprises a museum of pre-modern art, research and conservation institutes and administrative offices. Each is housed in a building of distinctive and contrasting form, coming together in plan as a kind of loose collage. It is accessed by stairs or via a small electric train running from the parking lot. Meier is known for his stylistic purity, and his pristine white buildings generally manifest a complex, abstract geometry that may appear removed from everyday life and the natural world. In this case the architect made certain concessions, using light-coloured stone cladding instead of his usual white steel panels. In positioning itself as a gleaming bastion of high culture on a hilltop, the Getty has found the suggestion of cultural elitism hard to avoid, but it quickly launched an aggressive campaign to make visitors from all backgrounds feel welcome. The finished center is rumoured to have cost over a billion dollars. It is open to the public with no admission charge.

979. **Peter Eisenman**, **Richard Trott** and **Laurie Olin**, *Wexner Center for the Arts*, Columbus, Ohio, 1983-1989 (U.S.A.)

980. **Helmut Jahn**, *United Airlines Terminal*, O'Hare International Airport, Chicago, Illinois, 1985-1988 (U.S.A.)

981. **Mario Botta**, *San Francisco Museum of Modern Art*, San Francisco, California, 1989-1995 (U.S.A.)

982. **Josh Schweitzer**, *Monument House*, Joshua Tree National Park, California, 1990 (U.S.A.)

983. **Venturi, Scott Brown and Associates**, *Seattle Art Museum*, Seattle, Washington, 1991 (U.S.A.)

984. **Frank Gehry**, *Walt Disney Concert Hall*, Los Angeles, California, 1989-2003 (U.S.A.)

985

985. **Ricardo Legorreta**, *Metropolitan Cathedral of Managua*, Managua, 1993 (Nicaragua)

986

986. **Bart Prince**, *Hight Residence*, Mendocino, California, 1992-1993 (U.S.A.)

987

987. **Ieoh Ming Pei**, *Rock and Roll Hall of Fame*, Cleveland, Ohio, 1993-1995 (U.S.A.)

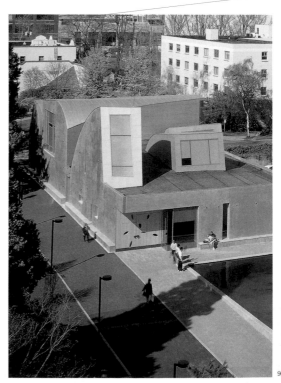

988. **Steven Holl**, *Chapel of St. Ignatius*, Seattle, Washington, 1994-1997 (U.S.A.)

989. **Herzog & de Meuron**, *Dominus Winery*, Yountville, California, 1996-1998 (U.S.A.)

990. **Frank Gehry**, *Experience Music Project*, Seattle, Washington, 1999-2000 (U.S.A.)

Devoted to the history of rock music, this museum was established in Jimi Hendrix's hometown by Paul Allen, co-founder of Microsoft. The anarchic and populist nature of its theme clearly inspired Gehry to come up with one of his most outrageous and uninhibited designs. Here his architectural forms are extraordinarily dynamic and flexible, and the building's free-form envelope seems more like a pile of multicoloured cloth blowing in the wind than a solid structure; Gehry was particularly inspired by the shapes and colours of Stratocaster guitars. The EMP's complex curves are animated by a rainbow of dazzling and unexpected colours, including gold, silver, dark red, baby blue and a shimmering 'purple haze'. The interior, formed from a giant steel frame of wildly irregular profile, is appropriately dark and cave-like, suitable for dramatic lighting effects suggestive of a rock concert. A central room known as the "sky church" features 21-metre tall video screens showing performances by Hendrix and others. Never a clear-cut critical or financial success, the building now also houses a science fiction hall of fame.

991

992. James Polshek, *Rose Center for Earth and Space, American Museum of Natural History*, New York, New York, 2000 (U.S.A.)

992

991. **Daniel Libeskind**, *Denver Art Museum extension*, Denver, Colorado, 2000-2006 (U.S.A.)

993

993. **Oscar Niemeyer**, *Museo Oscar Niemeyer*, Curitiba, 2002 (Brazil)

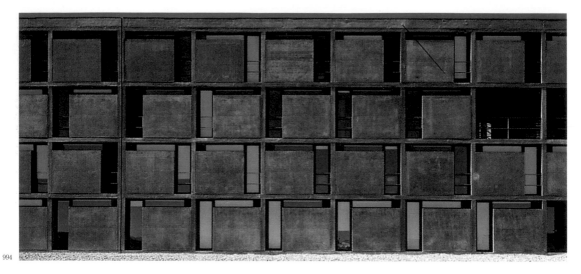

994. **Auer+Weber+Assoziierte**, *Eso Hotel*, Cerro Paranal, 2002 (Chile)

995. **Frank Gehry**, *Stata Center*, Cambridge, Massachusetts, 2004 (U.S.A.)

996. **Thom Mayne** of **Morphosis**, *Diamond Ranch High School*, near Pomona, California, 1999-2000 (U.S.A.)

997 **Rem Koolhaas**, *Seattle Public Library*, Seattle, Washington, 2004 (U.S.A.)

998. **Richard Meier**, *Crystal Cathedral International Center for Possibility Thinking*, Garden Grove, California, 1998-2003 (U.S.A.)

999

999. **Herzog & de Meuron**, *Walker Art Center*, Minneapolis, Minnesota, 2005 (U.S.A.)

1000. **Herzog & de Meuron**, *M. H. de Young Memorial Museum*,
Golden Gate Park, San Francisco, California, opened in 2005 (U.S.A.)

1000

BIOGRAPHIES

Alvar AALTO

(Kuortane, 1898 – Helsinki, 1976)

The Finnish architect Aalto represents a stream of Scandinavian humanism that continues to moderate the more technocratic urges of modernism, proposing an architecture that is technically and aesthetically progressive while remaining closely concerned with the real psycho-physiological needs of people. Aalto's undogmatic approach is summed up in his remark: "Nature, not the machine, is the most important model for architecture." Even before he attended a CIAM meeting in Frankfurt in 1929, Aalto's work had begun to reflect more advanced European ideas, and his *Turun Sanomat* newspaper plant in Turku (1927-28) is clearly informed by Le Corbusier's theories. The sunny and optimistic Paimio Sanatorium (n° 664) devoted equal attention to the technical and health-giving aspects of the building, while his Municipal Library in Viipuri (n° 662) attracted international acclaim both for its humane practicality (optimal reading conditions were ensured by the installation of light-diffusing conical skylights) and lyrical expression (the undulating wood ceiling of the auditorium, which was ostensibly justified by acoustic considerations). Aalto's approach was taken abroad in his Finnish Pavilions for the World's Fairs of 1937 (Paris) and 1939 (New York). After the war his favoured material was warm red brick, as in his Baker House dormitory for MIT (1947-48) and the Town Hall in Säynätsalo (1949-52). Aalto erected many large public buildings in Helsinki through the 1950s and 1960s, though his Church at Vuoksenniska, Imatra (n° 695) stands as an expressionistic highlight of his later period. Aalto was equally a pioneer in the design and production of bent plywood furniture, which are characteristic of his preference to use warm, natural materials to mitigate the coldness of a more doctrinaire functionalism.

Robert ADAM

(Kirkcaldy, 1728 – London, 1792)

Robert Adam was a British architect. Born in 1728, he certainly studied at the University of Edinburgh before spending three years in Italy studying Roman architecture. In 1757 he visited the ruins of Diocletian's Palace at Spalato in Dalmatia with the French architect C.L. Clérisseau and published the results in 1764 in *The Ruins of the Palace of Diocletian*.

In 1762 he was appointed sole architect to the King and the Board of Works where he stayed for six years. In 1768 he entered Parliament as member of the county of Kinross. The same year he and his three brothers leased the ground fronting the Thames and proceeded to erect the ambitious block of buildings called the Adelphi which is imperishably associated with their name.

As an architect, he was strongly under Italian influence, and his style and aims were exotic rather than native. He was able to mould and adapt classical models as to create a new manner of the highest charm and distinction.

In his view, the architect was intimately concerned with the furniture and the decoration of a building, as well as with its form and construction. In his furniture, he made lavish use of his favourite decorative motives: wreaths and paterae, the honeysuckle, and the fan ornament which he used so constantly. Thus his country houses like Kedleston House (n° 532) or Kenwood House are unique products of English art.

Leon Battista ALBERTI

(Genoa, 1404 – Rome, 1472)

Leon Battista Alberti was one of the outstanding personalities of the Renaissance. He employed the principles of mathematical perspective and developed a polished theory of art. Alberti came from an important Florentine family who had, however, been banned from the town in 1387. When his family returned to Florence in 1429, Alberti, under the influence of Brunelleschi, Masaccio and Donatello, dedicated himself to the studies of architecture and art. Alberti quickly became the protégé of the Rucellai Family, for whom he created two of his most significant pieces of art in Florence, the Palazzo Rucellai in the Via della Vigna (n° 382) (today the home of the Alinari Museum), and the elegant small Temple Santo Sepolcro (1467) in the Rucellai-Chapel near San Pancrazio (where the Marino Marini Museum is today). But the major part of his work as an architect was to take place in Rome: Alberti restored Santo Stefano Rotondo and Santa Maria Maggiore in Rimini, and built the unfinished Tempio Malatestiano (1450), the first building which he tried to build according to his architectonic principles. Until this time, Alberti's experience as an architect had been of rather theoretical nature. Finally, towards the end of his career, he worked in Mantua, where he anticipated the typical religious architecture of the counterreformation with the churches San Sebastiano (1460) and Sant'Andrea (n° 387). The façade of Santa Maria Novella (n° 388) is regarded as his most important work, as it unifies the already existing elements and the parts he added into a clear realisation of his new principles. Alberti was educated in the Latin and Greek languages, but never had a formal training as an architect. His architectonic ideas were therefore the result of his own studies and research. His two most important papers on architecture are *De Pictura* (1435), in which he emphatically supports the significance of painting as a foundation for architecture, as well as his theoretical masterpiece *De Re Aedificatoria* (1450). *De Re Aedificatoria* is divided into ten books, such as the ten books on architecture by Vitruvius. But unlike Vitruvius, Alberti told architects how buildings should be constructed, rather than focusing on how they had been built to date. *De Re Aedificatoria* claimed its importance as the classical treatise on architecture from the sixteenth to the eighteenth century.

Tadao ANDO

(Osaka, 1941 –)

While at first sight the often austere architecture of Ando might seem to embody a rigidly minimalistic approach, he in fact embraces much of the aesthetics of traditional Japanese buildings. Ando has an unusual background: he is self-taught as an architect, with no professional training or apprenticeship. Most of his early buildings are small houses in concrete which seek to reconcile the principles of modernism (abstraction, simple geometries, contemporary materials) with the specific sensibilities of Japanese architecture—restraint, privacy, respect for the nature of materials, connection to the natural world. The Koshino house in Ashiya (1979-84) consists of two parallel rectangular boxes, one private and one for entertaining, which are partly sunk into the earth; light enters through narrow slits in the walls and ceiling, with large windows in the living room facing the garden court. By withholding most sensory input, Ando directs our attention to the changing effects of light. His Rokko housing complex in Kobe (n° 173), with later additions) is a cubic composition set into a hillside to catch the view. Through the 1980s Ando produced a remarkable series of religious buildings whose elemental articulation creates a monastic focus on spiritual rather than material realities: these include the Chapel on Mount Rokko in Kobe (1985-86) and the Church of the Light in Ibaraki (1987-89); the latter consists of a simply furnished concrete box with glazed slits forming a cross of light behind the altar. Among his many museums and corporate buildings in Japan and elsewhere, the Fort Worth Museum of Modern Art in Texas (2002) is outstanding for its lyrical deployment of water. Though Ando's work is undeniably demanding, it possesses an unshakeable integrity, referencing basic architectural dualities of inside/outside, solid/void and darkness/light while proposing a balance of the man-made and the natural.

Luis BARRAGÁN
(Guadalajara, 1902 – Mexico City, 1988)

The simple but evocative buildings of the Mexican architect Barragán exemplify what is sometimes termed a 'critical regionalism,' in that he attempted to negotiate between international modernism and local traditions of place. Born in Guadalajara, Barragán was trained as an engineer and largely self-taught in architecture. Particularly inspired by the example of Le Corbusier, around 1940 his interests in contemporary landscape gardening and sculpture contributed to the formation of a distinctly personal aesthetic. Working for wealthy patrons in and around Mexico City, Barragán created a series of houses, stark, geometric volumes which recall not so much the industrial aesthetics of European modernism, but the plain, vernacular forms of traditional Mexican building. He placed particular emphasis on the primacy of the adobe wall, roughly textured and painted in bright, contrasting colours. Barragán was equally innovative in landscaping, and the extraordinary combination of buildings and outdoor space in such commissions as the El Pedregal district exhibit his love for the Alhambra. In 1947 Barragán built a remarkable house for himself in the Tacubaya district, using a peasant vernacular as the starting point for an exquisitely considered minimalism (n° 905). Like all his houses, it proposes a refuge from the outside world, an austere but serene enclosure for meditation. Barragán later took on the planning and urban design of the Las Arboledas residential district (1957-61). As highlighted by carefully staged photography, Barragán's work also has oneiric and surrealist elements, most notable in his poetic use of bodies of water in the horse stables of the San Cristobal estate near Mexico City (1967-68). Barragán's modernism ultimately rejected the impersonality of the machine in favour of emotion, imagination and a nuanced regionalism.

Peter BEHRENS
(Hamburg, 1868 – Berlin, 1940)

Behrens provides a crucial link between the 19th-century Arts and Crafts movement and the 20th-century machine aesthetic, and in the latter capacity he served as an important mentor to Gropius, Le Corbusier and Mies van der Rohe, all of whom passed through his Berlin office. Behrens began his career as a painter, graphic artist, book binder and furniture designer. His first large building was his own house in the artists' colony at Darmstadt (1901), for which he designed every detail, down to the furniture, towels and decorative items. His move to a more industrial expression came in 1907 with his appointment as official architect and house designer for the huge AEG Company in Berlin, which produced all kinds of industrial and electric products from light bulbs to armaments. Behrens created an entire branded image for the company, taking charge of everything from logos and letterhead to the architectural design of entire factories. His industrial structures for AEG were among the first to break from historical tradition to embrace—and even monumentalise—a new appreciation of industrial materials and techniques; the AEG Turbine Factory in Berlin (n° 634) nevertheless still betrays a lingering debt to Classicism in its heavy (and non-structural) quoins articulated as rounded corner piers, as well as the massy polygonal pediment. For his more formal commissions, notably the Germany Embassy in St. Petersburg (1911-12), Behrens made use of a geometrically simplified Classicism to impressive if austere effect. After the war Behrens embraced the current fashion for Expressionist design, as in his fanciful and appropriately polychromatic I.G. Farben offices in Höchst (1920-24). His most notable building outside Germany is the remarkable house in Northampton known as 'New Ways' (1926), which introduced international modernism to England.

Gian Lorenzo BERNINI
(Naples, 1598 – Rome, 1680)

Bernini was a master in the creation of magnificent spaces with a skilled eye for perspectival effects. This is displayed primarily in the square in front of St Peter's (n° 462) with its surrounding columned halls, or the Scala Regia of the Vatican (n° 472). After Maderno's death, Bernini completed the façade and front hall and created the famous bronze baldachin over the high altar for the inside (n° 454).

The speed of the change of mind, in which the admiration for the antique waned, is illustrated by the fact that the contemporaries of this tabernacle placed it as the high point of an independent artistic style. Bernini is also to be praised for the Palazzo Barberini (n° 455) with its masterful staircase, and for several smaller churches. The importance of the piazza design of this period can be seen by the positioning of the two small cupola churches Santa Maria di Monte Santo and Santa Maria dei Miracoli at the north entrance of the Corso that were designed by Carlo Rainaldi and executed by Bernini and his student Carlo Fontana. It was they who helped bring the Piazza del Popolo to its completion.

Bernini was most skilled in decorative sculpture and here, with his Triton fountain on the Piazza Barberini and the main fountain on the Piazza Navona (n° 461), he created an imperishable memorial. With this fountain and the gods it features, Bernini reached back into Antiquity, which was already the fundamentals in the three main works of his youth, Aeneas and Anchises, the stone-throwing David and Apollo and Daphne in the Villa Borghese in Rome which he created as a 17-year-old.

Mario BOTTA
(Mendrisio, 1943 –)

The dramatic mountain landscapes of Ticino, the southernmost canton of Switzerland, have been formative to the work of Botta, who is famous for a tough-minded regionalism that works more with the specifics of site and topography than with sentimental notions of the past. Characterised by simple, large-scale geometries, Botta's architecture is formally ordered and most often symmetrical, lending his buildings an unusual *gravitas* and monumentality, whatever their size. Born in Ticino, Botta studied architecture in Venice under Carlo Scarpa. During this time he worked briefly with Le Corbusier (1965) and Louis Kahn (1969), whose example suggested to Botta that the given conditions of a project can be crystallised in a specific and quasi-inevitable formal composition. Botta's first major commission was the school at Morbio Inferiore (1972-77), a late-Brutalist series of concrete units arranged in an emphatically linear manner. He then began a series of single-family domestic buildings in exposed concrete and brick: the house at Riva San Vitale (1971-73) is a blocky tower set on an incline and accessed by a metal catwalk, thus serving as a territorial marker between mountain and lake. The house at Ligornetto (1975-76) is a striped rectangular block with rectilinear cutouts sheltering windows, while the Casa Rotonda at Stabio (1980-82) is a three-storey cylinder sliced vertically on the north-south axis to allow carefully controlled views. Though Botta's idiosyncratic and repetitive geometrical strategies mean that he is sometimes pegged as a formalist, his motivation in fact comes from the idea of 'building the site,' in which works of architecture are positioned as emphatic markers in the landscape in order to allow their inhabitants a clear existential grounding, orientation and relationship to the natural world. By their insistent formality, his buildings further seem to propose a mode of organisation for any future construction on the site. Botta's larger and later works include the Cathedral of Évry (n° 749), the San Francisco Museum of Modern Art (n° 981), and the Cymbalista Synagogue and Jewish Heritage Centre in Tel Aviv, Israel (1996-98).

Donato BRAMANTE

(Monte Asdrualdo, 1444 – Rome, 1514)

Donato Bramante was born in Monte Asdruald (now Fermignano) near Urbino in 1444. We have little knowledge of his early training. He seems to have spent the largest part of his early career studying painting under Mantegna and Piero della Francesca.

We hear about him for the first time in 1477, when he was working on frescoes in the Palazzo del Podesta in Bergamo. Afterwards he settled down in Milan in the 1480s. Although he created some buildings at this time (Santa Maria Presso, San Satiro, Santa Maria della Grazie, the cloisters of Sant' Ambrogio), his paintings, especially his use of the trompe l'œil technique and the rigorous monumentality of his figures in solemn compositions, had a great influence on the Lombardic school. Bramante then moved from Milan to Rome in 1499, where he gained the favour of the future Pope Julius II. Here, Bramante began his exceptional new interpretation of classical antiquity. In November 503, Julius commissioned Bramante to renovate the Vatican. At first, Bramante dedicated himself to the basic new design of the Vatican palaces at the Belvedere. He worked on the new building of St Peter's (n° 401) from 1506 on, which was later continued by Michelangelo. Within a few years, Bramante had risen to the position the most important architect at the papal court. His historical significance lies not so much in his actual buildings, of which only a small part has been preserved, but rather that he constituted an important inspiration and a great influence with regard to later architects. Bramante died in 1514, a year later than his patron Pope Julius II.

Marcel BREUER

(Pécs, 1902 – New York, 1981)

Born in Hungary, Breuer studied briefly in Vienna before enrolling as one of the earliest students at the Weimar Bauhaus. Rapidly absorbing Gropius's lessons of functionalism and elementarism, Breuer was soon given charge of instruction in the Bauhaus's furniture department where he produced some of the modern movement's most iconic chair designs in bent tubular steel. When the Bauhaus moved to Dessau in 1926, Breuer was commissioned to produce all the furniture for Gropius's new buildings. Though meeting with only minor success as an

architect in Berlin, Breuer produced many innovative competition designs for large-scale projects and designed the famous Doldertal flats for the architectural historian Sigfried Giedion in Zurich (1935-36). He then moved on to London to establish a partnership with F.R.S. Yorke, and later followed Gropius to Massachusetts. Here Breuer and his former teacher formed an architectural partnership and served as mentors to a rising generation of younger American architects (notably Philip Johnson, Paul Rudolph and Ieoh Ming Pei) at Harvard. Breuer's American output consisted mainly of smaller houses, many of innovative character, until he was selected (with Nervi and Zehrfuss) to build UNESCO's new Paris headquarters in 1953 (n° 694). This launched a series of more prominent buildings, including St. John's Abbey and College in Minnesota (n° 921), the IBM Research Centre at La Gaude, France (1960-69) and the Whitney Museum of American Art in New York City (n° 942). Not much given to theorising, Breuer's clear-thinking approach to modern architecture nevertheless validated the play of contrasts, as often manifested in his use of textured rubble and concrete surfaces played off against smoothly planar or transparent walls. His later buildings in reinforced concrete became increasingly heavy and sculptural, contributing decisively to the rise of the Brutalist aesthetic of the 1960s and 70s.

Filippo BRUNELLESCHI

(Florence, 1377-1446)

Brunelleschi is regarded as the father of Renaissance architecture and one of the most famous Italian architects. Although he never worked as a painter, Brunelleschi was a pioneer in the art of perspective. In addition, he developed processes to transport building material to its required location, and constructed a self-supporting wall for domes.

Filippo Brunelleschi began his career as an apprentice to a goldsmith. He passed his examination six years after his apprenticeship and was accepted into the goldsmiths' guild as a master. He started his architectural career by renovating town houses and other buildings. He belonged to those artists who in 1401/02 were defeated in the competition for the new doors of the baptistery for Florence Cathedral (his two panels from the competition are in the Bargello) by another great goldsmith and sculptor, Lorenzo Ghiberti. This disappointment apparently made Brunelleschi give up sculpture and turn to architecture. Brunelleschi dedicated himself to architectural studies in Rome and developed the exceptional abilities which enabled him to build one of the most important buildings of Renaissance architecture in Italy – the unfinished Gothic Cathedral in Florence (1420-36). This became one of the first examples for architectonic functionality and exhibits architectonic reliefs, circular windows and a wonderfully proportioned dome. In other buildings, such as the Church of San Lorenzo (n° 369) built by the Medici, and the orphanage Ospedale degli Innocenti (n° 370), Brunelleschi employed a severe and geometrical style, inspired by the art of ancient Rome. Later Brunelleschi turned away from this linear, geometrical approach towards a more rhythmical style, more characterised by sculpture, especially in the unfinished Church Santa Maria degli Angeli (the building work started in 1434), the Basilica of Santo Spirito (n° 378) and the Cappelli di Pazzi (started approximately 1441). This style embodied the first step towards the Baroque style. Filippo Brunelleschi died at the age of sixty-nine and was laid to rest in the Cathedral of Florence.

Michelangelo BUONARROTI

(Caprese, 1475 – Rome, 1564)

Michelangelo, master of the Italian Renaissance, was born near the Tuscan city of Arezzo in 1475. He served an apprenticeship with a painter and enjoyed the patronage of the powerful Medici family early in his career. Already an established sculptor due to the popularity of his relief work and his iconic statue of David, Michelangelo famously accepted a papal commission to paint the ceiling of the Sistine Chapel in Rome when he was in his early 30s. While he is most remembered for sculpture and painting, his architectural accomplishments rival those of the greatest architects of the Renaissance in terms of aesthetic and structural sophistication. Many buildings now considered iconic symbols of Florence and Rome are examples of his craftsmanship.

The tomb of Pope Julius II at the church of San Pietro in Vicoli was an early commission for Michelangelo. Begun in 1505, the project was repeatedly delayed and reduced in splendour due to lack of funds, but finally completed in 1545. It remains a striking example of the artist's powerful use of sculpture in architecture. He designed the New Sacristy and Medici Chapel for the Basilica of San Lorenzo in Florence (n° 408); numerous members of the famous family are buried in its crypt. The Palazzo dei Conservatori (n° 383) on Rome's Capitoline Hill (n° 419) was in disrepair when Michelangelo designed its new façade: its massive Corinthian columns and flat roof are among the artist's architectural signatures. He is also responsible for the masterful remodelling of the palaces that surround the Piazza del Campidoglio, which he arranged ingeniously to compensate for the irregularities of the landscape. The bright grandeur of the Laurentian Library in Florence (n° 407), which Michelangelo designed in 1530, demonstrates the artist's Mannerist insistence on balance and idealised proportions.

Perhaps Michelangelo's most recognisable monument is the dome of St. Peter's Basilica in Vatican City (n° 401), designed in 1547. Refining and elaborating on the designs of then-deceased master builders Donato Bramante and Giuliano da Sangallo, Michelangelo devised an egg-shaped dome with an inner and outer shell, mounted on four enormous piers. The dome rises to a height of 136.6 metres, making it the tallest dome in the world.

Michelangelo died at the age of 89 on 18 February 1564 in Rome, before the completion of the cupola of St. Peter's. His remains were subsequently transported to Florence in his native Tuscany, and he was entombed in the Basilica of Santa Croce.

LE CORBUSIER
(La Chaux-de-Fonds, 1887 – Roquebrune-Cap-Martin, 1965)

Of Swiss origin but a French citizen by choice, Le Corbusier (real name: Charles-Édouard Jeanneret) remains the single most influential European architect of the 20th century. His fame rests in part on his relatively small built oeuvre, but equally on his many polemical books and articles. His massively influential *Vers une Architecture* (1923) proposed a new design mindset modelled on the rational calculations of the engineer: Le Corbusier urged architects to look at the products of industry — airplanes, automobiles, ocean liners and industrial buildings — for inspiration. In terms of domestic architecture, he famously postulated that the house should be seen as a "machine for living in." At the same time, Le Corbusier's texts betray an essentially mystical idealism based on the idea that the purity of Platonic solids and careful control of proportions can produce an aesthetic impact that verges on the spiritual. His early houses in and around Paris, pure white externally though animated by isolated walls of pure colour inside, made great innovations in the shaping of space, light and circulation, and remain the epitome of early modernist design; of these, the Villa Savoye (n° 666) is the most famous. After the Second World War, Le Corbusier's production took on a radically different cast, now espousing complex curves, rougher surfaces and a generally sculptural approach. This is best represented by his pilgrimage chapel at Ronchamp (n° 688), whose dramatically battered walls, irregular fenestration and organic forms were conceived as a subjective response to the mountainous

locale and the spiritual demands of the commission. Le Corbusier's most imitated building is certainly his Unité d'Habitation at Marseille (n° 685), a huge housing block of crudely molded concrete that attempted to give its inhabitants the feeling of sailing in a self-sufficient vessel through a sea of greenery. Though often critiqued for hubris and reductive thinking, Le Corbusier's creative and intellectual approach to design continues to inspire many architects today.

Johann Bernhard Fischer VON ERLACH
(Graz, 1656 – Vienna, 1723)

The son of a sculptor, Johann Bernhard Fischer von Erlach was born in Graz in 1656. At the age of 11, he left home to serve as an apprentice in Rome, where he studied architecture in the studio of Carlo Fontana. There, he met Gian Lorenzo Bernini and enthusiastically discovered the works of Borromini and Guarini.

He quickly gained a reputation as a gifted architect, which earned him commissions from Austrian aristocracy and also caught the attention of the Holy Roman Emperor Joseph I and the Church. Solicited everywhere, he divided his time between Vienna, Salzburg and Prague, before permanently settling in Vienna in 1686. He was ennobled by the Emperor Leopold, who appointed him Royal Engineer and added the aristocratic "von Erlach" to his name.

His most famous achievement is possibly the Schönbrunn Palace (n° 482). This magnificent palace, just outside of Vienna, claims to be "Austria's Versailles."

Fischer von Erlach built several Viennese structures, including the Winter Palace of Prince Eugene of Savoy, Count Batthyány's palace, and the Karlskirche (n° 492), dedicated to Saint Charles Borromeo.

Fischer von Erlach is considered one of the creators of the late German Baroque style. He knew how to combine elements from different architectural periods, synthesising Baroque and early classical techniques to develop his own style.

Hassan FATHY
(Alexandria, 1900 – Cairo, 1989)

A pioneer in the field of socially and climatically sensitive architecture, the Alexandria-born Fathy deliberately eschewed many of the technical and material innovations of mainstream modernism in favour of reviving traditional methods of construction, notably that of adobe or mud brick. Trained as an architect in Cairo, Fathy began to explore the possibilities of this technique in 1937. From 1946-53 he was employed by the Egyptian government's Department of Antiquities to supervise the construction of the village of New Gourna (n° 69), near Luxor, which was to provide a new home for a colony of resettled tomb robbers. Fathy taught the inhabitants to construct their own dwellings, yet despite attracting much press attention the experiment was not particularly successful. Fathy then designed a series of schools for the Egyptian Ministry of Education, and later went on to work in Greece, Iraq, Pakistan and several countries in Africa. He returned permanently to Cairo in 1963 and was for many years the Head of the Architecture faculty at the University of Cairo. Fathy also investigated the layout, aesthetics and climatic functioning of traditional Arab houses, particularly their passive cooling through the use of thick walls, courtyards and rooftop ventilation. Fathy's example demonstrates that architecture need not be overtly innovative or glamorous to fulfill the most pressing social needs, which continue to include the provision of much-needed housing and well-functioning architecture for underprivileged populations. Fathy's book *Architecture for the Poor* (1973) gave international prominence to his search for an economical, energy-frugal and socially appropriate architecture for indigenous populations on rural sites, and appears increasingly relevant in the present day.

Norman FOSTER

(Manchester, 1935 –)

One of the most high-profile and prolific of contemporary architects, Foster is unashamedly excited about new technology, though he is equally sensitive to such issues as form, light, context, human use and ecological footprint. Though he is often termed a High-Tech architect, Foster justifiably claims that he is interested only in using appropriate technology to create the most efficient, comfortable and inspiring surrounding for his clients. Born in Manchester, Foster studied architecture at Yale. He then formed the short-lived Team 4 with Richard Rogers, Su Rogers, and his first wife Wendy Foster; like Rogers, Foster began with the idea of creating neutral space envelopes, though his buildings rapidly presented a sleeker appearance than those of his former partner. His breakthrough project was the Willis Faber & Dumas Headquarters in Ipswich (n° 717), which re-imagines the typical office building as a low, spreading envelope of amoeboid plan; its walls of sheer plate glass passively reflect the urban surroundings by day and reveal the interiors by night. The Sainsbury Centre for the Visual Arts at the University of East Anglia (n° 724) is a vast hangar-like shed using deep trusses to create a completely free interior. The gridded cladding of its outer envelope allows standardised elements to be replaced at will. Foster's more high-profile Hong Kong and Shanghai Banking Corporation headquarters in Hong Kong (n° 170), rumoured to be the most expensive building per square metre ever constructed, makes use of an exposed steel structure inspired by bridge engineering. Five vertical zones, each visibly suspended from a 'coat-hanger' truss, were conceptualised as vertically-stacked villages. Foster continues to take charge of many of the largest and most technically advanced architectural commissions of our time, all inevitably privileging energy efficiency and user-friendliness: the long list includes the Commerzbank tower in Frankfurt (n° 766), Stansted Airport (opened 1991), Chek Lap Kok Airport in Hong Kong (n° 183), 30 St. Mary Axe in London (n° 785), London City Hall (n° 767), Wembley Stadium in London (2002-07), the Hearst Tower in New York City (2006) and Beijing Capital International Airport (2007).

Richard Buckminster FULLER

(Milton, 1895 – Los Angeles, 1983)

Often seen as more of a visionary engineer and tinkerer in the mode of Edison than as a professional architect, Fuller's fully engaged approach to technology was to provide a key ingredient in the formation of the so-called 'High-Tech' architects of the 1970s. Having little success with formal education at Harvard and elsewhere, Fuller worked in a variety of industrial occupations before attracting critical interest with his proposal for a radically new kind of dwelling, known as the 'Dymaxion House' (1927). To be built of aluminum and glass, the house would be suspended by cables from a central mast, which would also contain essential services. Fuller's goal was to create a prototype for mass-production along the line of cars or airplanes, but he met with little practical success. Now focused more fully on structural studies, Fuller made his next major contribution with the invention of the Geodesic Dome, a system that allows a maximum volume of space to be covered with a minimum amount of materials. The first experiments with this structure were carried out in the late 1940s during his residency at the famous Black Mountain College in North Carolina. Though dramatically put into material form in the American Pavilion at Expo '67 in Montreal (n° 948), the geodesic system proved to be of typologically minimal value, used largely for industrial, exhibition and scientific buildings as well as greenhouses and conservatories. During the 1960s and 70s, however, Fuller maintained a reputation as a charismatic lecturer, social visionary and prophetic futurist, and

his do-it-yourself domes enjoyed great popularity among students and hippies. Fuller's later writings, which deal with the largest existential questions of the future of human life on what he called 'Spaceship Earth,' are at once opaque, poetic and increasingly relevant.

Antoni GAUDÍ

(Riudoms, 1852 – Barcelona, 1926)

Antoni Gaudí i Cornet was born in the Spanish province of Tarragone, at Mas de la Caldera, his family's home in the town of Riudoms, in June of 1852. In 1870, he entered the architecture school in Barcelona, where he settled.

As a young architect, Gaudí was inspired by Viollet-le-Duc's neo-Gothic work, but quickly separated himself from this rather rigid style and developed greater originality and fantasy. Henceforth placing himself within the Art Nouveau movement, Gaudí unified architecture and furniture and would originate Art Nouveau's Spanish variant known as Modernista. Work on Barcelona's Sagrada Família began in 1882, when Joseph M. Bocabella purchased the land to build a temple dedicated to the Holy Family (n° 597). When disputes with the architect in charge of construction erupted, the commission was entrusted to Gaudí, who modified the original project and would continue throughout his life to make it ever more ambitious. In 1883, Gaudí was charged with building the Casa Vicens. A private commission from the industrialist and ceramist Manuel Vicens Montaner, this project already presaged Gaudí's style, highlighting the Oriental, Baroque, and Art Nouveau influences in his materials, trompe l'œil effects and arabesques. Two years later, the architect collaborated with textile manufacturer Eusebio Güell, for whom he built a palace and gardens. Afterwards, the wealthy industrialist would continue to support and finance Gaudí. Gaudí continued to undertake various private and public architectural commissions up until the early twentieth century. In 1900, he started work on a commission from Güell for a city garden on a hillside in Barcelona, the present-day Güell Park (n° 614). The industrialist's original pharaonic plan called for residences, studios, a chapel, and park – in other words, a small village within the Catalan capital. When it came to making the project a reality, skyrocketing costs only allowed for two houses and the park to be built. The project nevertheless allowed Gaudí to give free reign to his creativity and to his originality, which meant respecting the landscape's natural form.

A worthy representative of Art Nouveau, Gaudí is undoubtedly among those artists who made the most radical break with the past. His work, now under the protection of the UNESCO international heritage program, was greatly criticised during his time. Contemporaries dubbed the Casa Milà that Gaudí designed in 1905 La Pedrera (the Quarry) (n° 629), due to its overly organic appearance that seemed devoid of any rational architectural principle. The enveloping organic architecture of this man, who was then considered too eccentric to be an architect, was thought to be devouring the soul of beautiful Barcelona – the same Barcelona as today, whose soul everyone believes is the work of Antoni Gaudí.

Frank GEHRY

(Toronto, 1929 –)

Gehry's conception of architecture as a form of creative play meant that he was for many years known as a California eccentric, but in his late career he has been able to bring his unrestrained and exuberant approach to a variety of large-scale commissions in many countries, even to the extent that he now seems to have become a quasi-official foreign representative for American maverick individualism. In fact, Gehry was born in Toronto, Canada, though his family soon moved to California. He studied architecture at UCLA and Harvard before starting his own practise in Los Angeles in 1962. Gehry took some time to find his own expression, which was increasingly informed by a dialogue with contemporary artists: his strategies came to include collage, sculptural form, Surrealism and Pop irony. His own house in Santa Monica (with later alterations and additions, n° 965), a violent series of transgressions on an ordinary 1920s bungalow, seemed to break all the rules: layering 'cheapskate' materials — stud framing, corrugated sheet metal, chain-link fencing, plywood — and remaining in an apparent state of suspended construction, it served as the prototype for a series of off-beat residences of similar character. From the later 1980s Gehry's works became more fully sculptural, characterised by flowing, undulating and colliding forms. Among his more prominent commissions in this later mode are the Walt Disney Concert Hall in Los Angeles (n° 984), American Center in Paris, (1994), the Dancing House in Prague (n° 752), the Guggenheim Museum in Bilbao (n° 765), the DG Bank Building in Berlin (2000), the Experience Music Project in Seattle (n° 990), the Stata Center at MIT (2004), and the Pritzker Pavilion in Chicago (2004). Gehry's complex and unconventional structures have only been made practicable with the introduction of computer modeling, which has now opened up an almost unlimited scope for formal play in contemporary architectural design.

James GIBBS

(Aberdeen, 1682 – London, 1754)

James Gibbs was a British architect. Born in Scotland, he studied in Rome with the architect Carlo Fontana before moving to London in 1708. There he was noticed by Edward Harley, Earl of Oxford, who helped him to become joint surveyor in 1713, with Nicholas Hawksmoor, for the new churches to be built under the Act for Fifty New Churches. Gibbs's first church was St. Mary-Le-Strand. His daring and innovative masterpiece, St. Martin-in-the-Fields in Trafalgar Square, London (n° 498), became the most influential church in the English-speaking world of the eighteenth century. James Gibbs was under the influence of the Italian Baroque but also inspired by the works of British architects like Inigo Jones and Christopher Wren. Architectural historian John Summerson even describes his work as the fulfillment of Wren's architectural ideas, which were not fully developed in his own buildings. It should be noted that Gibbs was a Roman Catholic and a Tory, and was therefore not part of the Palladian movement which was prevalent in English architecture of the period. In 1728, he published *A Book of Architecture*, which included his building designs, which became a reference.

James Gibbs is also known for the Cambridge University Senate House (1722-1730), the nave of All Saint's, Derby (now Derby Cathedral, 1725) and the cylindrical Radcliffe Camera in Oxford (n° 514).

Michael GRAVES

(Indianapolis, 1934 –)

One of the leading architects of the Postmodern school of the 1970s and 1980s, Graves's stated goal has been to reintroduce a sense of 'figuration' (as opposed to modernist abstraction) into contemporary architecture; thus he has posited that such elements as a window, a column or a ceiling must 'read,' semiotically, as culturally recognisable entities rather than purely geometric inventions of no historical pedigree. Graves was born in Indianapolis and educated at the University of Cincinnati and at Harvard. In 1960 he was awarded the prestigious Prix de Rome, allowing extended study in Italy. His early buildings self-consciously featured a pastiche of Corbusian references, but his interest in Classicism soon asserted itself in the unbuilt project for the Fargo-Moorhead Cultural Center Bridge between North Dakota and Minnesota (1977-78), which made playful use of keystone and arch motifs. His Portland Public Services Building in Oregon served as an early test case to see if ornamentation and historicism had really returned to contemporary architecture: though deploying few literal historical quotations, Graves turned each façade of the boxy tower into a colourful, decorative pattern, again playing with the forms of columns and giant keystones. These experiments were carried forward in the more grandiloquent Humana Building in Louisville (n° 973), Kentucky (1985), while the remarkably over-the-top Dolphin and Swan Hotels at Disneyworld in Orlando, Florida (1988-90) apotheosised Graves' frank embrace of colourful ornamentation: two huge luxury hotels connected by a bridge across a crescent-shaped lake, the complex has been described as "entertainment architecture." His later buildings, such as the Central Library of Denver, Colorado (1995-96) and his museums, cultural institutions and government buildings in Washington, D.C., have served to recoup some of the critical standing that his more exuberant creations had at one time threatened.

Eileen GRAY

(Enniscorthy, 1878 – Paris, 1976)

Along with furniture designer Charlotte Perriand, Gray is an all-too-rare instance of a woman who played an important role in early modern design. Born to an aristocratic Irish family, Gray studied art at the Slade School in London and later at the Académie Julian in Paris. Having mastered the labour-intensive craft of Japanese lacquering from the master Seizo Sugawara in London, she launched a successful career as a furniture designer. After the First World War, Gray's exquisitely handcrafted screens and other items of luxury interior décor in a fashionable Classical-Art Deco mode were marketed to a select clientele through her store in Paris, which she called Jean Désert. From the 1920s her approach took on the more industrial character of the Bauhaus school, as epitomised by her famous 'Bibendum' armchair, its tubular curves of padded leather recalling the famous Michelin mascot. Her most important architectural commission was the now-derelict house known as E-1027 near Roquebrune on the Côte d'Azur (n° 667), designed for and in collaboration with the architectural publisher Jean Badovici. Influenced by the theories of Le Corbusier and in the forefront of modernist aesthetics, E.1027 was remarkable for the care that Gray devoted to items of practical use, such as tables, built-in closets and storage areas. In her later life Gray became more reclusive and her work and career remained largely forgotten until recent years. Before her death at the age of 98, however, she was able to appreciate the adulation of a new generation of design enthusiasts and feminist scholars who again revealed her originality to public notice. Gray's furniture designs remain modern classics.

Walter GROPIUS

(Berlin, 1883 – Boston, 1969)

Perhaps more influential as an educator and a polemicist than as a practising architect, Gropius played a crucial role in promulgating international modernism throughout Europe and North America. After an apprenticeship with Peter Behrens from 1907-10, Gropius formed a partnership with Adolf Meyer and built the Fagus factory at Alfeld-an-der-Leine (n° 635). This manifested all the ingredients of the new architecture, including an exposed structure, use of industrial materials, extensively glazed curtain walls, and a stripped-down aesthetic of pure rectilinear geometry. Convinced that the 20th century would belong to the masses, Gropius's concerns were also economic and social, for he hoped to provide healthier working and living conditions for the laboring classes. After service in the war, Gropius was put in charge of a new school of art and design which he called the Bauhaus. Later housed at Dessau in Gropius's custom-designed buildings (n° 653), the Bauhaus had an influence far beyond its relatively small number of students and brief period of operation. Starting from an allegiance to Arts and Crafts principles, the Bauhaus moved to promulgate a simplified machine aesthetic that was seen to be compatible with industrial mass production. At the same time, this made use of the vocabulary of elemental geometry pioneered by abstract artists, many of whom were teachers at the school. In the 1930s, Gropius practised in England and then in the United States, where he was to take up the influential position of the director of Harvard's Graduate School of Design. Here, an entire generation of American architects would come to absorb Bauhaus doctrines. Gropius was later active with his architectural firm TAC (The Architects' Collaborative), which put into practise his ostensible preference for communal or team-based design work over individualistic self-expression.

Zaha HADID
(Baghdad, 1950 –)

Probably the most prominent woman architect now working in the world, Hadid was born in Baghdad, Iraq. As a child she was inspired by the beauty of ancient Sumerian cities and the reed villages of the marshes of southern Iraq. After her studies at London's Architectural Association, she worked for Rem Koolhaas's Office of Metropolitan Architecture, where she became a partner in 1977. Establishing her own practise in London in 1980, Hadid produced a largely theoretical and unbuilt body of work while teaching at the AA and elsewhere. The densely layered and explosively fragmented nature of her designs led to her being identified with Deconstructivism. And since many of these appeared to be largely conceptual or experimental in nature, she was able to build very little before the mid-1990s, despite winning several international competitions; her well-publicised projects for the Peak Club, Hong Kong (1982) and the Cardiff Bay Opera House in Wales (1994) are among these unbuilt projects. Hadid's first realised building to attract international attention was the small but agressively angular Vitra Fire Station in Weil am Rhein, Germany (n° 754). More recent works include the Rosenthal Center for Contemporary Art in Cincinnati (1998), the Phaeno Science Centre in Wolfsburg, Germany (n° 782), and the Bridge Pavilion for Expo 2008 in Zaragoza, Spain, which spans the river Ebro. Hadid will also build the London Aquatics Centre for the 2012 Olympics. Her desire to invest architecture with dramatic qualities of light, form and colour inevitably produces visually striking results. She also works as an abstract sculptor. In 2004 Hadid was the first female recipient of the Pritzker Prize.

Victor HORTA
(Gand, 1861 – Brussels, 1947)

In 1878, he made his first trip to Paris for the Universal Exposition and completed a period of training with the architect and decorator Jules Debuysson. In 1880, fate led him back to Belgium right after his father died.

Married the next year, he moved to Brussels and enrolled in the Académie Royale. During this period he commenced training under Alphonse Balat, the official architect of Leopold II.

In 1884, Horta submitted a plan for Parliament that earned him the first place in the Godecharle architecture competition. The next year he built three houses in Gand. In 1887, his plan for the Museum of Natural History won the triennial alumni competition launched by the Académie des Beaux-Arts in Brussels.

In 1889, Horta returned to Paris to attend the new Universal Exposition. Upon his return to Belgium, his wife gave birth to a daughter Simone, and in 1892 he was hired to teach at the Faculté Polytechnique of the Université Libre of Brussels

where he was appointed professor in 1899. The next year, Horta designed a private residence for the physicist-chemist Emile Tassel. Today, Tassel House remains a key Art Nouveau monument. Set on a deep and narrow lot, the structure's principle element is a central staircase covered by a frosted lantern. Bathed in light, and supported by thin cast-iron columns sprouting botanical arabesques that are continued in the paintings and mosaics that cover the walls and floors, the staircase is the townhouse's principal architectural feature. Horta's nod to architecture marked the beginning of a lengthy series of commissions that continued until the first decade of the twentieth century, among which the majority were for townhouses, mainly in the Belgian capital. The following private residences are among Horta's most famous: Tassel (n° 606), Solvay (n° 608), Van Ettvelde (n° 607), Aubecq (1899) and Max Hallet (1902). In 1898 Horta also completed a house and studio for his own use on the rue Américaine. Victor Horta lent his talent to public projects as well. In 1895, he built the Maison du Peuple for the Belgian Socialist Party, largely with Solvay's financing. He also worked on department stores: the Brussels department store chain called A l'Innovation (1900), the Anspach stores (1903), Magasins Waucquez (1906) and Magasins Wolfers (1909). In 1912, Horta was entrusted with the reorganisation of the Académie des Beaux-Arts of Brussels. The next year he agreed to serve as the institution's director for three years. At the end of his term directing the Académie des Beaux-Arts, Horta was forced to exile himself to the United States until 1919.

Upon his return, he sold his premises on the rue Américaine and started working on plans for the Palais des Beaux-Arts in Brussels. In 1925, Horta completed the Pavillon d'honneur for the first International Exposition of Decorative and Industrial Modern Arts in Paris and became the Principal of the Fine Arts class at the Académie Royale de Belgique.

Horta was elevated to the title of Baron in 1932. Five years later, he submitted his final project: the Gare Centrale de Bruxelles (Brussels Central Train Station). Fortunately, he died without having to witness the destruction of his works, such as the Magasins Anspach and the Maison du Peuple, which were demolished in 1965-1966. In 1969, his house and studio on the rue Américaine were turned into the Musée Horta (n° 611), in the end serving to consecrate his work as an artist.

Thomas JEFFERSON
(Shadwell, 1743 – Monticello, 1826)

Thomas Jefferson was the third President of the United States. Born in 1743, he studied law and was admitted to the bar in 1767. He began his public service as a justice of the peace and parish vestryman; he was chosen a member of the Virginia House of Burgesses in 1769 and entered the Continental Congress in 1775. He is famous for being one of the writers of the Declaration of Independence from 1776. Between 1784 and 1789 Jefferson visited France and served as Minister there. After returning from France he became secretary of state under George Washington and then Vice President before being elected as a President in 1800. Jefferson was one of the greatest political managers his country has known, and he was President of the United States until 1809. His importance as a maker of modern America can scarcely be overstated, for the ideas he advocated became the very foundations of American republicanism. His administration ended the possibility of the development of Federalism in the direction of class government; and the party he formed fixed the democratic future of the nation.

Jefferson was not only a politician but also an architect. He designed his house in Monticello (n° 836) which was very modern for the time with automatic doors and the first swivel chair. After he retired from his political career, he devoted his last years to the establishment of the University of Virginia at Charlottesville (n° 845). He planned the buildings, gathered its faculty and shaped its organisations. He died on the 4th of July 1826, the fiftieth anniversary of the Declaration of American Independence.

Philip JOHNSON
(Cleveland, 1906 – New Canaan, 2005)

Sometimes called the dean of American architects, the long-lived Johnson played a pivotal role in introducing modern architecture to America. His reputation is nevertheless ambiguous, for while he commanded respect for his behind-the-scenes influence, few of Johnson's buildings are seen as unequivocal masterpieces and both his personal life and professional philosophy proved controversial. Drawing on an extensive knowledge of architectural history, particularly Neoclassicism, Johnson's approach was essentially aesthetic and artistic rather than intellectual, and he repeatedly disavowed having any firm convictions. A child of Midwestern privilege, Johnson studied history and philosophy at Harvard before taking an interest in architecture. In 1932, in collaboration with the architectural historian Henry-Russell Hitchcock, he mounted an exhibition at the Museum of Modern Art on recent modern buildings, later published in book form as *The International Style*. In his 30s Johnson went to study architectural design under Gropius and Breuer at Harvard. Soon afterwards he erected his most widely admired building, his own Glass House, in New Canaan, Connecticut (n° 911): an elegantly detailed glass box on a low plinth, its minimal aesthetics are those of Mies van der Rohe. Johnson's work in the 1960s became increasingly free, eclectic, decorative and even hedonistic, establishing itself as part of a 'New Formalism.' His New York State Theater at Lincoln Theater at Lincoln Centre (1960-64), which recalls Classical motifs, is a typical example. Working with John Burgee from 1967, Johnson designed many large-scale corporate buildings, notably the conventionally modernist Pennzoil Place, Houston (1970-76) as well as the groundbreakingly historicising AT&T Building, New York City (n° 972), whose stone cladding, broken pediment and monumental entrance lobby launched American Postmodernism. Always in the forefront of the latest trends, Johnson spent his last years experimenting with Deconstructivism and computer modeling. As this brief list indicates, Johnson's ever-changing approach confirms his frank admission that his only fundamental belief was relativism

Inigo JONES
(Smithfield, 1573-1652)

Inigo Jones, English architect of Spanish origin, was the first to introduce Renaissance architecture to Great Britain.

Born into a modest family (his father was a master tailor), it was through his numerous trips to Italy, particularly Venice, that Jones was introduced to art. Upon his return to England, he was accepted into the court of King Charles I, where he became renowned not only for his architectural talents, but also as a painter, engineer, geometrician, stenographer, and playwright. Founder of mask theatre at the court, Jones was also named Geometrician to the King and General Steward to the Buildings of the Crown. It was in this position that he was charged in 1612 with the responsibility of scouring Italian museums and private anthologies in order to put together a collection of the most remarkable drawings inspired by Antiquity.

Jones's best-known works – Covent Garden (n° 459), the Queen's House in Greenwich (n° 451), and the Banqueting House in Whitehall (n° 453) – are strongly inspired by Italian architecture. Jones cultivated the appreciation of uncluttered, sober and solid construction. Using the Italian architect Andrea Palladio as a

reference, he attached great importance to mathematical proportions, and established the model of the cubic building as an architectural principle. His designs for Covent Garden, including the church, square, and surrounding streets, are considered the first work of London urbanism.

Filippo JUVARRA
(Messine, 1678 – Madrid, 1736)

Filippo Juvarra is considered one of the representative artists of early Rococo, who marked the period with his elegant and sophisticated creations.

Born in Messina in 1685 into a family of goldsmiths, he learned the family business before joining the studio of Carlo Fontana in Rome. There, he studied antique architecture, as well as the works of Michelangelo, Bernini, Borromini and Pietro da Cortona. His efforts were crowned with success, and Juvarra came away with several awards, including that of the Academy in 1705.

In 1724, he was summoned to Lisbon, where he elaborated on the plans of the Sé Patriarchal Cathedral. Upon his return to Italy, he found himself entrusted with the dome of the Basilica di Sant'Andrea in Mantua and the design of the cathedral cupola in Como, as well as the façade of the Santa Cristina church in Turin.

In Turin, he specialised in religious architecture and earned the affection of Victor Amadeus II, the prince of Piedmont, who commissioned Juvarra's two most beautiful creations: the Basilica of Superga (n° 497), a round, sepulchral church topped with a dome that is considered a masterpiece of Baroque art, and the royal hunting pavilion of Stupinigi (n° 507), which Juvarra transformed into a true palace.

In 1735, the King of Spain asked him to draw the plans for the new Royal Palace of Madrid. Unfortunately, this order, like so many others, never came to fruition: his designs were so ambitious that his financial partners were often intimidated by the elevated cost of the construction.

Louis KAHN
(Kuressaare, 1901 – Manhattan, 1974)

Sometimes categorised as a Brutalist, Kahn certainly favoured the bold, large-scale forms in brick and concrete characteristic of that vaguely-defined approach, but his work was informed largely by an idiosyncratic personal philosophy and by historical tradition. Possessing great personal charisma, Kahn remains something of a cult figure among architects, though his often austere buildings seem to hold less appeal for the general public. Kahn was born in Estonia, but his family soon settled in Philadelphia. After a traditional fine arts education at the University of Pennsylvania, he worked for the City Planning Commission. It was only in the early 1950s that he was able to synthesise his love of ancient buildings with more progressive approaches. In searching for an architecture that could communicate on the deepest levels, Kahn began by rethinking the practise first from principles, positing elemental categories of structure, form, space, light and order. His early extension to the Yale University Art Gallery (n° 917) was an elegantly Miesian brick and glass box, though the Richards Medical Research Center at the University of Pennsylvania (n° 930), assembled from prefabricated concrete parts, is deliberately complex and varied: he here famously proposed a separation of "served" and "servant" areas, articulating the latter (including circulation and mechanical systems) as towers. The Salk Institute for Biological Studies in La Jolla (n° 928), conceived as a poetic retreat for research and meditation, has a formal, axial plan: its two wings frame a dramatic view of the Pacific. The Kimbell Art Museum in Fort Worth (n° 949) is a series of parallel concrete vaults of unique light-diffusing configuration, though the interiors are less compartmentalised than this might suggest. Finally, Kahn's monumental government complex at Dhaka, Bangladesh (n° 166) deployed his stark geometries on the grandest possible scale. Kahn can be seen to have reinvigorated modern architecture by using Classical or Beaux-Arts strategies to reinfuse drama and meaning into abstract geometry and by reintroducing a mythic element at a time when sterile functionalism or social determinism seemed to have the upper hand.

Rem KOOLHAAS
(Rotterdam, 1944 –)

The forcefully progressive architecture of the Rotterdam-born Koolhaas actively embraces aspects of contemporary capitalism, consumerism and globalisation – notably dehumanisation, chaos, placelessness and unprecedented scale – that many find disturbing. Both cynical and realistic, Koolhaas celebrates the speed and disorder of modern urban life. Though clearly allied to earlier modernism, he has effectively questioned older dogmas concerning functionalism and rigid adherence to a pre-established program. Koolhaas studied film in Amsterdam and architecture at London's AA and at Cornell before forming the Office for Metropolitan Architecture (OMA) in 1975. A pure theoretician for much of his early career, Koolhaas published his first manifesto, *Delirious New York*, in 1978. This carefully researched but passionate study of the phenomenon of 'Manhattanism' launched his career-long interest in the notion of 'bigness,' which he realised could be exploited as an aesthetic option rather than simply tolerated as a necessary evil of an overcrowded planet. His early fantasy projects for New York skyscrapers were imaginative and colourful, reflecting a further interest in Russian Constructivism. Among Koolhaas's first realised projects were the Netherlands Dance Theatre in The Hague (n° 732) and the Rotterdam Kunsthal (1992-93). His influential and monumentally large book *SMLXL* (1995, with Bruce Mau and Hans Werleman) is a dense collage of imagery, essays, diaries, fiction, and coverage of OMA projects; its overall message was to reinforce the extent to which architecture must now move with the speed of modern transportation, electronic media, and changing fashion; his later books have been written in collaboration with his Harvard students. Koolhaas's recent designs, including the Dutch Embassy in Berlin (2004), Seattle Public Library (n° 997) and the CCTV Headquarters, Beijing (2004), all betray his characteristically angled and faceted geometries, embodying a resolutely unsentimental attempt to meet the intimidating challenges of contemporary society with creative enthusiasm.

Louis LE VAU
(Paris, 1612-1670)

Louis Le Vau was one of the founders of French classicism (the "Louis XIV" style), which he managed to blend elegantly with the Baroque style.

The son of a master mason, he began his career amongst a wealthy, private clientele, for whom he constructed numerous private mansions and castles. During his apprenticeship, Le Vau was so bold as to exercise great creative freedom: leaving behind his academic education, he adopted a very personal style. His specialities were panelled ceilings, alcove rooms and rooms inspired by Italian architecture, all of which garnered him so much aclaim that he was appointed First Architect to the King by Louis XIV in 1654.

Between 1656 and 1661, he built his most famous monument, the castle of Vaux-le-Vicomte (n° 467), which was commissioned by the Superintendent of Finances, Nicolas Fouquet. Constructed in a grandiose style, the château was built according to the designs of Mansard and Le Nôtre. *(See commentary.)*

Taken under the wing of Louis XIV, Le Vau participated in the transformation of Paris into the magnificent, radiant capital of the King's dreams. In addition to

the expansion of the castle at Versailles (n° 468), he helped to embellish the Château de Vincennes, the Tuileries Palace, the Louvre (n° 477), and the Pitié-Salpêtrière Hospital. He also designed the College of the Four Nations (n° 469), now the principal seat of the Institut de France, at the request of Cardinal Mazarin. This structure demonstrates the skilful combination of Baroque and Classic styles, the two disciplines loved by the architect, and also shows the particular influence of Bernini's work.

Daniel LIBESKIND
(Lódź, 1946 –)

The spectacularly angled forms of American architect Libeskind, who at one point was classed as a Deconstructivist, were for many years seen as so speculative and expressionistic as to be unbuildable; in recent years they have nevertheless achieved material form in several cities. Of Polish ancestry, Libeskind is the son of Jewish holocaust survivors and grew up in New York City. He studied architecture at the Cooper Union and later at Essex University, England. After very brief stints with Richard Meier and Peter Eisenman, Libeskind embarked on an international career characterised largely by teaching and theorising. His first realised building, finished in 1998 when he was 52 years old, was the Felix Nussbaum art museum in Osnabrück, Germany. His breakthrough commission, however, was the well-regarded Jewish Museum in Berlin (n° 747), which opened in 1999. Its violently angular and scored geometries, derived through a process of conceptual mapping, provides an appropriately unsettling container for anguished memories. It is now Germany's most visited museum. In 2003 Libeskind won the competition for the reconstruction of the World Trade Center in New York City. His entry, entitled 'Memory Foundations,' proposed a series of tall, crystalline forms flanking a central 'Freedom Tower' of unprecedented height; this will no longer be built as designed, however. Libeskind has since erected Jewish museums in several other cities, as well as the Imperial War Museum North in Manchester (1997-2002) and an extension to the Royal Ontario Museum in Toronto (2002-07); his famous design for a spiral extension to the Victoria and Albert Museum in London was cancelled due to lack of funding. Libeskind's studio is two blocks north of the World Trade Center site.

Adolf LOOS
(Brno, 1870 – Vienna, 1933)

Austrian architect and writer Adolf Loos was born in Brno, Czechoslovakia, in 1870. After finishing his studies in architecture in Dresden, he spent three years in the U.S. There, Loos discovered the creations of American architect Louis Sullivan, leader of the Chicago School, an architectural movement that profoundly influenced him.

He settled in Vienna in 1896, where he began to work for the architect Carl Mayreder before establishing himself independently in 1897. In 1920, he was named the Chief Architect of the Housing Department of Vienna. At the same time, he pursued his theoretical research, which he revealed in the form of several essays; the most famous of these, "Ornament and Crime" (1908), was published by Le Corbusier in his periodical, *Esprit Nouveau*.

Adolf Loos is known for his opposition to the Viennese Secession movement and his virulent criticism of ornamental construction as envisioned by supporters of Art Nouveau. An independent herald of change, he continued the thought movement launched by Otto Wagner and advocated a style based on refinement and function.

Loos conceived several houses and villas in Vienna, but also in Paris, notably the residence of Dadaist Tristan Tzara. Some of his most famous works are the

Goldman and Salatsch store building (n° 637), also called the "Looshaus" (1912), the Steiner House (n° 636), one of his most radical constructions in reinforced concrete, and the Villa Moller (n° 668). The purity of his style made Adolf Loos a pioneer of modern architecture. He had a direct influence on later artists and on the architecture of the 20th century.

Charles Rennie MACKINTOSH

(Glasgow, 1868 – London, 1928)

Producing his greatest works in a few short years around the turn of the century, Mackintosh stands at the intersection of older Arts and Crafts traditions and the search for a uniquely modern style that was associated with the Art Nouveau movement. Mackintosh's formal creations are unmistakably his own, characterised by long, elegant vertical lines terminating in floral or vegetative motifs. Drawing inspiration from Art Nouveau designs published in *The Studio* magazine, Mackintosh began his career largely as a graphic and furniture designer in conjunction with his friend J H. McNair and the sisters Frances and Margaret Macdonald (the latter of which he later married). While working as a draughtsman for the firm of Honeyman & Keppie, Mackintosh won the competition for a new building for the Glasgow School of Art (n° 610), where he had earlier studied. The result was a unique hybrid of Art Nouveau, Scottish castle motifs and an artistic use of wrought iron. The large and asymmetrically disposed studio windows, influenced by factory architecture, would later be seen as forerunners of the machine aesthetic of the 1920s. Much of Mackintosh's mature work is notable for its characteristically aestheticised mode of interior decoration: his domestic and commercial interiors were generally white and airy, with lacquered furniture and selected points of exquisite floral decoration. He designed a chain of tearooms in Glasgow, whose visual purity was intended to mirror their intended goal of providing a healthier alternative to alcoholic drinking establishments. Mackintosh's two major houses, both near Glasgow, were Windyhill (1899-1901) and Hill House (n° 618). Already known in Vienna, he achieved further international prominence when his designs for 'the house of an artistic connoisseur' were published as part of a competition organised by a German magazine in 1901. (These were finally realised in Glasgow in 1996.) His last years were spent painting stylised landscapes and still lifes. In the later 20th century, Mackintosh's work was rediscovered, and his buildings are major tourist attractions in Glasgow and its vicinity.

Richard MEIER

(Newark, 1934 –)

Among late-modern architects, Meier is perhaps the pre-eminent flagbearer for the expressive potential of abstract, sculptural form. Almost invariably employing white as his sole colour, Meier's intricate buildings evince a purity that may seem detached from mundane realities. But while his formal language is often so abstract as to seem self-referential, Meier's deployment of elements is nevertheless governed by a rigorous conceptual plotting of the interplay of form, structure, site, circulation and social elements. After studying at Cornell, Meier sought unsuccessfully to work for his idol Le Corbusier in Paris, but instead began his career with Skidmore Owings & Merrill and Marcel Breuer in America. Opening his own practise in 1963, Meier's early work consists of a series of detached dwellings in natural settings, notably the Smith house in Darien, Connecticut (1965-67) and the Douglas house in Harbor Springs, Michigan (n° 964). Meier exhibited with the New York Five from 1969, eventually turning out to be the most mainstream and prolific member of that intellectual and sometimes arcane group. His Athenaeum at New Harmony,

Indiana (n° 967), which serves as an orientation centre at the site of an early 19th-century utopian colony, again deploys a Corbusian vocabulary of ramps, columns and planes while privileging the notion of circulation; its white enamel cladding ensures a maximal contrast between nature and man-made geometry. The High Museum of Art in Atlanta, Georgia (n° 975) is focused around a huge top-lit atrium, its long ramp improving on that of the Guggenheim by being kept rigorously separate from display areas. In 1984 Meier was chosen to design the new Getty Center in Los Angeles, a monumental complex of buildings set on a hilltop, with gallery spaces, library and study facilities, and conservation labs (n° 978). Though each wing of this lavish and expensive complex is articulated differently, the whole comes together as a kind of collage, a medium which Meier in fact embraces in his secondary role as an artist.

Erich MENDELSOHN

(Olsztyn, 1887 – San Francisco, 1953)

Mendelsohn's work is characterised by a sculptural curvilinearity that introduced a new dynamism into early modern architecture even as it sometimes underplayed functional considerations. This tendency first emerged in a series of tiny sketches of imaginary buildings that he produced while serving in the trenches in the First World War. Following the lead of the German Expressionist painters, Mendelsohn's goal was to convey a sense of energetic spontaneity. The earliest material manifestation of this expressionistic approach can be seen at the Einstein Tower (n° 649), an observatory built at Potsdam (1919-21). The Tower's organic curves were originally to have been built in reinforced concrete, but practical considerations forced him to achieve the desired effect using plaster over brick. Through the 1920s Mendelsohn designed a series of industrial buildings of unusually diverse and imaginative form, while his large department stores in Stuttgart and Chemnitz deployed sweeping curves for their façades. Sensing the coming troubles for Jewish architects, Mendelsohn left Germany in 1933 to form a partnership in London with Serge Chermayeff. Their most notable collaboration is the De La Warr Pavilion at Bexhill-on-Sea (n° 675), an elegantly modernistic entertainment centre characterised by smooth white surfaces, large areas of glass and a dramatic spiral staircase. In the later 1930s Mendelsohn was active in Palestine, erecting a house for Chaim Weizmann in Rehovot and the Hadassah University Medical Centre on Mount Scopus in Jerusalem. Seeking further commissions, Mendelsohn moved to the United States in 1941. His Maimonides Hospital in San Francisco (1946-50) contains reminiscences of his youthful expressionism in the form of rounded balconies and staircases, and his last works were a series of synagogues in the American Midwest.

Charles MOORE

(Benton Harbor, 1925 – Austin, 1993)

The multi-faceted Moore succeeded in bringing many forgotten elements back to modern architecture, including colour, ornamentation, humor and a sensitive awareness of historical typologies. Moore studied at the University of Michigan and at Princeton, where he acted as a teaching assistant for Louis Kahn. Based largely in Berkeley, California from 1959, Moore moved around America constantly and hence worked with many partners, including Donald Lyndon, William Turnbull and Richard Whitaker. He served as Dean of the Yale School of Architecture from 1965-70, went to teach at UCLA in 1975, and finally came to Austin in 1985 to teach at the University of Texas. Moore's own house in Orinda, California (1962) attracted attention for its conceptual identity as a series of nested aedicules. The wooden-clad geometries of his innovative condominiums at Sea Ranch on the northern California coast (1964 and later, with landscape architect

Lawrence Halprin) respond to the bleak, windswept setting as well as to older buildings (barns, the Russian settlement at Fort Ross) nearby. Kresge College at UC Santa Cruz (1971) is articulated a fanciful version of an Italian hill town. Moore's later works appear even more theatrical and scenographic: the famous Piazza d'Italia in New Orleans (n° 969), a collection of dislocated Classical elements reproduced in incongruous materials, introduced Postmodern humor and historical pastiche to American architecture. Moore's last building, the Washington State History Museum in Tacoma (1996), features huge arched gables. Eclectic, extroverted and colourful, Moore's approach may at first seem superficial, but his fruitful dialogue with older architectural typologies, as well as his influential and thoughtful books, makes Moore one of the pre-eminent architectural thinkers of the 20th century.

Julia MORGAN
(San Francisco, 1872 – San Francisco, 1957)

Morgan's career represents a series of firsts in the all-too-brief story of women in the architectural profession. Raised in the San Francisco Bay Area, Morgan took a degree in engineering at UC Berkeley before making the unprecedented step of going to Paris to study architecture at the famed École des Beaux-Arts. Morgan thus not only received the best possible architectural education, but went on to establish one of the most prolific and successful architectural practises in California. By the time of her death she had designed (and in most cases actually erected) between 700 and 800 domestic, religious, educational, commercial and public buildings. Much of her early work was residential: in the first decade of the 20th century she became famous for her many shingle-clad Arts and Crafts houses in Berkeley, Oakland and San Francisco. Morgan in fact worked simultaneously in many different styles, including English half-timbered, Mediterranean, Spanish Colonial and Classical. In 1915 she was made the official architect for the national YWCA in the West, and her subsequent career was to include much patronage from female clients and organisations. All such commissions were inevitably overshadowed by her role as architect for the palatial hilltop estate that newspaper tycoon William Randolph Hearst built for himself on a remote part of the California coast (n° 882). For the main building of San Simeon (begun 1919), Morgan combined allusions to California missions, reminiscences of medieval and Renaissance architecture, and many other points of reference. This eclecticism was in part necessary in order to incorporate the many fragments of historical buildings — doorcases, ceilings, paneling, tapestries and large pieces of furniture — that Hearst had purchased in Europe; many of these still remain in warehouses. When she finally closed her office, Morgan destroyed many of her blueprints and documentation, making the reconstruction of her long and groundbreaking career a difficult task.

Richard NEUTRA
(Vienna, 1892 – Wuppertal, 1970)

Neutra was instrumental in bringing the innovations of European modernism to North America. Born and educated in Vienna, he was influenced early on by the architect and theorist Adolf Loos, who instilled in him the need to reject the ornamentalism of the earlier Secessionist school. This tendency was reinforced by his discovery of the work of Frank Lloyd Wright. Neutra trained as an urban planner in Switzerland and worked for Erich Mendelsohn in Berlin before moving to the United States in 1923. Here he had a position in a large commercial firm in Chicago and studied under Wright at Taliesin before moving on to start a practise in Los Angeles. Neutra's early domestic buildings in

California, exemplified by his 'Health' house for Dr. Philip Lovell (n° 885), were radically modern in form, materials and ideology: set atop a steep hillside, the Lovell house used an innovative system of steel framing and cable suspension to create a stack of planar, partially transparent and seemingly weightless terraces. Neutra's influence was to be decisive for the later 'Case Study' house program in southern California and for modernist house design in general. Neutra also took an interest in larger-scale social projects, including the design of mass housing complexes and innovative school typologies. After the war, his most prominent masterwork was the Kaufmann House in Palm Springs (n° 904), an elegant series of glass-walled spaces arranged according to a 'pinwheel' plan (recalling those of Wright) and focused outwards to the spectacular desert landscape. Neutra's later and larger buildings in Los Angeles are less memorable, but his writings, such as *Survival through Design* (1947), lay out an intriguing theory of the role that psychological factors should take in the shaping of architectural space.

Oscar NIEMEYER
(Rio de Janeiro, 1907 –)

The remarkably long-lived Niemeyer will be remembered not only for bringing European modernism to South America, but for modulating a sometimes puritanical approach to suit a distinctive vision of Brazil's regional character. Niemeyer's vocabulary remains that of international modernism, but is crucially inflected by his preference for expressive and sensual forms: he has often stated his belief that rectangular design is unnatural, hard and inflexible, and that he prefers the sensuality of the curves to be found in natural and organic forms. Niemeyer's decisive influence came from Le Corbusier, who visited Rio in 1936 to assist in the design of the new Ministry of Health and Education, a building for which Niemeyer acted as design head in succession to Lucio Costa. His first internationally recognised commission was a series of pavilions of varied and sculptural forms for the resort at Pampulha (1942-44). Through the following decade he designed factories, schools, houses and apartment blocks in Brazil, all of which recast the typologies of modernism into a more lyrical and curvilinear idiom. In 1957 Niemeyer embarked on the project that would come to occupy him for the rest of his life: the new national capital of Brasilia, master-planned by Costa (n° 924). Here each widely-spaced building, including the Presidential Palace, Supreme Court, National Congress and National Cathedral, is of unique form and simple elegance, the keynote again provided by repeated curves; his most recent buildings in the capital were added as recently as 2006. Niemeyer's staunchly Communist politics may seem at odds with his work for élite and establishment clients, but the beauty of his forms, as epitomised by the Sambadrome parade ground in Rio (1984), is meant to bring joy to all social classes and to embody national pride. His more recent works, equally striking in form, include the Niterói Art Museum (1996) and the Oscar Niemeyer Museum in Curitiba (n° 993) (2002).

Jean NOUVEL
(Fumel, 1945 –)

Nouvel's architectural output is of such diversity that it resists summation, but it is held together by his incessant creative experimentation with new forms and technologies, and in this he may be seen to continue the legacy of French engineering running from Viollet-le-Duc through Contamin, Eiffel, Freyssinet, Perret and Prouvé. He is particularly enamoured of complex effects of light, transparency and screening. Born in Fumel, France, Nouvel studied at the École des Beaux-Arts in Paris before working for the architects Claude Parent and Paul Virilio (1967-70). He gained an international following with his Arab World Institute in Paris (n° 731), which recasts traditional Arabic symbolism in a High-Tech language: though the cultural centre presents a curving glass screen to the Seine, the south façade comprises a grid of titanium and steel diaphragms of complex geometrical character; equipped with photoelectric cells, each opens and closes in response to changing conditions of ambient light. They are meant to recall, in fact, the pierced wooden screens that shade windows in traditional Middle Eastern and North African houses. Nouvel's Nemausus housing complex at Nîmes (1987) is more uncompromisingly industrial, with many metallic elements. The unbuilt project for an 'Endless Tower' at the La Défense district of Paris (1989) proposed a tall cylinder whose progressive vertical articulation in granite, aluminium, stainless steel and glass would cause it to appear to vanish into the sky. Nouvel's Cartier Foundation for Contemporary Art in Paris (n° 760) is partly concealed behind a series of free-standing glass screens. His more recent work includes the bullet-shaped Torre Agbar in Barcelona (2005) and the new branch of the Louvre in Abu Dhabi, a domed building presently under construction. Nouvel won the Pritzker Prize for architecture in 2008, and his practise is presently one of the largest in France.

Andrea PALLADIO

(Padua, 1508 – Vicenza, 1580)

Andrea Palladio was an important artist, architect and author for the entire development of Western architecture. His original name was Andrea di Pietro. Palladio, the name he adopted, refers to the Greek goddess of wisdom Pallas Athena. At the age of thirteen years we find him in the stonemasons' guild of Vicenza as an assistant. Then he met the amateur architect Giangiorgio Trissino, who looked after him and changed his name to Andrea Palladio. After a number of commissions in the classical tradition, he dedicated himself primarily to the construction of palaces and villas for the aristocracy. In the 1560s he took up designing religious buildings. He completed the refectory of the Benedictine monastery San Giorgio Maggiore, the cloister of the monastery Santa Maria della Carita (now the Galleria dell'Accademia), and the façade of the church of San Francesco della Vigna. His Venetian work culminated in three magnificent churches which have been preserved to this day: San Giorgio Maggiore (n° 434), Il Redentore (n° 437) and "Le Zitelle" (Santa Maria della Presentazione). Surprisingly, in spite of numerous attempts, Palladio never managed to get commissions for worldly buildings in Venice. In 1570 he published his theoretical paper *I Quattro Libri dell 'Architettura*. In the same year he was appointed architectonic consultant of the Venetian Republic. Although he was influenced by a number of thinkers and architects of the Renaissance, he developed his conceptions quite independently from most contemporary ideas. Palladio's work slightly lacks the splendour of other Renaissance architects, but instead he established a successful method, which survived the times, of invoking the architecture of classical antiquity as a source of inspiration. His loggias, equipped with colonnades, constituted an innovation which was later taken up in the whole of Europe.

Ieoh Ming PEI

(Guangzhou, 1917 –)

Chinese-American architect Ieoh Ming Pei's work validates the idea that modernist abstraction and Classical monumentality can be successfully reconciled. Born in Guangzhou (Canton), China, where his family can trace its roots back to the 15th century, Pei was schooled in Hong Kong and Shanghai before arriving in America at the age of 18. There he studied architecture at the University of Pennsylvania, at MIT, and finally at Harvard's Graduate School of Design under Gropius. Establishing his practise in New York, Pei worked closely for many years with developer William Zeckendorff. Much of his early work, such as the Mile High Center in Denver, Colorado (1954-59) or the Place Ville Marie in Montreal (1962), consisted of large-scale commercial projects in a conventionally modernist idiom. The National Center for Atmospheric Research in Boulder, Colorado (n° 940), however, featured bold sculptural forms in concrete to match the scale and power of the mountain setting. His mature style, owing much to Brutalist aesthetics, became increasingly reliant on simple geometries deployed on a grand scale; the Dallas City Hall (1972) is a good example. Pei's high-profile East Wing of the National Gallery in Washington, D.C., (n° 955) made use of massive triangulated forms that nevertheless succeed in creating a respectful dialogue with the older Classical monuments of the capital, an effect in part achieved through cladding with white stone sourced from the same quarries that had been used by its historic neighbours. Pei's greatest professional coup, however, was undoubtedly his selection by French President François Mitterrand to design the massive renovation and expansion of the Louvre museum in Paris (n° 741); Pei's self effacing approach was to sink almost all of the new construction under the main courtyard, allowing public access through a large but minimal glass pyramid. Many of his later works were created in collaboration with James Ingo Freed and Henry N Cobb.

Auguste PERRET

(Ixelles, 1874 – Paris, 1954)

Though his reputation has been somewhat eclipsed by the subsequent fame of his one-time pupil Le Corbusier, Auguste Perret is today best remembered for bringing the hitherto utilitarian material of reinforced concrete into use for formal and domestic structures, including churches. In this regard, his technical innovations are perhaps more notable than his architectural aesthetics, which generally remained anchored to historical precedent. Working in partnership with his two brothers, Perret erected his first major building: a block of flats at 25b rue Franklin in Paris (n° 620), whose façades of floral tile served as an external expression of its concrete framing. The now-demolished garage in the rue Ponthieu (1905) exposed its reinforced concrete structure even more openly while including such decorative flourishes as a large rose window in its façade. Perret again used reinforced concrete for his Théâtre des Champs-Elysées (1911-14), but here the rigorously rectilinear forms and decorative bas-relief sculptural panels recall a more conservative Classical idiom. His church of Notre-Dame du Raincy (n° 650) essentially reinterprets the Gothic tradition in terms of concrete, using the structural possibilities of the new material to draw out the older style's innate tendencies toward skeletonisation and the dematerialisation of walls into fields of luminous colour. Perret's post-war rebuilding of the cities of Le Havre and Amiens made use of his favoured material on a huge scale, most dramatically for the tall skyscraper at Amiens (1947) and the impressive but lugubrious church of St. Joseph (1951-58) with its 106 metre spire, though here again his vocabulary is that of a rationalised Neoclassicism. In 2005, UNESCO declared Perret's reconstruction of Le Havre to be a World Heritage Site.

Renzo PIANO

(Genoa, 1937 –)

Sometimes labeled as a High-Tech architect, Piano has in fact used technology in a nuanced and not always overt manner, and his career can more fairly be characterised by its diversity of formal approach and responsiveness to context and user needs. Piano studied and later taught in Milan, and worked with Louis Kahn from 1965-70. He formed a partnership with Richard Rogers from 1970-77 to design and build the Pompidou Centre in Paris (n° 716), his first major commission. This great cultural complex famously appears as a giant factory or machine, but its design was largely predicated on notions of flexibility and user-friendliness. Its exposed steel exoskeleton was meant to free up the internal spaces, while its equally emphatic display of services, all colour-coded, creates a busy, decorative patterning on the outside of the building. Many of Piano's subsequent projects were erected in Italy, but notable among his work in other countries is the Menil Collection (n° 971) in Houston, Texas (1981-87 and later), an art museum housed in a self-effacing series of wood-clad pavilions in a domestically-scaled neighbourhood, with internal toplighting controlled by curving concrete leaves. Piano's Kansai International Airport (n° 179), Osaka (1987-94), built on an unprecedentedly large scale on an artificial island, has a linear arrangement that is conceptually and visually simple, and its subtly curved silver roof aids in the circulation of fresh air. His many later museum projects include the remarkable Jean-Marie Tjibaou Cultural Centre (n° 186) in Noumea, New Caledonia (1991-98), a series of wooden, egg-like forms arranged in a shallow arc to suggest a lagoon-side village. The Nasher Sculpture Center in Dallas, Texas (opened 2003), as well as the Morgan Library expansion, New York (2003-06), are notable for their lightness, transparency and elegant restraint. His most recent project, the *New York Times* Building (2008), has been praised as a rebirth of innovative skyscraper form in Manhattan.

Henry Hobson RICHARDSON

(St. James Parish, 1838 – Brookline, 1886)

Henry Hobson Richardson was an American architect born of a rich family. He graduated from Harvard University in 1859 and entered the École des Beaux-Arts in Paris. After returning, he established himself in New York where he soon made his way into practise as an architect. In 1878, he moved to Boston where he passed the remaining years of his life.

Richardson's career was short (he died at the age of forty-seven), and the number of his works was small compared with the attention they attracted and the influence he left behind him. One of the most important and characteristic is Trinity Church in Boston (n° 854). In Trinity Church, his first monumental work, he broke away from the prevailing English Gothic fashion. The style, though mixed, shows his surrender to the attraction of the European Romanesque and particularly of the churches in Auvergne, which furnished the material for the design of the apse.

Among other monuments that he designed, one can note the Allegheny County Courthouse in Pittsburgh (n° 856) and Glessner house in Chicago (n° 857). Richardson's uncommon personality so embodied itself in his works that it cannot be overlooked. He had an inexhaustible energy of body and mind, an enthusiasm more genial than combative, but so abounding and at times vehement that few men could resist him.

He found American architecture restless, incoherent and exuberant; his example did much to turn it back to simplicity and respose.

Richard ROGERS

(Florence, 1933 –)

In our present era of computers, cybernetics and unending technological innovation, it may well be asked why we continue to build with heavy, archaic materials like bricks and concrete when we could be using light, precision components of metal and glass. Rogers has taken such experiments further than most designers, though his aims are not merely technical. After training at the Architectural Association in London and at Yale, Rogers formed Team 4 with Norman Foster, Wendy Foster and his wife Su Rogers. Their Reliance Controls factory in Swindon (1967), a modest industrial structure with exposed diagonal bracing, highlights most of Rogers' later strategies: the building's skin (cladding), structure and services are kept distinct and visually evident, creating a free and flexible internal space. This approach was repeated on a monumental scale for the Centre Pompidou in Paris (1971-77, with Renzo Piano), whose structural frame and service elements—air, water, electricity, circulation—are moved to the exterior and brightly colour-coded. Rogers' headquarters for Lloyds of London (n° 722), based around a tall interior atrium, privileges the idea of future change: he reasoned that the frame of the building (in reinforced concrete) has a long life expectancy, but that individual service elements—toilets, kitchens, elevators, stairs, etc.—may not; hence they are plugged into the exterior as prefabricated units, accessible for cleaning or replacement. Externally, Lloyds is picturesquely defined by six servant towers with cranes, with many elements clad in stainless steel. Among Rogers' many other large-scale commissions are Heathrow's Terminal 5 (1989-2008), the European Court of Human Rights, Strasbourg (1995), the Millennium Dome, Greenwich (n° 770), and the Law Courts in Bordeaux (1992-98) and Antwerp (1998-2005). Increasingly concerned with urbanistic issues, Rogers is as an impassioned advocate for a technologically progressive architecture with a social and ecological conscience, as laid out in his book *Architecture: A Modern View* (1991).

Aldo ROSSI

(Milan, 1931-1997)

The work of Aldo Rossi has a richness, poetry and historical resonance rare in modern architecture. Equally active as an artist, Rossi developed a repertoire of imagery that was at once repetitive, eclectic and personal. Based in Milan for most of his life, Rossi was originally classified as a Neorationalist, meaning that he continued the tradition of earlier Italian modernism ('rationalism') and utilised a minimal vocabulary of stark geometry. In fact, Rossi often made reference to the traditions of Classicism, as well as to purely personal reminiscences of religious, domestic and industrial buildings encountered in his earlier years; the melancholic mood of his renderings further reveals a specific debt to the Metaphysical painter Giorgio di Chirico. Rossi first gained prominence as a historian and theorist of urbanism, and his influential treatise *The Architecture of the City* (1966), strongly informed by linguistics, proposed a typological reading of urban form: focusing mainly on traditional Italian towns, he posited that building types assume typical configurations whose usage nevertheless changes over time. His thought was also analogical, drawing scalar comparisons between a street and a corridor, a house and a city. Some of these ideas can be sensed in the Gallaratese housing complex in Milan (1970-73): stark, linear row housing raised above ground level to create a continuous covered street, it is both uncompromisingly modern and evocative of traditional Italian architecture. Rossi's formal, axial design for the San Cataldo Cemetery in Modena (1971 and later) deployed giant geometries to haunting effect: the hollow cube of the columbarium, conceived as a 'house of the dead,' is notably affective. His Theatre of the World, a floating wooden construction built for the 1980 Venice biennale, recalled Renaissance precedents and created a dialogue with the towers and domes of the city. Rossi's ironically titled *Scientific Autobiography* (1981) reveals the essentially poetic nature of his motivation.

Eero SAARINEN

(Kirkkonummi, 1910   Ann Arbour, 1961)

Born into an artistically distinguished Finnish family, Saarinen studied sculpture in Paris and architecture at Yale. His first buildings were done in Michigan in collaboration with his father, Eliel, though he first rose to public attention with his simple and distinctive design for the Jefferson National Expansion Memorial in St. Louis (n° 910). Saarinen rapidly assimilated the forms and aesthetics of Miesian modernism, as demonstrated on a monumental scale in the elegant rectilinear pavilions that make up the General Motors Technical Center in Warren, Michigan (n° 906). Centred on a giant lagoon, the complex was feted as an 'industrial Versailles' at the time of its construction. After this time, Saarinen's career took an imaginative and eclectic turn, and his subsequent projects each betray a distinctive appearance, form, structure and use of materials. His expressive, sculptural manner is best represented by the Ingalls Hockey Rink at Yale (n° 927) and the TWA Terminal at Idlewild, New York (n° 926). In the latter, four intersecting shells of reinforced concrete are supported by Y-shaped columns, the whole composition irresistibly recalling an eagle about to take flight; Saarinen said only that his aim was to express "the drama and specialness and excitement of travel." In contrast, the façades of his John Deere administration centre in Moline, Illinois (n° 941), appear as densely layered grids of rusted steel. Though Saarinen's untimely death cut short this intriguing and diverse series of experiments, a number of prominent American architects, such Cesar Pelli and Roche & Dinkeloo, first found their creativity in Saarinen's office, and the expressive innovations in modern architecture that Saarinen had set in motion became irreversible.

Jacopo SANSOVINO

(Florence, 1486 – Venice, 1570)

The Italian sculptor and architect Jacopo Sansovino's original name was Jacopo Tatti. He took the surname Sansovino as a sign of respect for the Florentine sculptor Andrea Sansovino, to whom he was apprenticed. He spent the years from 1506 to 1511 and from 1516 to 1527 in Rome, where he took part in theoretical and practical debates on architecture. His early sculptures were mainly influenced by classical antique art. Having dedicated himself to sculpture in his early years, he then designed several buildings in Rome as an architect and went to Venice in 1527, introducing the classical style of Roman architecture of the High Renaissance there. In 1529 he was appointed the highest master builder in the town, designing palaces, churches and public buildings. The style of these buildings was characterised by the merging of the classical tradition of the Florentine master Bramante with the more decorative Venetian approach. His building work in Venice began with four notable buildings: the high altar of the Scuola Grande di San Marco (approximately 1533), the new Scuola Grande di Misericordia (building started 1533), the church of San Francesco della Vigna (started 1534) and the Palazzo Corner a San Maurizio (designed in 1532). In addition to these masterpieces, he built the Palazzo Corner della Ca' Grande (n° 416), the mint, the hall at the foot of the great campanile and several churches. When the Venetian town government made the decision to renew the town centre (the Piazza San Marco), in order to express municipal liberty symbolically, Sansovino was entrusted with the construction of the most important buildings of the new urban complex: Biblioteca Marciana, Zecca and Loggetta del Campanile. Sansovino achieved a wonderful balance between classicism and Venetian tradition as a result of the successful studies of the urban complex. Another one of his masterpieces was the Villa Garzoni (n° 424), laid out like a small factory, in Pontecasale (building started approximately 1540). Sansovino deserves the artistic importance of being the most significant figure in Venetian art of the sixteenth century. His designs became the fundamental model of Venetian palaces in the entire century. His outstanding masterpiece, the Libreria Vecchia (1536-88) (n° 409) at the Piazzetta San Marco follows the antique Roman theatre of Marcellus: Doric columns frame the arcade on the ground floor and Ionic columns the one on the first floor, so that there is a long majestic façade. As with all his buildings, the architecture is richly decorated with impressive free-standing sculptures and friezes.

Sansovino had a great influence on the future Venetian architects Andrea Palladio and Baldassare Longhena.

Karl Friedrich SCHINKEL

(Neuruppin, 1781 – Berlin, 1841)

Karl Friedrich Schinkel was a German architect and painter, and professor in the Academy of Fine Arts at Berlin. He was a pupil of Friedrich Gilly, the continuation of whose work he undertook when Gilly died in 1800. In 1803 Schinkel went to Italy, returning to Berlin in 1805. The Napoleonic wars seriously interfered with his work as an architect, so he took up landscape painting, displaying a talent for the romantic delineation of natural scenery.

In 1810 he drew a plan for the mausoleum of Queen Louise and in 1819 a brilliant sketch for the Berlin cathedral in Gothic style. From 1808 to 1814 he painted a number of dioramas for Gropins. From 1815 he devoted much time to scene painting, examples of his work are still in use in the royal theatres of Germany. Schinkel's principal buildings are in Berlin and its neighbourhood. His merits are, however, best shown in his unexecuted plans for the transformation of the Acropolis into a royal palace, for the erection of the Orianda palace in the Crimea and for a monument to Frederick the Great.

Sir John SOANE

(Goring-on-Thames, 1753 – London, 1837)

Sir John Soane was an English architect and art collector born of a humble family. His talent as a boy attracted the attention of George Dance the Younger, the architect, who with other friends helped him on. He won the Royal Academy's silver (1772) and gold (1776) medals, and a travelling studentship and went to Italy to study. Upon returning to England, he got into practise and married a rich wife. He became architect to the Bank of England (n° 547), his best-known work which he practically rebuilt in its present form, and did other important public work such as the Dulwich Picture Gallery. His architectural works are distinguished by their clean lines, careful proportions and skilful use of light sources. He became an Associate Royal Academician (A.R.A.) in 1795, then Royal Academician (R.A.) in 1802, and professor of architecture to the Royal Academy in 1806. In 1831 he was knighted. In his house in Lincoln's Inn Fields, he brought together a valuable antiquarian museum (now the Sir John Soane's museum in London (n° 560)), which in 1835 he presented to the nation with an endowment; and there he died in 1837.

James STIRLING

(Glasgow, 1926 – Edinburgh, 1992)

One of the more influential architects of the second half of the 20th century, Stirling was of a generation that began to question the achievements and assumptions of the pioneering modernists of the 1920s. His critique of modernist orthodoxies ultimately allowed him to recoup the past history of Western architecture, which had previously been repressed. Born in Glasgow, Stirling studied architecture at the University of Liverpool, where he was particularly marked by the teachings of the historian and theorist Colin Rowe. From 1956 he practised in London with James Gowan. Their Engineering Building at Leicester University (1959-63), a violent collision of blocky geometries featuring red bricks, extensive glazing, dramatic cantilevering and sawtooth skylights, was seen as brazenly industrial, and its ostensible refusal to make any concession to conventional notions of taste secured Stirling's reputation as a proponent of Brutalism. The History Faculty Building at Cambridge (1964-67) was in a similar vein, though its extensive glazing turned out to be functionally defective. Collaborating with Michael Wilford from 1971, Stirling had little success in getting his projects built during this period. But with the stone-clad Clore Gallery at the Tate, London (1980), Stirling began to reveal a hitherto unsuspected interest in historical and Classical forms: entered through a large triangular opening, the façade evinced a non-specific monumentality that presaged much postmodern architecture. This was equally true of the new Staatsgalerie, Stuttgart (n° 721), whose brilliantly hued high-tech elements could not disguise its overall reading as a colossal ruin recalling both Roman and Neoclassical precedent. Ironically, however, Stirling's exuberant office building at No.1 Poultry in London (1986-96) was specifically criticised for historical insensitivity in replacing a listed Victorian structure.

Louis Henry SULLIVAN

(Boston, 1856 – Chicago, 1924)

In the later 19th century Sullivan was the leading figure of the Chicago School, which strove to develop a new kind of architecture suited to the socio-geographic conditions of the American Midwest. His architectural education consisted of a one-year stint at the Massachusetts Institute of Technology, though he later worked with engineer William LeBaron Jenney in Chicago and at the Académie Vaudremer in Paris. He partnered with the engineer Dankmar Adler from 1881. Sullivan was strongly influenced by the rugged neo-Romanesque style of H.H. Richardson, as can clearly be seen in the firm's breakthrough building, the colossal Auditorium in Chicago (1886-90), a multi-use facility housing a theatre, hotel and office space. Even in this early commission, Sullivan's trademark decorative motifs make an appearance: vegetative and prolific in character, they bear a coincidental resemblance to European Art Nouveau of the same date, but were intended to reference Sullivan's theory of an 'organic' architecture growing naturally from its environment. Sullivan went on to design a series of early skyscrapers, notably the Wainwright Building in Saint Louis (1890-91) and the Guaranty Building in Buffalo (1895). After the Carson, Pirie, Scott Department Store in Chicago (n° 861), Sullivan's career was largely spent, and apart from a few small Midwestern banks of astonishing originality his last years were marked by alcoholism and critical neglect. His book *Kindergarten Chats* (1901), uniquely idealistic and sardonic in tone, sets out his architectural philosophy. Sullivan's famous but much misunderstood dictum that "form ever follows function" does not advocate a Spartan utilitarianism; he in fact remained obsessed with the possibilities of a symbolic system of ornamentation, which formed the subject of his last, unfinished treatise. Many of Sullivan's ideas were carried forward in the work of his brilliant pupil Frank Lloyd Wright.

Kenzo TANGE

(Sakai, Osaka, 1913 – Tokyo, 2005)

The pre-eminent Japanese modernist of the post-war years, Tange was able to assimilate the latest innovations in European architecture while maintaining a regard for traditional Japanese forms, structures, and traditions. Tange studied (and for many years taught) at the University of Tokyo. Specialising in urbanistic projects, he first worked in the office of Kunio Maekawa, a pupil of Le Corbusier. In 1949 Tange won the prestigious competition to build the Hiroshima Peace Memorial Park: here his modern post-and-beam structures recall both older Japanese wooden construction as well as the more robust Brutalist aesthetic of Le Corbusier. His Kagawa Prefectural Government Building (1955-58) again has emphatically trabeated façades. In 1960, Tange proposed a massive redesign of Tokyo, which would have seen the city expand onto the water in grids of repeated modular units; though never built, this proved remarkably influential, eventually even finding an echo in the late work of Le Corbusier himself (his unbuilt project for the Venice Hospital, 1965). Its rationale is essentially that of Structuralism, which had great impact in architecture and other intellectual fields at the time. The swooping forms of Tange's Olympic stadium (n° 164) for the Tokyo Olympics of 1964 brought him international recognition, while the massively sculptural Yamanashi Press and Broadcasting Centre (n° 168) again deployed Brutalist aesthetics to powerful emotional effect. Notable among Tange's many later projects, which have been built in Bahrain, America, Nigeria and Singapore, is the colossal Tokyo Metropolitan Government building (1991), which at 243 metres was until recently the tallest building in the capital. His mannered and memorable Fuji Television Building (n° 182) is an asymmetrical composition of two blocky towers linked by an openwork grid of suspended corridors that intersect a huge silver sphere in mid-air. Tange's students have included some of the most prominent Japanese modernists, including Kisho Kurokawa, Arata Isozaki and Fumihiko Maki.

Ludwig Mies VAN DER ROHE

(Aachen, 1886 – Chicago, 1969)

Mies van der Rohe appears at once as one of the most characteristic and one of the most conservative of all modern architects. His famous dictum "less is more," as well as his dedicated investigations into the nature of materials, served as guiding principles in all of his mature work. Despite his later influence, Mies van der Rohe had no formal training in architecture. After an apprenticeship in furniture design and construction, he worked as an assistant to Peter Behrens in Berlin, thus cementing his love of careful craftsmanship and launching his search to find an appropriate means of expression for the Machine Age. At the same time, he was strongly influenced by Neoclassical tradition as exemplified by his German predecessor K.F. Schinkel, and even in his most uncompromisingly modern compositions we can still trace the Classical virtues of precision, elegance, carefully considered proportions and the deployment of simple trabeated construction in repeated bays. From 1919, following contemporary Constructivist influences, Mies's projects and brick houses became both free-form and elementarist. At the same time, he began to envision the erection of tall glass-clad skyscrapers, a vision he would only be able to realise after his move to America in 1937. His most notable intervention in German architecture before the war was his management of the Weissenhof housing exhibition in Stuttgart (n° 655), where the uniformity of the prototype houses built by Europe's leading modernists indicated to many visitors that a new 'style' had been born. Once in America, Mies van der Rohe took up a teaching post at (and designed a new campus for) the Illinois Institute of Technology in Chicago (n° 922). His later masterworks, such as the glass-walled Farnsworth House (n° 912), captured the imagination of many architects but failed to impact the design of post-war housing, though his skyscrapers, such as the Lake Shore Drive apartment towers in Chicago (n° 914) and Seagram Building in New York City (n° 916), set clear typological and stylistic precedents for much modernist production over the next two decades.

Robert VENTURI
(Philadelphia, 1925 –)

Sometimes described as the 'godfather' of Postmodernism, Venturi was for many years better known as a polemical theorist than as an architect. His work reflects both his academic knowledge of architectural history and an ironic appreciation of popular culture, an attitude derived from Pop Art. Born and based in Philadelphia, Venturi studied at Princeton and worked for Saarinen and Kahn before entering into a series of professional partnerships with John Rauch, Denise Scott-Brown and others. His first major commission, the Guild House retirement home in Philadelphia (1960-63), illustrates his validation of a non-heroic, even 'ordinary,' architecture which nevertheless foils convention in subtle ways and includes covert, coded references to historical forms calculated to appeal to a select audience of architectural insiders. Built for his mother, the Vanna Venturi house in Chestnut Hill, Pennsylvania (1960-64) appears at first sight to be a conventional suburban tract house, though its many ambiguous and unresolved elements exemplify the principles set out in Venturi's *Complexity and Contradiction in Architecture* (1966). This influential manifesto questioned such basic modernist tenets as simplicity and clarity while championing a new plurality and hybridity. Venturi later published *Learning from Las Vegas* (with Scott Brown and Steve Izenour, 1972), which proposed an embrace of the commercial 'vernacular' of ordinary American landscapes. Some of Venturi's later commissions work more directly with history: his Franklin Court in Philadelphia (1972-76) uses hollow steel members to outline a hypothetical 'ghost' of Benjamin Franklin's original house and outbuildings, while the Sainsbury Wing of London's National Gallery (1986 on) plays with Classical elements to humorous effect. Breaking further modernist taboos, the Seattle Art Museum (n° 983) is unabashedly decorative and colourful. Venturi's most important contribution is perhaps his recognition that architecture is inevitably a matter of signs and symbols, as well as his validation of a "messy vitality" in urban design.

Otto WAGNER
(Vienna, 1841-1918)

Otto Wagner was an Austrian architect. Accepted to the Polytechnic Institute of Vienna at the age of sixteen, he continued his studies at the Royal Academy of Construction in Berlin, ultimately graduating from the School of Fine Arts in Vienna. He built his first structures in a resolutely classical style until 1890, when he found himself entrusted with the urban management of the city of Vienna. Wagner abandoned the historicist style and introduced a decorative and ornamental architecture that lent distinction to the thirty or so stations that he built for the new subway (n° 612). He was so successful that in 1894 he was appointed Director of the Academy of Architecture in Vienna.

In 1896, he published a book entitled *Modern Architecture*, in which he revealed his ideas about the role of the architect, then in 1897 he co-founded the Viennese Secession movement with a group of artists including Gustav Klimt, Joseph Maria Olbrich, Josef Hoffmann and Koloman Moser. This movement, breaking away from the preferred artistic tastes of the time, aimed to renew interest in the applied arts. Wagner's most significant project associated with this movement is the Austrian Postal Savings Bank (n° 626), built in reinforced concrete, decorated with marble and topped by an ornate victory balustrade.

Otto Wagner's style, placing him at the crossroads of historicism and modernity, had a strong influence on modern architecture.

Sir Christopher WREN
(East Knoyle, 1632 – Hampton Court, 1723)

Christopher Wren was an English architect. He first studied geometry and applied mathematics in Oxford before becoming professor of astronomy. It is as an architect that Wren is best known, and the great fire of London, by its destruction of the cathedral and nearly all the city churches, gave Wren a unique opportunity as he made designs for rebuilding them.

St. Paul's Cathedral in London (n° 473) is one of his greatest achievements. As a scientific engineer and a practical architect, Wren was perhaps more remarkable than as an artistic designer. The construction of the wooden external dome, and the support of the stone lantern by an inner cone of birchwood, quite independent of either the external or internal dome, are wonderful examples of his constructive ingenuity. Wren was an enthusiastic admirer of Bernini's design and designed a colonnade to enclose a large piazza forming a clear space around the church, somewhat after the fashion of Bernini's colonnade in front of St Peter's (n° 462).

Among Wren's city churches the most noteworthy are St. Michael's, Cornhill; St Bride's, Fleet Street and St Mary-le-Bow, Cheapside. Wren was very judicious in the way in which he expended the limited money at his command; he devoted it chiefly to one part or feature, such as a spire or a rich scheme of internal decoration. The other buildings designed by Wren are very numerous, including Trinity College in Cambridge, the Royal Naval Hospital (n° 483) in Greenwich and the reconstruction of Hampton Court (n° 480).

Wren was knighted in 1673 and elected President of the Royal Society in 1681. He was in Parliament for many years before dying in 1723.

Frank Lloyd WRIGHT
(Richland Center, 1867 – Phoenix, 1959)

The prolific and often prolix Wright remains the most famous American architect of the 20th century. Coming from a background of Transcendentalist idealism, Wright was largely self-taught, though his work under Louis Sullivan was to prove decisive for his later architectural philosophy. Like Sullivan, Wright was preoccupied with the need to develop a radically new kind of architecture suited to his vision of America, which necessarily meant rejecting all past stylistic allegiances. Having spent his youth on a farm, Wright desired to create an 'organic' architecture that would emerge naturally from the soil. His solution was the 'Prairie House,' a new typology characterised by emphatic horizontality, as manifested in a low podium (instead of a basement), deep eaves, and extended strips of clearstorey windows. Wright at the same time tacitly embraced the principles of the Arts and Crafts movement, notably the emphasis on natural and local materials and the unified design of all elements within a given interior. His early houses also embody a radical rethinking of the ground plan, allowing a freer flow of space between rooms. After a relatively fallow spell working in Japan and Los Angeles, Wright's career staged a spectacular comeback in the 1930s, when he produced such unquestioned masterpieces as Fallingwater (n° 896) and the Johnson Wax administrative headquarters (n° 894). Wright's very late works, like the Guggenheim Museum (n° 925) and the Marin County Civic Center (n° 932), have been criticised for their formalistic and decorative mannerisms, and his most lasting legacy may well prove to have been in the field of inexpensive modern house design, as epitomised by the first Herbert Jacobs house in Wisconsin (1936). Wright's architectural school, Taliesin, continued to operate for many years after his death, but his philosophy of organic architecture has found only sporadic adherence among later architects.

CHRONOLOGY

– 3000-2000 BCE –

AFRICA	4500 BCE:	Domesticated cattle, sheep and goats in North Africa as well as hunter-gatherer societies
	3300 BCE:	First writing systems (Egypt)
	c. 3100 BCE:	Unification of Egypt under Egyptian Pharaoh Menes who founds the 1st dynasty
	2620-2500 BCE:	Construction of Giza pyramid complex in Egypt, 4th dynasty
	2790-2181 BCE:	Old Kingdom of Egypt

n° 4: *Great Pyramids of Giza* (Egypt)

ASIA	14000-400 BCE:	Jomon period in Japan, Jomon Pottery, cultural interchange between Japan and China, China conquers Korea
	From 4th millennium BCE on:	Eurasion nomads domesticate horses and camels on the steppes of Central Asia, Mongolia, and Eastern Europe
	4000-3100 BCE:	Uruk period, beginning of urban life in Mesopotamia (The Sumer contributed essentially to the first Mesopotamian civilisation): emergence of the cuneiform script, potter's wheel and clay brick
	c. 3200-1850 BCE:	Longshan culture in China (central and lower Yellow River), famous for its highly polished black pottery
	3000 BCE:	The Semitic peoples begin to dispread in Southwest Asia
	3000-1500 BCE:	Harappa and Mohenjo Daro culture in Indus Valley

EUROPE	3200-2700 BCE:	Civilisation of the Cyclades (Greece)
	2700-1200 BCE:	First European civilisation, of the Minoan in Crete, appears; Celts spread in Central Europe up to Spain and Turkey
	2500 BCE:	Proto-Indo-Europeans arrive in Europe and intermingle with settled farming peoples

n° 191: *Stonehenge* (United Kingdom)

AMERICAS	c. 3000-1500 BCE:	Mound builders in North America

– 2000-1000 BCE –

AFRICA	2040-1640 BCE:	Middle Kingdom of Egypt
	1570-950 BCE:	New Kingdom of Egypt
	c. 1500 BCE:	Cultivation of plants in the Sahel

nº 7: *Funerary Temple of Queen Hatshepsut* (Egypt)

ASIA	2nd millenium BCE:	Cultivation of wheat, barley, and legumes from China/Central Asia in Deccan (India)
	c. 1500 BCE – 6th century BCE:	Vedic period: Aryan tribes bring their culture to the Indus Valley Civilisation and have a large impact on Hindiusm
	2200-1700 BCE:	Oxus civilisation (Bactria-Margiana Archaeological Complex) in Central Asia
	1894-1830 BCE:	Foundation of Babylonia by the Semitic Amorites
	1894-1881 BCE:	First King of the First Dynasty of Babylon Sumu-abum (also Su-abu)
	1600 BCE:	First Bronze Age and script culture at the Yello River during Shang Dynasty in China (1600-1046 BCE)
	1200 BCE:	Usage of iron around the Mediterranean Sea
	1045-256 BCE:	Zhou Dynasty in China

EUROPE	Second millenium BCE:	Appearance of the Germanic peoples (British Isles)
	1800 BCE:	Use of bronze
	1000 BCE:	Beginning of the Iron Age (Iberic Peninsula)

nº 192: *Palace at Knossos* (Greece)

AMERICAS	From 2000 BCE:	Maya civilisation
	2000 BCE:	Cultivation of manioc in South America
	2000 BCE:	Agrarian village communities in the Andes

AFRICA	814 BCE: 332 BCE: 146 BCE: 30 BCE:	The Phoenicians found Carthage Alexander the Great enters Egypt Destruction of Carthage by the Romans Egypt falls under the rule of the Romans	 nº 15: *The Treasury* (Jordan)
ASIA	728-559 BCE: 625-549 BCE: 6th-5th century BCE: 551-479 BCE: 550-330 BCE: 476-221 BCE: 6-5th century BCE: 320-185 BCE: 326 BCE: 300 BCE-300 CE: 250-125 BCE: 221 BCE: 206 BCE-220 CE: 180 BCE-10 CE: 185-73 BCE: 1st century BCE-7th century A.C.:	First Persian Empire Median Empire Siddhartha Gautama teaches Buddhism in India Life of Confucius, whose philosophy influenced a great part of Asia Achaemenid Empire in parts of Greater Iran Warring States Period in China: challenge of the Zhou Dynasty, proliferation of iron work replaces bronze Magadha, kingdom in north-east India Maurya Empire in India, expansion of Buddhism Alexander the Great invades India Yayoi period in Japan, technological progress (metal working, culivation of rice) Greco-Bactrian Kingdom in Central Asia: Buddhist art and culture prospers Unification of China under the First Emperor Qin Shi Huang, beginning of Imperial China Han Dynasty: China prospers (agriculture, handicrafts, commerce, invention of paper) Indo-Greek Kingdom Sunga Empire in North-central and Eastern India Three Kingdoms of Korea	nº 86: *Great Stupa*, Sanchi (India)
EUROPE	800 BCE: 753 BCE: 750-480 BCE: 750 BCE: 660 BCE: 597 BCE: 575 BCE: 561 BCE: 510 BCE: 510-323 BCE: 508 BCE: 490-479 BCE: 449 BCE: 443-429 BCE: 431-404 BCE: 338 BCE: 336-323 BCE: 331 BCE: 323-146 BCE: 264-241 BCE: 218-201 BCE: 168 BCE: 166 BCE: 150 BCE: 149-146 BCE: 146 BCE-330 CE: 52 BCE: 44 BCE: 31 BCE: 31 BCE: 27 BCE:	Intensification of Greek trade towards the Middle East, then Italy. Beginning of the Etruscan civilisation in Tuscany Foundation of Rome Archaic Greece Beginning of Greek colonisation towards the East Foundation of Byzantium. Splendour of Nineveh Destruction of the Temple of Jerusalem by Nebuchadnezzar Height of the power of the Estruscan kings over Rome. Tarquin the Elder imposes himself on the Latins, dries the site of and installs the forum. Servius Tullius builds the city fortifications Pisitratus becomes the tyrant of Athens. Autocracy in all Greek Cities Pisitratides are chased out of Athens. Installation of the Republic Classical Greece Installation of democracy in Athens by Clysthen Medic War. Destruction of the Acropolis by the Persians. Victory of the Greeks Ratification of peace between Greece and Persia Pericles in Athens rebuilds the Acropolis War of the Peloponnese: Sparta beats Athens Defeat of Athens and its last allies to Philip II of Macedonia Reign of Alexander the Great. Conquest of Greece and Persia Foundation of Alexandria Hellenistic Greece First Punic War: Rome takes Carthage from Sicily, Sardinia and Corsica Foundation of Cartagena in the Iberian Peninsula Second Punic War: Hannibal crosses the Alps and threatens Rome, which finally spreads its control all the way to the Iberian Peninsula and Northern Africa Rome triumphs over Macedonia Overthrow of the last Macedonian king by the Romans. Rome dominates the entire Mediterranean region Sack of Corinth by the Romans Third Punic War: destruction of Carthage Roman Greece Victory of Caesar over the people of Gaul in Alesia Assassination of Julius Caesar (Italy) Battle of Actium: defeat of Mark Antony and Cleopatra Beginning of the Empire Octavius is proclaimed Augustus. Beginning of the Roman Empire	nº 199: *The Heraion* (Greece)
AMERICAS	c. 1000 BCE:	Beginning of Maya ceremonial architecture	nº 814: *Pyramid of the Sun* (Mexico)

– 0-550 CE –

AFRICA	2nd-3rd century: 429:	Christianity in North Africa Vandals arrive in Africa
ASIA	230 BCE – 220 CE: c. 250-538: c. 250-710: 265-420: 280-550: 386-535: 5th century: 534-550: c. 538-710:	Satavahana Empire in Southern and Central India Kofun period in Japan: Chinese script, introduction of Buddhism Yamato period in Japan Jin Dynasty in China Gupta Empire in regions of Northern India, Golden Age of India due to scientific and artistic efforts, Hinduism Northern Wei Dynasty in China: Unification of northern China in 439, Buddhism The Huns Hephtalites attack Gupta Empire in Northern India, end of Golden Age Eastern Wei Dynasty in China Asuka period in Japan: Artistic, social, and political transformations
EUROPE	9: 64: 70: 79: First century: c. 126: 293: 306-337: 313: 330: 375: c. 400: 406: 451: 455: 476: 496:	Battle of the Teutoburg Forest, victory of the Germanic tribes over the Romans (Central Europe) Great Fire of Rome and first Christian persecutions by Nero Destruction of the Jerusalem Temple by Titus Disappearance of the cities of Herculaneum and Pompeii after the eruption of Vesuvius Appearance of Christianity in Greece Construction of the Pantheon, Rome Diocletian establishes the Tetrarchy, dividing the government of the Empire between West and East Reign of Emperor Constantine. Unity of Empire established Edict of Milan authorises Christians to practise their religion Constantine I founds Constantinople Invasion of the Huns in Central Europe, beginning of the migration period Beginning of the Barbarian Invasions (Italy) Beginning of the Great Invasion in Gaul after the freeze of the Rhine Invasion of Gaul by Attila the Hun Invasions of the Vandals. Sack of Rome Emperor Romulus Augustus abdicates in favour of the German vassal chieftain Odoacer – end of the Roman Empire Clovis I, King of the Francs (480-511), converts to Christianity
AMERICAS	250-900:	Classical Maya era: predominance of the city of Tikal and Calakmul

n° 89: *Ise shrine* (Japan)

n° 231: *The Colosseum* (Italy)

AFRICA	7th century: c. 790-1076: 800:	Arabians conquer North Africa, Christianity disappears Ghana Empire, due to trans-Saharan trade rich in gold and salt Appearance of the Arabic numerals 606-647: Harshavardhana rules in Northern India, Buddhism flourishes again

n° 29: *Dome of the Rock* (Israel)

ASIA	618-907: 655: 7th century: 8th century: 8th-10th century: 710-794: 794-1185: 9th-13th century: 907-960: 918-1392: 960-1279:	Tang Dynasty in China, economic and cultural influences in East and South Asia Korean kingdom of Silla allies with Chinese Tang Dynasty, then conquers the other Korean kingdoms and reigns until 9th century Richness of philosophical and social structure under the Yamato government in Japan, Chinese calendar, Confucianism and Taoism Islam in Central Asia and India Rashtrakuta Dynasty, Pala Empire and Pratihara share power in India, stagnancy of culture, philosophy and social structure, repression of Buddhism Nara period in Japan: Economic, administrative and cultural boom (roads, taxes, coins) Heian period in Japan: Confucianism, peak of the Japanese imperial court and arts Chola Dynasty in Southern India Five Dynasties and Ten Kingdoms Period in China, beginning in the Tang Dynasty and ending in the Song Dynasty: Time of political overthrow Goryeo Dynasty in Korea united the Later Three Kingdoms in 936 Song Dynasty in China, reunification of China

n° 104: *Borobudur* (Indonesia)

EUROPE	511-751: 532: 568-572: 596: 634: 711: 715: 718: 730-787: 732: 756: 785: 825: 834-841: 846: 862: 866-910: 887: 909: 919-936: 926: 962-1806: c. 976: 976-1025: 987-996: 989:	Merovingian dynasty (Central Europe) Reconquering of the Roman Empire by the Emperor Justinian (527-565). Ravenna becomes the capital Invasion of the Italian peninsula by the Lombards Toledo becomes the capital of the Visigoth kingdom Umar unifies Araby and launches the first wave of Muslim conquest (Hijra) Arab conquest of the Visigoth kingdom St Boniface evangelises Frisia (Northern Europe) Creation of the Christian kingdom of the Asturias (Spain) First iconoclasm in the Byzantine Empire Charles Martel halts the Arab invasion in Poitiers Abd-ar-Rahman founds the Umayyad dynasty of the Cordova emirate Pippin the Younger delivers Rome from the Lombard Siege. Creation of Church States Beginning of the construction of the Mezquita in Córdoba First unification of the Christian-Anglo-Saxon kingdoms Settlement of the Normans in Frisia Sack of St Peter's in Rome by the Saracens. Pope Leon IV builds the fortifications of the Vatican Arrival of the Viking Rurik who founds the first Russian dynasty Reign of Alfonso the Great, King of Asturias and León Abdication of Charles III, end of Carolingian Empire Fundation of the Cluny Abbey in Bourgogne Reign of Henry I, King of Germany Raids of the Magyards, halted in Lechfeld (955) by Otto Holy Roman Empire Arabic numbers are introduced in the Western world Reign of Basil II, golden age of the Byzantine Empire Hugh Capet becomes first King of France of the eponymous Capetian dynasty Baptism of Vladimir of Kiev, conversion of Russians to Christianity

n° 254: *Hagia Sophia* (Turkey)

AMERICAS	982: c. 1000:	Viking settlers arrive in Greenland The Inuit migrate to the Arctic section of North America

n° 823: *El Castillo* (Mexico)

– 1000-1500 –

AFRICA	1299-1923: Middle of 15th century: 15th century:	Ottoman Empire (Southeastern Europe, the Middle East and North Africa) Europeans begin slave trade Beginning of colonialism in Africa, rise of Christianity

n° 43: *Great Mosque* (Mali)

ASIA	1185-1333: 1207: 1299-1923: 13th century: 1333-1568: 1336/46-1565: 1347-1527: 1392-1897:	Kamakura period in Japan The Mongols spread xylography in eastern Europe (Russia) Ottoman Empire (Southeastern Europe, the Middle East and North Africa) Islam reaches Southeast Asia Marco Polo's voyage to China Muromachi period in Japan Vijayanagara Empire in Southern India, conquered by Muslim generals Muslim state Bahmani Sultanate in Central India Joseon Dynasty in Korea

n° 111: *Angkor Wat temple complex*
(Cambodia)

EUROPE	1054: 1066: 1095: 1099: 1138-1152: 1146: 1152-1190: 1168-1362: 1180-1223: 1190: 1200: 1204: 1212: 1214: 1215: 1223: 1226-1270: 1232-1492: 1233: 1238: 1242: 1275: 1309-1423: 1337-1453: 1369: 1378: 1384: 1385: 1417: 1429: 1453: 1455-1485: 1456: 1469: 1478: 1479: 1480: 1485: 1485-1509: 1487: 1492: 1493: 1494: 1498:	Schism between the Orthodox and Catholic church (Rome and Constantinople). Birth of Orthodoxy (Greece, Italy) Battle of Hastings: conquest of England by William the Conqueror, Duke of Normandy First Crusade Sack of Jerusalem by Godefroi de Bouillon Reign of Conrad III, King of Germany. Dynasty of the Hohenstaufen Second Crusade preached by St Bernard of Clairvaux, with Louis VII Reign of Frederick I, called Barbarossa, King of Germany Grand Princes of Vladimir-Suzdal King Philip Augustus II of France Third Crusade with Philippe Auguste, Frederick I, called Barbarossa and Richard the Lionheart Venice, Pisa and Genoa dominate trade with the East Sack of Constantinople by the crusaders (Italy) The combined armies of Aragon and Castile defeat the Almohads at the Battle of Las Navas de Tolosa (Iberic Peninsula) Philip Augustus of France wins the Battle of Bouvines. Starts a long period of French control (Belgium, Netherlands) King John forced to sign the Magna Carta. Council of the Lateran (British Isles) Invasion of Russia by Mongols King St Louis of France (Louis IX). Last Crusade The Nasrid dynasty rules Granada (Iberic Peninsula) Pope Gregory IX starts the Papal Inquisition. Extirpation of the Cathars in southern France The Moors set their last refuge in Grenada (Iberic Peninsula) Alexandre Nevski begins unification of Russia Marco Polo reaches China Avignon becomes the residence of the Pope, starting by Clement V (France) England and France start the Hundred Years' War Marriage of Philip the Bold, duke of Burgundy, to Margaret of Flanders, beginning of Burgundian rule in the Low Countries (Belgium, Netherlands) Two popes are elected, Pope Urban VI in Italy, Pope Clement VII in France. Beginning of the Great Schism Creation of the Burgundy states by Philip the Bold Victory of Juan I of Portugal over the Castilians End of the Great Schism (Italy) Saint Joan of Arc leads the French to victory against the English (France) Turkish conquest of Constantinople, end of the Byzantine Empire (Italy) War of the Roses in England between the Houses of York and Lancaster The Portuguese discover Cape Verde Reign of the Catholic Monarchs (Ferdinand of Aragon and Isabella of Castille) (Iberic Peninsula) Sixtus IV issues the Bull establishing the Spanish Inquisition (Iberic Peninsula) The Treaty of Alcaçovas settles the union of Ferdinand of Aragon and Isabelle of Castile: beginning of the reign of Catholic Monarchs Ivan III Vasilevich frees Russia from Mongol domination Reconstruction of the Moscow Kremlin Reign of Henri VII Tudor, King of England Bartolomeu Dias sails around the Cape of Good Hope Moors driven out of Grenada and Spain. End of 800 years of Islamic presence in Spain Maximilien I establishes the Habsburg family as a major international power (Central Europe) Beginning of Italian Wars with the expedition of Charles VIII, King of France Vasco de Gama discovers the sea route to India (Italy)

n° 306: *Notre Dame Cathedral* (France)

AMERICAS	1492: 1497:	Columbus reaches the New World (claims the land for the kings of Spain), beginning of intensive European colonisation of America John Cabot explores the east coast of the northern part of America (today Canada)

n° 826: *Fortified city of Machu Picchu*
(Peru)

– 1500-1700 –

AFRICA	1652:	The Dutch found first durable white colony in South Africa

ASIA	15th-16th century:	Spice trade in Asia by European navigators
	15th-17th century:	Sengoku period in Japan: Christianity arrives in Japan
	1526-1857:	Muslim Mughal Empire on the Indian Subcontinent
	From 1540:	Christian missionaries in India and other Asian countries
	1592:	Japan conquers Korean Joseon Dynasty until expelled by Chinese Army
	End of the 16th century:	Acts of piracy and encroachment of Western countries result in the reduction of oversea trade in whole East Asia
	1600:	East India Company
	1602:	Dutch East India Company
	1603-1868:	Edo period in Japan
	1644-1911:	Qing Dynasty in China, extension of areas under cultivation
	1664:	Foundation of the French East India Company

n° 66: *Shah Mosque* (Iran)

n° 147: *Taj Mahal* (India)

EUROPE	1494-1559:	Italian wars
	1500:	First Portuguese (Pedro Alvares Cabral) explorers disembark in Brasil
	1508-1519:	Reign of Maximilan I, emperor of the Holy Roman Empire. Spreads the Habsburgs' reign to Burgundy, the Netherlands, Franche-Comté, Hungary and Bohemia
	1513:	Pacific Ocean discovered by Vasco Nuñez de Balboa (Iberic Peninsula)
	1515:	Battle of Marignan, victory of France against the Swiss
	1515-1547:	Frances I, King of France
	1517:	Luther posts his 95 theses. Protestant Revolt, beginning of the Reformation (Central Europe)
	1519-1555:	Charles V, Holy Roman Emperor (Iberic Peninsula; Belgium, Netherlands)
	1520:	Revolt of Gustave Vasa, King of Sweden (1523-1560), against Denmark
	1520:	Magellan sails across the Pacific Ocean, discovers a strait and names it after himself (Iberic Peninsula)
	1521-1557:	Reign of Juan III, King of Portugal
	1526:	Victory of the Turks in Mohács, Hungary
	1527:	Sack of Rome by the troops of Charles V
	1529:	Turkish invasions, Ottoman Siege of Vienna
	1530:	End of the Florence Republic (1500-1530). Under the reign of Cosimo de' Medici, Tuscany acquires the title of Grand Duchy
	1533:	Henry VIII is excommunicated by the Pope (British Isles)
	1533-1584:	Ivan IV of Russia (Ivan the Terrible) first ruler of Russia to assume the title of tsar
	1534:	Adoption of the Act of Supremacy by England: birth of the Anglican Church
	1545-1563:	Council of Trent. Counter-Reformation (Italy)
	1553-1558:	Reign of Marie Tudor, Queen of England. Return to Catholicism
	1555:	Abdication of Charles V. His son, Philippe II, is crowned King of Spain and Sicily (1555-1598) Ferdinand I, his brother, becomes emperor of the Holy Roman Empire
	1558:	Protestantism established in the Church of England
	1559-1603:	Reign of Elizabeth I, Queen of England. Anglicanism becomes the official religion of the kingdom
	1568:	General revolt in the Netherlands
	1571:	Battle of Lepanto, Ottomans defeated by the Venetian and the Spanish: end of the Ottoman hegemony on the Mediterranean Sea
	1572:	St Bartholomew's Day massacre: massive, brutal killings of Protestants in France
	1579:	Union of Utrecht: creation of the Dutch Republic (Independence of the Northern provinces from Spain)
	1581:	Creation of the Dutch Republic (Independence of the Northern provinces from Spain)
	1588:	Spanish Armada defeated by England. End of Spanish commercial supremacy
	1592-1598:	Wars of Religion (France)
	1598:	Edict of Nantes proclaimed by French king Henry IV (1589-1610). End of the French Wars of Religion
	1598-1621:	Philip III rules Spain, Naples, Sicily, Southern Netherlands and Portugal
	1609:	Twelve Years Truce, Spain acknowledges the Independence of the United Provinces
	1610-1643:	Louis XIII, King of France
	1613-1645:	Reign of Michel III, Tsar. Romanov Dynasty (1613-1917)
	1618-1648:	The Thirty Years War
	1619-1637:	Reign of Ferdinand II, emperor of Holy Roman Empire
	1621-1665:	Reign of Philippe IV, King of Spain
	1621:	Victories against the French and Dutch (Iberic Peninsula)
	1640-1660:	English Revolution. Led by Oliver Cromwell (1599-1658)
	1648:	Defeat of Spain against France, peace of Westphalia, concession of the Flanders' territories
	1653:	Oliver Cromwell, Lord Protector of England
	1660-1685:	Reign of Charles II Stuart, King of England
	1661-1715:	Louis XIV, the "Sun King", King of France
	1666:	Great fire in London
	1668:	Spain acknowledges Portugal's independence
	1672-1678:	Dutch War comes to an end with the Treaty of Nijmegen; Louis XIV becomes the Europe "arbiter"
	1675-1700:	Charles II of Spain, last Spanish king from the House of the Habsburgs
	1683:	Last siege of Vienna by the Ottomans
	1685:	Revocation of the Edict of Nantes, Protestantism declared illegal in France
	1688-1697:	War of the "Augsburger Allianz"
	1696:	Fischer von Erlach: Castle of Schonbrunn, Vienna
	1697-1718:	Reign of Charles XII, King of Sweden

n° 401: *St. Peter's Basilica* (Vatican)

AMERICAS	1500:	First Portuguese explorers disembark in Brasil
	1506:	The conquistador Hernán Cortés defeats the Aztecs: beginning of three centuries of Spanish colonisation
	1521:	The Spanish defeat the Mexicans. A 300 year colonial period starts
	1524:	Giovanni da Verrazzano explores the East Coast of North America
	1531-1534:	Pizarro conquers the Inca Empire
	1588:	Spanish Armada defeated by England. End of Spanish commercial Supremacy
	1607-1675:	British colonisation of North America
	1608:	Beginning of British colonisation in Northern America. Samuel de Champlain founds Quebec
	1619:	First Africans brought to English North America (Virginia)
	1622-1898:	American Indian Wars
	1624:	Dutch set in Manhattan and around
	1681:	King Charles II of England grants a land charter to William Penn for the area that now includes Pennsylvania
	Late 17th century:	Harsh slave codes are introduces in the US

n° 833: *Independence Hall* (U.S.A.)

– 1700-1800 –

AFRICA	1794: 1798-1801:	Convention in France votes for abolition of slavery Napoleonic Campaign in Egypt, beginning of scientific research of the Pyramids
ASIA	18th century: 1788:	Extension of British power in India Colonisation of Australia by the United Kingdom

n° 151: *Summer Palace and gardens* (China)

EUROPE	1700-1746:	Reign of Philippe V, King of Spain
	1701-1713/14:	War of the Spanish Succession and Treaty of Utrecht (Iberic Peninsula)
	1703:	Uprising of Hungary, which breaks free from the Habsburgs. Foundation of St. Petersburg by Peter the Great
	1707:	Act of Union merges the Kingdom of England and the Kingdom of Scotland in the "United Kingdom"
	1709 and 1748:	Discovery of the ruins of Herculaneum and Pompeii (Italy)
	1710:	Thomas Newcomen develops his steam engine, combining the ideas of Thomas Savery and Denis Papin
	1714-1727:	Reign of George I, first Hanoverian King of England
	1721-1725	Reign of Peter I of Russia, first emperor of the Russian Empire
	1738:	Vienna Treaty. End of the war of Polish Succession
	1740-1786:	Frederic II, King of Prussia
	1741:	Beginning of the Austrian War of Succession
	1748:	Discovery of the ruins of Herculaneum and Pompeii
	1756-1763:	Seven Years War between Europe and the American colonies
	1759-1788:	Reign of Charles III, King of Spain
	1762-1796:	Reign of Catherine II, Empress of Russia
	1764-1795:	Reign of Stanislaw August Poniatowski, King of Poland
	1765-1790:	Reign of Joseph II, emperor of the Holy Roman Empire
	1768:	The Royal Academy is founded, with the painter Joshua Reynolds (British Isles)
	1768-79:	James Cook explores the Pacific (British Isles)
	1770:	Nicolas-Joseph Cugnot builds the first automobile (France)
	1774-1792:	Reign of Louis XVI, King of France
	1780-1810:	First Industrial Revolution in England
	1783:	First flight in hot air balloon (France)
	1788:	Colonisation of Australia by the United Kingdom
	1789:	Lavoisier publishes studies of chemistry (France)
	1789:	Beginning of the French Revolution
	1792-1815:	Napoleonic Wars
	1792-1804:	First Republic established (France)
	1793-94:	Reign of Terror led by Robespierre (France)
	1793:	Louis XVI executed (France)
	1793:	Opening of the Musée du Louvre (France)
	1794:	Southern Netherlands conquered by the French
	1796:	Italy Campaign of Bonaparte.
	1798-1799:	Expedition of Bonaparte in Egypt (France)
	Late 18th/early 19th centuries:	Industrial Revolution (Western Europe, North America), early capitalism

n° 513: *Trevi Fountain* (Italy)

AMERICAS	Early 18th c.:	Benjamin Franklin invents the bifocal lens and performs experiments involving electricity
	1763:	Treaty of Paris. France cedes Canada and all its territory east of the Mississippi River to England
	1775:	American War of Independence begins
	1776:	Declaration of Independence of the United States: Official founding of the United States
	1789:	Election of George Washington
	Late 18th-early 19th centuries:	Industrial Revolution (Western Europe, North America), early capitalism

n° 844: *The White House* (U.S.A.)

AFRICA	1802: 1833: 1848: 1859-1869: 1880-1881: 1880-1914: 1884-1885: 1899-1902:	Napoleon reintroduces slavery Abolition of slavery in the British colonies Second abolition of slavery in the French colonies Suez Canal First Boer War (First Anglo-Boer War) Scramble for Africa: Europeans compete for African territory Berlin Conference: Partition of African territorial by the colonial powers Second Boer War
ASIA	19th century: 1839-1842/ 1856-1860: 1857-1858: 1861: 1868-1912: 1869-1948: 1876: 1885: 1894-1895:	France takes territories in Indochina Opium Wars between China and the British Empire, China's ports open for European powers Indian Rebellion of the Sepoys Emancipation of the serfs (China) Meiji period and Restoration in Japan: modernisation and westernisation of Japanese society, rapid economic growth Life of Mohandas Karamchand Gandhi, who stands up for India's Independence Victoria of the United Kingdom becomes the first Empress of India of the British Raj Hindus and Muslims found Indian National Congress for India's independence First Sino-Japanese War, defeat of China
EUROPE	1801: 1802: 1804: 1804-1815: 1805: 1806: 1811-1820: 1812: 1814: 1814: 1815-1848: 1815: 1825-1855: 1830: 1831: 1837-1901: 1848: 1848: 1848/49: 1853-1856: 1855-1881: 1860: 1860s: 1861-1878: 1861: 1866: 1867: 1869: 1869: 1870-1871: 1871: 1871-1918: 1875-1940: 1888-1918:	Assassination of Tsar Paul I. Alexander I is brought to power Treaty of Amiens (end of the wars with France) Civil War in France Reign of Napoleon I, French emperor Victory of Nelson at Trafalgar. Victory of Napoleon at Austerlitz Dissolution of the Holy Roman Empire Regency period. Flowering of the arts and literature (British Isles) Napoleon invades Russia Abdication of Napoleon defeated by the armies of Britain, Russia and Austria. Louis XVIII ascends the throne (France) Vienna Congress. Restoration of the Bourbons in Spain Restoration of the French Monarchy with Louis XVIII (1814-1824) and Charles X (1824-1830) Defeat of the French army against Prussia and England at Waterloo (Belgium, Netherlands) Nicolas I, Tsar of Russia, enforces military discipline, censorship and traditions of the Orthodox Church London Protocol: The sovereignty of Greece is confirmed, foundation of a small, independent Greek kingdom Belgian independence from the Netherlands Reign of Victoria I, Queen of the United Kingdom of Great Britain and Ireland and the first Empress of India (1876-1901) Year of revolutions: revolts in France, Italy, Austria and Hungary Napoleon III is Emperor of the 2nd Empire (France) Revolutions of 1848 in the German states War of Crimea. United Kingdom and France declare war on Russia Tsar Alexander II of Russia Beginning of the Second Industrial Revolution Russian populist movement (the Narodniki) Reign of Victor-Emmanuel II, King of Italy Italian Kingdom is proclaimed. Victor-Emmanuel II is crowned. (Italy) Battle of Sadowa: Prussia excludes Austria from the new German Confederation Bismarck becomes Chancellor of the North German Confederation Charles Cros invents a process for colour photography (based on three colours) (France) Inauguration of the Suez canal Franco-Prussian War. Fall of the Second Empire in France Repression of the Commune in Paris German Empire (II Reich) Third Republic (France) Reign of William II, German emperor and King of Prussia
AMERICAS	1803: 1810-1821: 1812: 1834: 1848: 1848-1896: 1857-1861: 1860: 1861-1865: 1862: 1879: 1890: 1898:	Louisiana sold to the United States by Napoleon Mexican War of Independence. By 1826, Mexico conquers the Spanish colonies of America, except for Cuba and Puerto Rico, and gains its independence War with Great Britain Thomas Davenport makes the first commericaly successful electric motor James W. Marshall discovers gold in California Gold Rush in Western America The War of Reform (Mexico) Election of Abraham Lincoln American Civil War Emancipation Proclamation (end of slavery) First incandescent lamp (Thomas Alva Edison and Joseph Wilson Swan) Halifax first city to be totally lit with electricity Spanish-American War

n° 602: *Eiffel Tower* (France)

n° 855: *The Brooklyn Bridge* (U.S.A.)

– 1900-2002 –

AFRICA		
	Beginning of 20th century:	Whole African continent (except for Ethiopia and Liberia) under European dominance
	1914-1918:	Germany loses its colonies
	1948:	National Party governs South Africa, Apartheid begins
	1951:	Independence of United Kingdom of Libya from France and United Kingdom
	1956:	Independence of Morocco from France and Spain, Indpendence of Tunisia from France
	1960:	Independence of nearly all French colonies
	1962:	Evian Accords: independence of Algeria. Cuban missile crisis. Second Vatican Council
	1973:	Yom Kippur War
	1974-1975:	New Portuguese gouvernement decides independence of all its colonies (except Macau)
	1994:	Rwandan Genocide
	1994:	Election of Nelson Mandela in South Africa, first Black President

n° 82: *Burj al Arab hotel*
(United Arab Emirates)

ASIA		
	1904-1905:	Russo-Japanese War. Rivalry for dominance in Korea and Manchuria
	1910:	Japan annexes Korea, Korea becomes Japanese colony
	1914-1918:	World War I
	1919:	Treaty of Versailles, Japan takes the German colonies in China
	1937-1945:	Pacific War in the Pacific Ocean, its islands, and in East Asia
	1939-1945:	World War II
	1945:	Atomic bombs drop on Hiroshima/ Nagasaki. Japan capitulates. USSR takes North Korea, USA South Korea
	1945:	Potsdam Agreement between the USSR, USA and UK: reduction of Japanese territory
	1947:	Independence of India
	1948:	Independence of Korea from Japan, foundation of Cummunist North Korea (Democratic People's Republic of Korea) and South Korea (Republic of Korea)
	1949:	People's Republic of China is established by Mao Zedong
	1950-1953:	Korean War
	1951-1952:	Treaty of San Francisco, signed by 49 nations
	1965-1975:	Vietnam War
	1966:	Great Proletarian Cultural Revolution (China)
	1960s-1970s:	Rapid economic growth in Japan. Japan among the G7 countries

n° 184: *Petronas Towers* (Malaysia)

EUROPE		
	1905:	First Russian Revolution
	1911:	Assassination of the Archduke Franz Ferdinand and his wife the Duchess of Hohenberg at Sarajevo (Central Europe)
	1914-1918:	World War I
	1915:	Vittorio Emanuel III declares war on Austria-Hungary (Italy)
	1917:	October Revolution in Russia, the Bolsheviks take power. Russian Revolutions. Abdication of Tzar Nicolas II
	1919:	Treaty of Versailles (Official end of World War I)
	1919:	Creation of the League of Nations in Geneva
	1919-1933:	Weimar Republic (Central Europe)
	1922-1953:	Stalin General Secretary of the Communist Party of the Soviet Union
	1922:	Benito Mussolini's march on Rome. Creation of the U.S.S.R. Joseph Stalin becomes General Secretary of the Communist Party
	1922-1943:	Mussolini leads Italy, creation of a fascist state
	1931:	Attempted coup by Franco; Spanish Civil War (1936-1939)
	1933:	Adolf Hitler becomes Chancellor of Germany. Beginning of the Third Reich
	1936:	Beginning of the Civil War in Spain
	1938:	Annexation of Austria by Germany (Anschluss)
	1939-1945:	World War II
	1945:	Yalta Conference. Untited Nations Charter
	1945:	Execution of Mussolini. End of fascist state
	1945:	Potsdam Agreement between the USSR, USA and UK: Agreement on policy for the occupation and reconstruction of Germany and other nations
	1946:	Beginning of the Cold War/Indochina War
	1946-1949:	Greek Civil War
	1947-1991:	Cold War (Central Europe)
	1948:	Establishment of the Marshall Plan. Israel declares itself a state
	1949:	North Atlantic Treaty (NATO). Republic of China declared
	1949:	Foundation of Federal Republic of Germany (West) and German Democratic Republic (East)
	1953:	Khrushchev, leader of Soviet Union, starts destalinisation
	1953:	James Watson and Francis Crick discover the structure of DNA (British Isles)
	c. 1955:	German "Wirtschaftswunder" ("economic miracle")
	1957:	Treaties of Rome
	1958:	Fifth Republic (France)
	1961:	Erection of the Berlin Wall
	1961:	First cosmonaute Youri Gagarine flies around the world
	1968:	Student revolts in Paris, Los Angeles and Berlin. Prague Spring
	1972:	Strategic Arms Limitation Treaty between the United States and Soviet Union
	1973:	Oil Crisis. Military Coup in Chile
	1975:	Death of Franco. Restauration of the Spanish monarchy
	1978:	Election of Pope John Paul II
	1980:	Outbreak of Iran-Iraq War
	1985:	Schengen Agreement
	1986:	Beginning of Perestroika in the Soviet Union. Explosion at the Tchernobyl nuclear power plant
	1989:	Fall of the Berlin Wall. Collapse of Communism. Ceausescu is overthrown in Romania
	2002:	Introduction of the Euro

n° 785: *Swiss Re building*
(United Kingdom)

AMERICAS		
	1914:	Henry Ford mechanises mass-production
	1914:	Inauguration of the Panama canal
	1917:	U.S.A. enters the First World War
	1929:	Wall Street Crash
	1939-1945:	Second World War
	1941:	Attack of Pearl Harbor by the Japanese
	1951-1952:	Treaty of San Francisco, signed by 49 nations
	1959:	Revolution of Fidel Castro in Cuba
	1960:	First satellite for telecommunication created by NASA
	1963:	Martin Luther King's "March on Washington"
	1964:	Guerrilla war lead by par Ernesto Che Guevara in Latin America
	1965-1975:	Vietnam War
	1969:	Neil Amstrong and Edwin Aldrin walk on the moon
	1972:	Strategic Arms Limitation Treaty between the United States and Soviet Union
	1973:	Oil Crisis. Military Coup in Chile
	1981:	First space shuttle launched by the States

n° 886: *Chrysler Building* (U.S.A.)

GLOSSARY

Abbey	A monastery, or conventual establishment, under the government of an Abbot or an Abbess.
Altar	A base or pedestal used for supplication and sacrifice to gods or to deified heroes.
Amphitheatre	A building in which the seats for spectators surround the scene of the performance.
Aqueduct	A term properly including all artificial works by means of which water is conveyed from one place to another, but generally used in a more limited sense.
Baldacchino	Canopy of state over an altar or throne.
Baptistery	A separate hall or chapel, connected with the early Christian church, in which catechumens were instructed and the sacrament of baptism administered.
Barrière	French for 'fence' or 'barrier.'
Basilica	In ancient Rome, a large covered building that could accommodate a considerable number of people. It had a central nave with an apse at one or both ends and two side aisles formed by rows of columns, which was used as a courtroom or assembly hall. It is also a Christian church building of a similar design.
Baths	Places that feature thermal springs.
Belfry	A tower which contains one or more bells.
Bibliothèque	Library in French.
Caravanserai	A public building for the shelter of a caravan and of wayfarers, generally in Asiatic Turkey.
Casa	Spanish for house.
Catacomb	An underground system of tunnels and chambers with recesses for graves, used in former times as a cemetery; a subterranean tunnel system used for burying the dead, as in Paris or ancient Rome.
Cathedral	The church that contains the official "seat" or throne of a bishop.
Cave	A hollow extending beneath the surface of the earth.
Château	Castle in French.
Choragic Monument	Small decorative structures erected in ancient Greece to commemorate the victory of the leader of a chorus in the competitive choral dances.
Condominium	A building or complex in which units of property, such as apartments, are owned by individuals and common parts of the property, such as the grounds and building structure, are jointly owned by the unit owners.
Convent	A term applied to an association of persons secluded from the world and devoted to a religious life, and hence the building in which they live, a monastery or (more particularly) nunnery.
Crematorium	A structure in which the bodies of the deceased are cremated.
Dormitory	Llarge bedroom with a number of beds, in schools and similar modern institutes.
Fortress	Fortified structure intended for the reception of a garrison and for the defence of a certain part of a country.
Forum	In Roman antiquity, any open place used for the transaction of commercial, judicial or political business, sometimes merely as a promenade.
Foundation	The act of building, constituting or instituting on a permanent basis, especially the establishing of any institution by endowing or providing it with funds for its continual maintenance.

Hospici	Hospice in English; the name usually given to the homes of rest and refuge kept by religious houses for pilgrims and guests.
Kondo	The building in which the sanctuary is located in a Buddhist monastery.
Krak	Fortified building constructed by crusaders in Palestine and Syria.
Madrasa	A centre for Islamic cultural and religious studies.
Manor	A large country house and its lands.
Mausoleum	A monument erected to receive the remains of a deceased person, which may sometimes take the form of a sepulchral chapel.
Memorial	Something, such as a monument or holiday, intended to celebrate or honor the memory of a person or an event.
Mission	House inhabited by an order of clergy who perform missionary work.
Monastery	The residence of a religious community.
Mosque	The house of prayer in the Muslim religion.
Mound	A pile or heap of earth, artificial or natural, especially such a pile raised over a grave or burial-place, a tumulus, or a means of defence.
Pagoda	An Eastern term for a temple, especially a building of a pyramidal shape common in India and the Far East and devoted to sacred purposes.
Peristyle	A gallery of columns lining the interior or exterior of a building and distinct from its surrounding wall.
Sacristy	The term in ecclesiastical architecture given to the room or hall in a large church in which vestments and utensils used in services and celebrations are kept.
Sanatorium	Institution in which ill or weak people are treated and strengthened.
Schloss	Castle in German.
Shrine	A holy place dedicated to the worship or veneration of a specific deity, ancestor, hero, martyr, saint or similar figure of awe and respect.
Stele	A slab of stone or wood, usually bearing inscriptions (plural **stelae**).
Stoa	In Ancient Greek architecture; covered walkways or porticos, commonly for public usage.
Stupa	(From Sanskrit and Pâli: *stûpa*, literally meaning "heap") a dome-shaped monument, used to house Buddhist relics or to commemorate significant facts of Buddhism or Jainism.
Synagogue	A building or place of meeting for worship and religious instruction in the Jewish faith.
Tholos	The term given in Greek architecture to a circular building; with or without a peristyle.
Tumulus	A Latin word meaning a heap or mound, also used in classical writings in the secondary sense of a grave.
Viaduct	An elevated bridge, usually formed by a series of arches, that serves to transport running water across a valley or chasm.
Ziggurat	A temple tower of the ancient Assyrians and Babylonians, having the form of a terraced pyramid of successively receding stories.

LIST OF ILLUSTRATIONS

Q

R

S